Writing About WORLD LITERATURE

and Supplemental Texts for English 231 and 232

KAREN M. GOCSIK
Dartmouth College

ROBERT KIRSCHEN
University of Nevada, Las Vegas

W. W. NORTON & COMPANY
New York • London

W. W. Norton & Company has been independent since its founding in 1923, when William Warder Norton and Mary D. Herter Norton first published lectures delivered at the People's Institute, the adult education division of New York City's Cooper Union. The firm soon expanded its program beyond the Institute, publishing books by celebrated academics from America and abroad. By midcentury, the two major pillars of Norton's publishing program—trade books and college texts—were firmly established. In the 1950s, the Norton family transferred control of the company to its employees, and today—with a staff of four hundred and a comparable number of trade, college, and professional titles published each year—W. W. Norton & Company stands as the largest and oldest publishing house owned wholly by its employees.

Editor: Peter Simon
Custom editor: Katie Hannah
Project editors: Kate Feighery, Sophie Hagen
Copyeditor: Michele Lansing
Production managers: Benjamin Reynolds, Ashley Horna, Diana Spiegle
Composition: Westchester Book Group
Manufacturing: Courier—Westford, MA

Library of Congress Cataloging-in-Publication Data has been applied for.

ISBN: 978-0-393-91879-3

W. W. Norton & Company, Inc., 500 Fifth Avenue, New York, NY 10110-0017
wwnorton.com
W. W. Norton & Company Ltd., Castle House, 75/76 Wells Street, London WIT 3QT

1 2 3 4 5 6 7 8 9 0

Brief Contents

Contents

Contents

Contents

4   Researching World Literature 63

5   Developing Your Thesis 75

Contents

Contents

Contents

Contents

1

What Is Academic Writing?

This short guide to writing about world literature provides information about the nature and process of academic writing in general, as well as information about the specific challenges involved in writing about world literature. Whether or not you've already taken a writing course, you should find guidance here that will help you complete whatever writing assignments you receive in your world literature class. The first topic we should tackle is the most general of all: What is academic writing?

Simply put, academic writing (sometimes called "scholarship") is writing done by scholars for other scholars—and that includes you. As a college student, you are engaged in activities that scholars have been engaged in for centuries: you will read about, think about, argue about, and write about great ideas. Of course being a scholar requires that you read, think, argue, and write in certain ways. You will need to make and support your claims according to the customary expectations of the academic community.

How do you determine what these expectations are? The literary theorist Kenneth Burke has famously described scholarship as an ongoing conversation, and this metaphor may be helpful. Imagine you have just arrived at a dinner party. The discussion (which in this case is about world literature) has already been going on for quite a while when you arrive. What do you do? Do you sit down and immediately voice your opinions? Or do you listen, try to gauge the lay of the land, determine what contribution you might make, and only then venture to make it?

The etiquette that you would employ at the dinner party is precisely the strategy that you should use when you write academic papers. In short, listen to what other scholars are saying. Familiarize yourself with the scholarly conversation before jumping in. Pay attention to both *what* is said and *how* it is said. A book like *The Norton Anthology of World Literature* is the perfect "dinner companion" for scholarship about world literature, getting you up to speed and filling you in on the conversation that preceded you. But you should make use of other resources, too. Your professor, for instance, is a living, breathing expert on what scholars of world literature care about. Books, journals, and even credible Internet sites also offer an opportunity to eavesdrop on the ongoing scholarly conversation about world literature. Once you understand the substance of that conversation, you can begin to construct informed arguments of your own.

Getting Started

CONSIDER WHAT YOU KNOW

When you sit down to write an academic paper, you'll first want to consider what you know about your topic. Different writing assignments require different degrees of knowledge. A short paper written in response to an episode from Murasaki Shikibu's *The Tale of Genji*, for example, may not require you to be familiar with the history of eleventh-century Japan.

However, if you're asked to write an academic paper on the novel, you'll want to know more. You'll want to have a sense of the basic outlines of medieval Japanese history and culture, as well as some knowledge of the author's biography. You'll want to familiarize yourself with the poctic tradition that preceded the novel so that you can understand the themes that were important to Murasaki and her contemporaries. Finally, if you're writing a research paper on this novel, you may be asked to be aware of different critical perspectives on *The Tale of Genji* so that you can place your argument within the ongoing critical conversation.

CONSIDER WHAT YOU THINK

The aim in thinking about your topic is to come up with fresh observations. After all, it's not enough to summarize in a paper what's obvious, what's already known and discussed. You must also add something of your own to the conversation.

Understand, however, that "adding something of your own" is not an invitation to allow your own personal associations, reactions, or experiences to dominate your paper. To create an informed argument, you must first recognize that your writing should be analytical rather than personal. In other words, your writing must show that your associations, reactions, and experiences of a work of literature have been framed in a critical, rather than a personal, way.

This is not to say that your personal responses to a work of literature are irrelevant. Indeed, your personal responses are often a good starting point for the academic work to come. For instance, being puzzled by the unfamiliar cultural assumptions of characters in *The Iliad* can be the first step on the way to a strong analysis. Interrogate your gut reaction. Why are you puzzled? Can you imagine what it would be like to value the things that these ancient warriors value? Does your interpretation of the work change as you learn more about the world from which this epic emerged?

Interrogating your personal responses is the first step in making sure that your argument will be appropriately academic. To help ensure that your responses are critical rather than personal, subject them to the following critical thinking processes: summary, evaluation, analysis, and synthesis.

SUMMARIZE

The first step in thinking critically about any work of literature is to summarize what it is saying. You can construct several different summaries, depending on your goals, but beware: even the most basic of summaries—the plot summary—isn't as simple as it seems. It's difficult to write both economically and descriptively, to discern what's essential to your discussion and what's not.

Consider this: William Shakespeare's *Hamlet* has a very complex plot—the play has a cast of more than thirty characters, and it takes well over four hours to perform it onstage. Perhaps the most widely performed, read, and studied play in English, *Hamlet* is nonetheless notoriously puzzling to first-time readers (or viewers) and well-informed scholars alike. In short, *Hamlet* is one of the most difficult plays to "sum up," and yet the following plot summary does an excellent job:

> Hamlet, a young Danish prince, returns to his home in Elsinore from his university studies abroad to find that his father, the king, is dead. Making matters worse, his uncle has married his mother and assumed the throne. Late one night, a ghost appears to Hamlet, claiming to be his father. The ghost announces that he was murdered—by his own brother, who stole both his wife and his crown. Hamlet vows revenge. However, whether plagued by doubts about the truth of what he has seen, or troubled by the implications for his immortal soul if he kills the new king, Hamlet

becomes lost in a fog of mental turmoil. In his uncertain course toward revenge, Hamlet berates his mother, accidentally kills the king's chief advisor, drives the advisor's daughter (whom he had previously courted) to suicide, and thereby provokes a duel with the advisor's son that eventually leaves the entire court of Elsinore dead. Arriving on the scene as Hamlet utters his last words, the crown prince of Norway claims the Danish throne.

What makes this summary effective? The writer of this summary traces the conflict without being sidetracked by too many of the plot's complications (of which there are many). He sticks to the theme and to the basic conflict/resolution structure. He also makes sure that his sentences are clear. In the end, he produces a summary that is faithful to the play but that doesn't overwhelm the reader with details.

Although you will rarely be asked to include a plot summary in a paper, the exercise of summarizing a literary work in this manner is a useful one. It hones your writing skills, alerts you to gaps in your understanding of the work, and helps you see the structure, conflicts, and themes of the work. But when thinking critically about literature, you needn't limit yourself to plot summary. Equally useful, depending on your purpose, are summaries of a particular work's origins, the author's life and times, similarities to other texts, and the work's reception by its audience and critics (reviews, scholarship, and so on). The point is that summarizing is useful in helping you clarify what you know about a work of literature, laying the foundation for the more complex processes to come.

EVALUATE

Evaluation is an ongoing process. You can evaluate a text the moment you encounter it, and you can continue to evaluate and to reevaluate as you go along. It's important to understand that evaluating a work of literature is different from reacting to it. When you evaluate for an academic purpose, you must find and articulate the reasons for your personal response. What in the text is leading you to respond a certain way? Which influences that are not in the text might be contributing to your response? Watching a performance of *Hamlet*, for instance, you might find yourself becoming impatient with the play's protagonist. What is making you feel this way? The words that Hamlet speaks? The actor's gestures and expressions? The sequence of scenes? Something else? Can you point to a moment in the play when you felt particularly impatient? In asking these questions, you are straddling two intellectual processes: experiencing your own personal response, and analyzing the play.

Evaluation also encourages you to compare a text with other texts that you've read. In a world literature course, this often means comparing texts from all corners of the globe. If you've just read Voltaire's *Candide*, you might ask yourself how it is similar to or notably different from Jonathan Swift's *Gulliver's Travels*. After all, they're both fictional travel narratives written in roughly the same period, though in different countries. You might also ask how either of those texts compares to Chikamatsu Monzaemon's *Love Suicides at Amijima*, written at roughly the same time, but several thousand miles away. Comparisons across time periods can be equally fruitful, especially since most world literature courses cover several centuries. For example, how does *Candide* compare to Molière's *Tartuffe*, both written in France about 100 years apart? Or how does Voltaire compare to twentieth-century French writers like Proust? The possibilities are many, and this process of evaluation will help you discover which aspects of the text are most interesting to you as you investigate them further. Remember: you only need to find one eye-catching idea to put you on the path toward writing a great paper.

ANALYZE

In the analysis stage of constructing an informed argument, your first task is to consider the parts of your topic that most interest you, then examine how these parts relate to one another or to the whole. To analyze *Hamlet* you will want to break the play down by examining particular scenes, particular characters, and particular actions. In short, you'll want to ask: What are the components of this play? How do these components contribute to the work as a whole? To analyze

Kalidasa's *Sakuntala and the Ring of Recollection*, you'll go through a similar process of asking questions that break the play down into its various components.

Ask about the play's structure: What is the purpose of the epigraph in praise of Shiva, or of the prologue at the beginning of Act I?

Ask about the characters and the role they play in the plot: What role does King Duyanta play in the story line? Is he an active player or a passive victim?

Ask about themes: What is the purpose of the nature imagery (flowers, bees, etc.)? What do the curse and its resolution tell you about the relationship in this play between the human and the divine?

Ask about the play's contexts: How does the play reflect the Hindu culture that produced it? Is the play effective in evoking Rasa in its audience? How so?

By asking these questions, you are examining individual components of the play. Your goal is to think about how each of those components functions within the complete work. When you analyze, you break the whole into parts so that you might see the whole differently. When you analyze, you find things to say.

SYNTHESIZE

We've seen that when you analyze, you break a work into its parts. When you synthesize, you look for connections between those parts. In analyzing *Hamlet* you might come up with elements that initially seem disparate. You might have some observations that at first don't seem to jell. Or you might have read various critical perspectives on the play, some of them disagreeing with one another. Now would be the time to consider whether these disparate elements or observations might be reconciled, or synthesized. This intellectual exercise requires that you create an umbrella argument—a larger argument under which several observations and perspectives might stand.

The introductory headnote to *Candide* in *The Norton Anthology of World Literature* provides an excellent example of synthesis. The author of the headnote points out that Voltaire wrote *Candide* to be "deliberately entertaining." The author then discusses the role of humor in the text, and in doing so recounts a lengthy list of comical incidents. It also is pointed out in the headnote that, in spite of the often-outrageous humor, "reality keeps intruding." The author then observes that several comical incidents in the text were inspired by tragic events in real life, such as the 1775 Lisbon earthquake, which had actually killed over 30,000 people. Educated and informed readers therefore not only laugh but are also invited to think seriously about the social and political issues that arise from historical events and their parodies. The author concludes: "The extravagances of the story are therefore uncomfortably matched by the extravagances of real life, and despite the comic lightness of the telling, Voltaire demands that the reader confront these horrors." This conclusion synthesizes the author's many observations about humor and horror, transforming this list of observations into a powerful argument about why humor is an important aspect of *Candide*.

Adopting a Rhetorical Stance

When writing an academic paper, you must consider not only what you want to say but also the audience to whom you're saying it. In other words, it's important to determine not only what you think about a topic but also what your audience is likely to think. What biases does your audience have? What values, expectations, and knowledge do they possess? For whom are you writing, and for what purpose?

When you begin to answer these questions, you have started to reckon with what has been called the "rhetorical stance," which refers to the position you take as a writer in terms of both the subject and the reader of your paper.

CONSIDER YOUR POSITION

Let's first consider your relationship to the topic you're writing about. When you write a paper, you take a stand on a topic. You determine whether you're for or against it, passionate or cool-headed. Because few issues can be reduced to pro and con or black and white, you'll also want to consider the nuances of your position. Finally, you may wish to consider whether or not your position takes a particular critical perspective (e.g., feminist). All of these considerations will enable you to refine your stance on a topic.

To ensure that your stance is appropriately analytical, you should ask yourself some questions. Begin by asking why you've taken this particular position. For instance, why did you find some elements of the work of literature more important than others? Does this prioritizing reflect a bias or preconception on your part? If you dismissed part of the work as boring or unimportant, why did you do so? Do you have personal issues or experiences that might lead you to be impatient with certain elements? Might any part of your response to the literary work cause readers to discount your paper as biased or uncritical? If so, you might want to reconsider your position, or, if you feel strongly about the argument you're trying to make, you will want to carefully plan how you will support that argument with evidence from the text.

CONSIDER YOUR AUDIENCE

Your position on a topic does not, by itself, determine your rhetorical stance. You must also consider your readers. In the college classroom, the audience is usually the professor or your classmates—although occasionally your professor will instruct you to write for a more particular or more general audience. No matter who your readers are, you'll want to consider them carefully before you start to write.

What do you know about your readers and their stance toward your topic? What are they likely to know about the topic? What biases are they likely to have? Moreover, what effect do you hope to have on the readers? Is your aim to be controversial? Informative? Entertaining? Will the readers appreciate or resent your intention?

Once you've determined who your readers are, you will want to consider how you might best reach them. If, for example, you're an authority on a particular subject and you're writing to readers who know little or nothing about that subject, you'll want to take an informative stance. If you aren't yet confident about a topic and you have more questions than answers, you might want to take an inquisitive stance.

In any case, when you're deciding on a rhetorical stance, choose one that allows you to be sincere. You don't want to take an authoritative stance on a subject if you cannot be confident about what you're saying. On the other hand, you don't want to avoid taking a position on a subject; readers are very often frustrated by writers who refuse to take a clear stance. What if you are of two minds on a subject? Declare that to the reader. Make ambivalence your clear rhetorical stance.

Finally, don't write simply to please your professor. Though some professors find it flattering to discover that all of their students share their positions on a subject, most of us are hoping that your argument will engage us by telling us something new about your topic—even if that "something new" is simply a fresh emphasis on a minor detail. Moreover, it's impossible for you to replicate the ideal paper that exists in your professor's head. When you try, you risk having your analysis compared to your professor's own. Is that really what you want?

Considering Tone and Style

So now you understand what's required of you in an academic paper. You need to be analytical. You need to create an informed argument. You need to consider your relationship to the topic and to the reader. But what about finding an appropriate academic tone and style?

The tone and style of academic writing might at first seem intimidating. But that needn't be the case. Professors want students to write clearly and intelligently on matters that they, the students, care about. What professors don't want is imitation scholarship—that is, exalted gibberish that no one cares to read. If the student didn't care to write the paper, the professor probably won't care to read it. The tone of an academic paper, then, must be inviting to the reader, even while it maintains an appropriate academic style.

Remember that professors are human beings, capable of boredom, laughter, irritation, and awe. They have lives outside of their duties as teachers, and they don't appreciate having their time wasted any more than you do. Understand that you're writing to a person who will be delighted when you make your point clearly, concisely, and persuasively. Understand, too, that she will be less delighted if you have inflated your prose, pumped up your page count, or tried to impress her by using terms that you didn't take the time to understand. (For more on how to craft an appropriate but engaging academic tone and style, see Chapter 7, "Attending to Style," later in this guide.)

2

Kinds of Writing About World Literature

Now that you have a sense of what it means to write an academic paper, you can think about what you need to do to write successfully about world literature. The study of world literature is a diverse and fascinating field. Scholars who write in this discipline write not only about particular works of literature but also about the authors, the cultural and historical contexts surrounding those works, and the history of the various genres of world literature. Let's turn our attention now to some of the kinds of papers that you will be asked to write in a world literature course.

Textual Analysis of a Work of Literature

One of the most common approaches to writing about world literature is textual analysis. Textual analysis requires the reader to break down the work into its different parts and to discuss how each part adds up to create the whole. This process is similar to taking apart a tractor in a field: you lay out the parts, try to understand the function and purpose of each one, and then put the parts back together. After doing this, you will no doubt understand much better how the tractor works, and you will be able to talk about its workings with precision and clarity. When it comes to taking apart a literary text, the particular pieces you're dealing with depend on the text you're analyzing. In a short poem you may need to look at rhythm, rhyme schemes, and the poet's use of rhetorical figures of speech. In novels or short stories you'll want to look at the characters, settings, motifs, and conflicts. In plays you'll need to look at characters' behavior, stage directions, instances of dramatic irony, and possibly soliloquies or other lengthy speeches. In all cases, you should think about the themes of the work, as well as the overall effect of reading the text, but be aware: themes are often best understood and written about when you view them through one of the afore-mentioned textual elements. In other words, as the author of a textual analysis paper, your goal is to choose one of these elements and examine in detail how that element contributes to the major themes or overall effect of the text.

Although some professors provide detailed instructions in their assignments—which topic to cover, which elements to discuss, and possibly even which part of the work to analyze—others permit students to choose the literary work and the overall topic they wish to discuss. Thus you might write a paper about characterization in Anton Chekhov's *The Cherry*

Orchard or the portrayal of time and memory in Marcel Proust's *Swann's Way*. Each of these topics clearly focuses on describing and interpreting the effectiveness of a single element or technique in a single work.

Contextual Analysis of a Work of Literature

A literary work's concerns are almost always oriented toward society—humans living among humans. To thoroughly understand a literary work, you must therefore consider the work's social, cultural, and political contexts. Understanding the context in which a work of literature is produced and enjoyed is especially important in a world literature course, where you are being asked to interpret texts from cultures across the globe.

To uncover a work's cultural or political arguments, you will want to undertake a contextual analysis. Contextual analysis involves examining the relationship between a work and its contexts: the social norms and political environment of the culture in which it was written, the historical events before or during the author's life, the literary tradition and popular culture in the region at that time, and so on. Four useful questions you can ask yourself to find fruitful approaches to a contextual analysis paper follow:

1. How is this text a *product* of its historical or cultural context? In other words, what historical or cultural forces conspired to create this particular work of literature? For instance,

for almost a century before Chikamatsu Monzaemon wrote *Love Suicides at Amijima*, Japan had been experiencing a population shift toward urban centers. The relative prosperity of the middle and working classes created a demand for popular entertainment. Chikamatsu's *Bunraku* productions filled that demand, providing insight into the lives, customs, and values of the people of Osaka at that time.

2. How does the text *reflect* its cultural context? In other words, in what ways does the text serve as a historical document that allows readers to reconstruct the society in which it was composed? Consider *The Epic of Gilgamesh*, which exemplifies this idea quite well. Though most of its key events are clearly mythic, the text illustrates several cultural values that are important to the society that produced it: fraternal affection; the power of sexuality; the importance of the distinction between civilization and wild savagery; and the idea that since biological immortality is impossible, a form of immortality can be achieved by creating lasting works on earth.

3. How did the text *influence* future historical events or inspire social change? *Candide* (along with many other texts from the European Enlightenment period) is often credited with helping to inspire the American and French Revolutions near the end of the eighteenth century. If you peruse historical documents associated with those events—for example, *Common Sense*, the Declaration of

Independence, or the Declaration of the Rights of Man and Citizen—you might find similarities between those documents' ideologies and the ideas from *Candide*. Which specific parts of the novel provide this potential influence?

4. How does the text *comment* upon recent history? To what purpose? A classic example of cultural commentary is Chinua Achebe's novel *Things Fall Apart*, in which Achebe critiques the colonization of Africa. What, precisely, is Achebe condemning in the political systems that he critiques? How is this critique rendered in the novel?

Once you've determined how a work is speaking to, about, or from its historical and cultural contexts, you will want to consider the work's political views. Granted, not all literature expresses a clear political ideology. Nevertheless, even when a work avoids expressing overtly political or ideological messages, it cannot help but convey subtle attitudes about the social arrangements and problems portrayed within. As you try to sort out a work's political argument, you might consider the following questions:

Does the work of literature seem to espouse a particular set of beliefs and values?

Is the work bringing competing beliefs and values into conflict with each other? If so, what is the writer telling us, explicitly and implicitly, about these beliefs and values?

Does the work seem explicitly political? Or, is it more generally concerned with portraying a social problem?

Does any character in the work consistently embody a particular worldview? What happens to this character? Are we meant to sympathize with him or her?

Knowing what you know about the history of the work and the time in which it was written, can you say whether or not the work is responding to a major cultural crisis—for example, a war, a famine, a political revolution, a grave injustice—**that the author would have been concerned about?**

How was the work first received when it was published? What does this early reception tell you about the work's relationship to the prevailing values of the culture in which it was written and performed?

Comparison Papers

Sometimes a professor will ask you to do a formal analysis paper comparing and/or contrasting two or more works of literature. A comparative study requires that you look at specific elements in each text and compare or contrast their qualities. Two strategies tend to produce good results. First, you might take two things assumed to be very similar but then go on to show important differences between the two (for example, comparing the story "The Death of Atsumori" from the epic *Heike Monogatari* to Zeami Motokiyo's play *Atsumori*). Second, you might take two things assumed to be very dissimilar and show important similarities (for example, describing how an important religious text, the *Bhagavad Gita*, and a heroic epic, *Beowulf*, both dramatize the tensions between violence, loyalties, and revenge). Whatever strategy you choose, remember: for a compare/contrast paper to be effective, the writer must be sure to limit the comparison to the most salient points. A paper that articulates carefully a few important comparisons or contrasts and analyzes their significance will fare much better than a paper that simply presents a laundry list of similarities and differences with no analysis or commentary.

The following hypothetical paper assignments show how the comparative approach is well suited to producing insightful and interesting papers:

1. Compare Sophocles' *Oedipus the King* to Euripides' *Medea* with respect to human relationships and dynamics with the gods. How does Euripides' worldview differ from Sophocles' worldview?

2. Compare and contrast the central character in the *Bhagavad Gita* with the eponymous hero of *Beowulf*. What do the differences between these two heroes tell us about the cultures in which they were composed (India during the first century B.C.E. and ninth-century Anglo-Saxon England)?

3. Compare Derek Walcott's *Omeros* to Homer's *Odyssey* in terms of conventions of epic poetry. Which conventions does Walcott keep and which does he ignore? Of those that he retains, does he modify them in any way? How does the use of epic conventions suit the needs of this particular text?

Note that the first assignment asks you to compare between two works that were written within the same cultural milieu, by two playwrights who were alive at the same time and aware of each other's work. The differences between their two plays thus arise from the playwrights' individual styles and world-views. The second assignment asks you to use two heroic figures as windows into the respective cultures in which the works about them were composed. The third assignment asks you to compare particular textual elements from two works created thousands of years and thousands of miles apart. In this case you are being asked to examine the nature of literary influence and the way one author can build on such influence to make his writing relevant in a new social and geopolitical context.

Writing About Adaptation

Since works of literature resonate strongly with their readers, many works are adapted to new forms to reach new audiences. Although the most common mode of adaptation is turning a work of literature into a film, adaptation can take many unusual and interesting forms. Samuel Taylor Coleridge's poem "The Rime of the Ancient Mariner," for example, was adapted into a heavy metal song by Iron Maiden. *Candide* was turned into an opera by Lillian Hellman and Leonard Bernstein. The Brothers Quay created a stop-motion animation short film based loosely on the beginning to *The Epic Gilgamesh*.

Writing a paper about an adapted work is typically a form of comparison paper—you are comparing the original text to the adaptation (or, sometimes, to multiple adaptations). As with any comparison paper, merely writing a laundry list of similarities and differences won't be very interesting—for you or for your reader. Rather, you should try to examine the significance of the differences you've observed, particularly any differences produced by the new form. Iron Maiden's "Rime of the Ancient Mariner," for instance, includes a lengthy pause with a voiceover between two verses. What effect does this adaptation have on your impression of the story? How does it contribute to the presentation of the piece? Since it is a musical adaptation, the artists have control over tempo and volume in ways that Coleridge does not in his written version. Does the band successfully take advantage of the adapted form?

In addition to the differences, you should also pay attention to notable similarities. Most of the Iron Maiden adaptation tells the story of the mariner using words and phrases that do not actually appear in Coleridge's poem. Neverthe-less, a few sections quote the poem verbatim. Why is that? Why leave those sections entirely unchanged while modify-ing everything else?

Once you've determined the differences and similarities between the two works, ask yourself two key questions. First, is the adaptation true to the original text? For instance, if the original text has an underlying political, social, or moral mes-sage, does the adaptation successfully present a similar mes-sage? Second, what is the purpose of the adaptation? Is it merely a matter of reaching a different audience? Does the adapted version change or update the message of the original in some way? You'll want to articulate as clearly as possible what that particular adaptation is trying to accomplish.

The list of adaptations you could write about is long—especially when you consider that not every adaptation uses the same title as the original literary work. Disney's animated film *The Lion King* is an adaptation of Shakespeare's *Hamlet*. New versions of older works put into modern settings are sometimes not really adaptations but, rather, retellings or new visions of an older work. The film *Bedazzled* (2000) is essen-tially a retelling of the Faust myth, as are countless other books and films based on the notion of a Faustian bargain. The multiple adaptations and retellings of *Faust*—in forms as varied as stage drama, opera, film, and more—provide ample opportunities for comparison papers.

Translation

Translating a work from one language to another is really just a form of adaptation. In world literature courses, many of the texts you read are works that were originally written in languages other than English. Inevitably, any two translations of a work will be different, sometimes radically different, from each other. Evaluating a work of literature by comparing various translations can lead you to interesting, eye-opening discoveries. If you are able to read the text in its original language, you will be able to evaluate the relationship between the original and its English translation.

Essay Exams

Not everything you write in a world literature course will involve writing papers per se. In fact, in many world literature classrooms, there are no formal writing requirements. Instead, many courses use in-class "essay exams," where you are expected to write a short essay in class during a timed examination period. Most of the advice in this book still applies to essay exams, but you may need to make a few adjustments to your writing process.

There are two important differences between an essay exam and a take-home essay: you likely won't be able to do any research or use any outside sources, and you have a time limit. These differences require a slightly different approach to the assignment.

First you need to consider the type of essay you're writing. In some cases your professor will give a specific essay prompt on an exam, but you also might find that the prompt is so broad that you're basically coming up with your own topic. Take a moment and look back at the kinds of writing assignments described earlier. You'll probably notice right away that some of these types of papers lend themselves to in-class writing better than others. Textual analysis will work quite well, because all you need is your memory and your knowledge of the primary text. Comparative analysis is also a reasonable possibility, because you will surely have a strong working knowledge of more than one primary text that you read for the class.

Contextual analysis might work, but you need to keep in mind that you won't be able to do any research, so in this case you are limited to the knowledge of history, culture, or other relevant information that you already have when you enter the classroom. However, if you happen to know a lot about, for instance, early eighteenth-century Japan and for your final exam you have to write an essay on Chikamatsu Monzaemon's *Love Suicides at Amijima*, then you're in luck! You already have the tools to incorporate historical context into your essay.

Except in unusual circumstances, writing about adaptation is probably not a good choice for an essay test. Reading (or viewing, or listening to) the adapted form of the work is essentially a specific form of research, which you won't be able to perform during the exam. So unless you have an exceptionally strong knowledge of, for example, a film version of the primary text about which you are writing, it's probably better to choose a different essay form.

The other factor you need to consider for essay exams is the time limit, which should affect your preparatory work. You have two goals for your prep work: do it quickly, and make it effective so you can also write the essay quickly. Obviously when you're in a timed environment, you don't want to waste a lot of time generating and organizing your ideas before you actually start writing the essay. If you do, you run the risk of not having enough time to finish. On the other hand, you don't want to just jump right into the essay without any forethought. If you perform your preparatory work well, it should make the essay-writing process go much faster and will end up saving you time.

In the next chapter we will present some techniques for generating ideas: brainstorming, freewriting, a discovery draft, five Ws and an H, and so on. If you are taking a course in which the essay test is the primary writing requirement, read the descriptions of these idea-generating techniques with a critical eye. Some of these techniques are more useful for essay tests than others, mostly because of how long they will take you to perform. Brainstorming (page 41), for example, can be fairly quick, so it's a good strategy to employ when taking an essay test. The journalistic "five Ws and an H" technique (page 48) is also fast, and it gives you a specific goal. Even tagmemics (page 49) or a very brief run through the topoi (page 51) could prove useful. Use whichever method you've found to be quick and efficient.

After you come up with some ideas, it might be tempting to start writing—after all, you don't want to waste any time, right? But you should resist that temptation. You'll probably find that it's actually more time-efficient not to start writing until you have a plan. So take the ideas from your brainstorming or other exercises and organize them into a coherent outline. You needn't produce something fancy. Just make a quick sketch to see how the essay will take shape, and then start writing. With the outline to guide you, the writing process should go much more quickly, although the fact that it will end up saving you time is actually just an added bonus. The real reason to use an outline is that it will improve the quality (the coherence and the clarity) of your essay, and it will keep you from getting lost in your many good ideas.

It's important to keep in mind that even though in-class writing and essay tests will feel different from regular essay assignments, the differences we've just discussed are really the only major distinctions. Almost everything else is the same, and the other pieces of advice you'll read about in this book—such as developing your thesis, organizing your argument, arranging your paragraphs, and making your essay coherent—all still apply.

One final note: on an essay test, it's often a good idea to plan out how you'll spend your time at the beginning of the exam period. Let's suppose you have a mid-term exam in a 50-minute class session. Your professor gives you three prompts and tells you to choose one. Your plan for the exam might look like this:

2 minutes: think about the prompts and pick one

5 minutes: brainstorm

7 minutes: nutshell from the brainstorm; come up with a working thesis

7 minutes: create a detailed outline

25 minutes: write the essay

4 minutes: reread what you've written and make revisions

Whichever schedule you put yourself on, make sure you dedicate enough time to preparatory work and outlining. It will make writing the essay a lot easier.

In some situations, completing detailed preparatory work may also have a hidden benefit. If you unfortunately run out of time before completing the essay, your brainstorming notes and outline will help show your professor what you would have written if the exam period were longer. An outline, of course, is not a substitute for an actual essay. Nevertheless, some instructors may be more generous in their grading if your preparatory work shows that you understand the material and that you likely would have written a high-quality essay if you had had more time. Such grading decisions are up to individual instructors, and we cannot guarantee that your instructor will give partial credit for a good outline—but providing an outline probably won't hurt.

3

Generating Ideas

In some ways writing about literature is similar to writing on any subject: you must choose a topic, generate ideas, research your topic, craft a thesis, structure your argument, and find the proper tone. But each of these more general tasks requires you to perform some tasks that are specific to the study of world literature. For instance, you must know how to read literature imaginatively and analytically, how to use specialized language appropriately, and how to use research resources effectively. The following section combines general advice with suggestions specific to the study of world literature, with the aim of helping you produce better papers for your world literature class.

Reading Critically / Reading Creatively

As we've said earlier, literature is a social phenomenon. However, the act of reading is usually an individual pursuit. While there are many advantages to the individual nature of reading (you can read at your own pace, wherever and whenever you like), there are some disadvantages as well. When you have social interactions with other people, your communication will involve much more than just words; for example, hand gestures, facial expressions, tone of voice, and other behaviors convey meaning. When you read, however, you don't have the benefit of that additional information. Authors therefore use other techniques to help convey their meaning. It is your job as a reader to identify and decipher the clues the author leaves for you.

READING CRITICALLY

Critical reading is essentially looking beyond what a text *says* to discover what it *means*. Critical reading begins with the understanding that the words you see on the page are only a starting point, and that other information is available to you. You should examine the way those words are presented, as well as the choices the author makes in crafting the text: language and tone, figures of speech, humor, rhythm, and so on. You should also try to determine what purpose these textual elements serve. A few simple examples follow.

Identify irony

In the first chapter of Voltaire's *Candide*, the narrator provides Candide's thoughts about the home of Baron Thunder-ten-tronkch: "The Baron was one of the most mighty lords in Westphalia because his castle had a door and windows. His great hall was even hung with a tapestry." At first glance this description appears to be filled with high praise, especially since it begins by describing the baron as "one of the most mighty lords" of his region. However, if you read a little closer and think about the details of the passage, you'll notice that the text is actually implying the opposite—the baron is not particularly wealthy or powerful (at least not by aristocratic standards). The best thing the narrator can say about the castle is that it has a door and windows, just like every other castle in Europe. Its decorations are not described as including lavish artwork, jewelry, reliquaries, and the like. Rather, the castle has only one tapestry. Determining that the "praise" heaped upon the baron's home is ironic is an important part of understanding this chapter. Think about the purpose this irony serves. In this case the irony indicates that the protagonist is naively optimistic: he thinks the best of his situation regardless of any evidence to the contrary. Understanding this characterization of Candide will help you understand his thought process and decision making throughout the text. In this way the irony of the passage provides a key to help you read the rest of the work. You now know that the narrator often provides information ironically—and you can read accordingly.

Identify implied information
Very often, authors will provide information about characters or events via clues that you must decipher. In James Joyce's short story "Araby," the young narrator spends a few hours

35

waiting for his uncle to come home. The narrator describes his eventual arrival: "At nine o'clock I heard my uncle's latchkey in the halldoor. I heard him talking to himself and heard the hallstand rocking when it had received the weight of his overcoat. I could interpret these signs." Try a quick exercise and answer the following questions: Why is the narrator's uncle late coming home? Where was he? How can you tell?

READING CREATIVELY

Along with reading critically, you should also practice reading creatively. Often, texts will imply information or build on abstract ideas, and you must imaginatively interpret the contents of the work in order to understand it. Here are a few examples:

Interpret textual details imaginatively

Again in the first chapter of Voltaire's *Candide*, the Baron's daughter Cunégonde has an interesting experience: "One day, as Cunégonde was walking near the castle in the little woods that they called a park, she saw Dr. Pangloss in the underbrush; he was giving a lesson in experimental physics to her mother's maid, a very attractive and obedient brunette. As Miss Cunégonde had a natural bent for the sciences, she watched breathlessly the repeated experiments which were going on; she saw clearly the doctor's sufficient reason, observed both cause and effect, and returned to the house in a distracted and pensive frame of mind, yearning for knowledge and dreaming that she might be the sufficient reason of young Candide." If you read the first sentence of this passage critically, you'll find clues that show Pangloss is definitely having sexual intercourse with the maid in the bushes. The fact that he's in the underbrush to begin with indicates he's trying to hide, and the information about the maid's appearance would not be especially important if he were actually teaching her about experimental physics. Knowing what the characters are actually doing here, you can envision the scene as the rest of it is told through euphemisms such as "sufficient reason" and "cause and effect." You'll know exactly why Cunégonde goes back to the house looking for Candide.

Imagine the world of the text

Jorge Luis Borges's short story "The Garden of Forking Paths" involves a fictional book by the deceased writer Ts'ui Pen. In this passage a character explains how this book is unlike all others: "In all fictional works, each time a man is confronted with several alternatives, he chooses one and eliminates the others; in the fiction of Ts'ui Pen, he chooses—simultaneously—all of them. He *creates*, in this way, diverse futures, diverse times which themselves also proliferate and fork." The world of this fictional book is one in which multiple realities exist simultaneously. This world is very different from the world we all inhabit, and it requires creative thinking to understand it. But once you are able to imagine this world, you should be able to apply that same creativity toward analyzing its role within the text.

Immersing Yourself in the World of the Text

Many texts you read in a world literature class will come from countries or time periods you don't know much about. A little background information about the historical and cultural contexts of the work will help your understanding of it tremendously. This background investigation doesn't have to involve extensive, time-consuming research—even just a little bit of pertinent information will be useful. If you don't really know where to begin, a good starting point is to use the advice from the previous section and try to imagine the text. Start by finding basic information that will help you create that mental picture: *How should the characters dress?* Fashion choices might be different for wealthy characters than for poor characters, or they might differ due to the characters' jobs, social standing, and so on. *How do people in this society talk?* Consider the language characters are speaking, as well as the patterns and habits of discourse they exhibit. *What is normal behavior?* Investigate dominant social values or mores. Consider whether characters act in accordance with those values or whether they violate them.

If you want to delve further into the world of the text, you might want to look at some of the questions raised in the section "Contextual Analysis of a Work of Literature" in Chapter 2 in this guide. Or just start with anything that seems interesting and see where your research takes you. Try to have fun with it—one of the great pleasures of a world literature course is the opportunity to learn about far-off places and people you might otherwise never know anything about.

Using Specialized Language

Think back to the dinner party we talked about at the beginning of the book. Just as it's a good idea to familiarize yourself with the ongoing conversation before jumping in, it's also a good idea to make sure that when you start speaking, you understand the terms of this particular conversation. Virtually every industry, discipline, or activity has its own vocabulary, and literature is no different. Learning and using appropriate terminology will make your job as a scholarly writer much easier.

Start with the basics. If you're writing about a play, be sure to refer to it as a play, not as a novel or short story. Learn to recognize common, frequently used figures of speech such as metaphor, metonymy, and simile; learn the differences between them and when to use them. You certainly don't need to learn every literary term all at once (or ever), but as you read more, you'll be exposed to additional literary techniques, and you should make an effort to learn them as you come across them. Remember how they differ from terms you already know so you can use the correct terminology when you write.

For more complicated terminology, let your instructor guide you. If you read Zeami's play *Atsumori*, your instructor might tell you about Noh drama. You may use this term much less frequently than "metaphor" or "irony," but if you plan to write a paper about *Atsumori*, it's a good idea to have a basic understanding of Noh drama, and you may wish to do additional research. If you learn about the differences between various forms of Japanese drama, such as Noh, Kabuki, and Bunraku, then it will become easier to talk and write about each of them. The bottom line is you should learn whatever terms you need in order to sound persuasive when you join the conversation at the dinner party.

Generating Ideas

While reading a work of literature, you will usually come up with some ideas worth writing about. But what if you've read the work a few times and you still haven't found anything that you feel is worth exploring? Or what if you've found an idea for writing, but you haven't yet discovered how you might develop that idea? In any of these situations you might want to take the time to try one of the following strategies for generating ideas.

CONVERSATION

After experiencing cultural events on our own time—for instance, after seeing a movie or attending a concert—we typically talk about it with others as soon as we leave the venue. Those conversations often leave us thinking about the movie or concert in new and interesting ways. Similarly, conversations with your classmates about the works of literature that you've read for class can help you discover what's interesting about a particular work. Note, however, that the kinds of conversations that we have with our friends—which are often freewheeling, opinionated, and more emotional than intellectual—mark just the beginning of scholarly inquiry. Still, talking with friends can be useful in exploring differences of opinion and in encouraging you to articulate and back up your point of view.

BRAINSTORMING

Another way to formulate ideas is to brainstorm. Brainstorming is useful because it is a quick and efficient way of laying out what you know about a subject. By brainstorming, you might also see what you don't know about a topic, which might move you to read and think further.

Suppose you have decided to brainstorm for a paper on *The Epic of Gilgamesh*. You might make a list like the one that follows:

The Epic of Gilgamesh
- is an epic poem;
- is about an ancient Sumerian king;

- involves a lot of sex;
- involves battles with some crazy-looking beasts/ monsters;
- emphasizes the difference between gods and humans;
- emphasizes the difference between civilized people and wild barbarians;
- contains some interesting similarities to the Old Testament (the snake, the flood) but was written much earlier;
- involves a failed search for immortality;
- isn't as fun or interesting to read as Homer's *Odyssey*.

As this list illustrates, brainstorming is an informal strategy for invention in which you jot down, as quickly as you can, ideas concerning your topic. The ideas don't have to be connected—though sometimes looking for connections will yield a paper topic. For instance, you might want to write a paper arguing that while *The Epic of Gilgamesh* is very much of its time and calls attention to issues important to ancient Mesopotamian culture, it seems fresh and contemporary even now because one of the themes at the center of the work—coming to terms with one's own mortality—will always be with us.

Remember that you can also stop at any point in the writing process to brainstorm, especially when you feel that you're stuck or that you have to fill in some gaps in your argument. In short, when you brainstorm you freely explore your topic without the pressure of structure, grammar, or style. In the process, ideas for an essay (or a paragraph, or even a foot-note) can evolve unhindered.

FREEWRITING

Freewriting is similar to brainstorming in that it is a quick and informal way to develop an idea. But whereas brainstorming most often involves making a list of ideas, freewriting requires that you try to elaborate on these ideas by writing about them, without paying close attention to syntax or grammar. In this way, freewriting can get you "unstuck" when coming up with ideas is difficult.

Here's an example (and note that this freewriting, since it is meant for the writer's eyes only, is very informal—with spelling, grammar, and punctuation errors intact).

> OK, so I just finished Samuel Beckett's Endgame and, wow, I'm supposed to write a paper on it but I have no idea what I'm going to say. It was easy enough to read, but half the time I was wondering what the heck was the point of all the talking, and when was something going to happen. but still i gotta come up with something. where to start? maybe i should begin with the point in the play where I realized that it's supposed to be funny in places, like when Nagg tells Nell "Our hearing hasn't failed" and she replise "Our what?" Up to that point, I didn't know what to make of the play. I even worried that it was going to be a long, depressing play. And sure, it is depressing.

But it's also funny at times, in a dark way, but still funny. lots of the humor is about words and what they mean, and how the things we say don't connect to the things we do, like Clov always telling Hamm "I'll leave you," but he never does. Even at the end of the play he's dressed to go but he just stands near the door watching Hamm until the end. At the beginning of the play, I wouldn't know what to make of that. But after awhile, I actually laughed when Clov would say "I'll leave you, I have things to do." The end when he's just standing there is a little sad, though. So, it's funny in a way, but clearly it's dark, and words seem to be at the heart of what makes the play dark, too. And the "action" of the play is also a sad (but sometimes funny) parody of real action in the form of words. I didn't even realize it as I was doing it, but I just put quotation marks around the word "action". I guess that's becuse there's really not much action at all. Infact, most of the play seems like it's about inaction. Like Nagg and Nell—they cant move at all. The whole idea of not going anywhere seems like it's really important in the play. That must be why Clov keeps talking about leaving but never doing it. So maybe I can write about that—inaction, people not moving, not doing stuff. It's so different from most plays I've read. hmmmm. i guess this was a pretty successful freewrite. all i had to do was push buttons and some ideas popped out. pushing buttons is a lot more fun than just sitting and staring at a blank screen.

DISCOVERY DRAFT

A discovery draft is another strategy for coming up with or developing your ideas. A discovery draft is similar to freewriting in that you can write freely, with little thought to the structure and the development of your ideas for the time being. You can also forget about matters of syntax and style. However, writing a discovery draft is different from freewriting in that a discovery draft makes a conscious attempt to focus on and develop an idea or a cluster of ideas. In other words, a discovery draft is like freewriting with an agenda. And because you have an agenda, a discovery draft tends to be more structured than freewriting, and to be written more or less coherently, in complete sentences.

Think of writing a discovery draft as writing a letter to a friend about your paper. You might first summarize, for your friend's benefit, the literary work and the issues it presents. You might then raise questions about the work. You might challenge the author on certain points. You might point out a certain part of the work that you found compelling. You might address and then work out any confusion that you have about the work's plot or characterization. In writing the discovery draft you might have an aha! moment in which you see something you hadn't seen before and break off mid-sentence to explore it.

In a sense, the aha! moment is the point of the discovery draft. When writing the discovery draft, your thoughts are focused on your topic. You're giving language to your questions and observations. In this process, the mind almost always stumbles across something new—it makes a discovery. And with this discovery, a paper is often launched.

An example of the beginning of a discovery draft follows:

In Endgame, a lot of words and phrases are repeated very often throughout the play. Sometimes even entire mini-conversations are repeated. The most obvious repeated words are "end" and "finish," or variations of those words, like "ending," or "finished." This repetition must be connected to the title, Endgame. Both the title and the constant use of the words "end" and "finish" seem to suggest that the characters are just waiting for their lives to end, not really doing anything about it. In fact, they're not really doing much of anything at all.

Another repeated phrase is Clov's ongoing threat "I'll leave you." Sometimes he follows it up with "I have things to do." Hamm always seems skeptical. He's skeptical both that Clov will leave and that he has anything he needs to do.

The phrase that really sticks out is Hamm asking for his pain-killer, which he does a lot. Clov always responds that it's not time for it yet, until the last time Hamm asks. Then Clov tells him there aren't any pain-killers left. It seems like a metaphor—there's no way to escape the pain.

All of this repetition must mean something. Let's look closer at one of the examples. As I already said, Clov is always telling Hamm he's going to leave because he has "things to do," but he never really does anything except talk to Hamm. Even at the end of the play, when he finally acts like he might actually leave, he just stands by the door, watching and waiting. He never really does much of anything, and neither does Hamm. Furthermore, since it seems like there aren't any other people anywhere, the situation Hamm and Clov find themselves in seems to represent Beckett's view of the human condition: everyone is waiting to die. That's why the characters keep using the words "end" and "finish:" they're just waiting to die. The pain-killer incident really hammers home the point: There's no point in doing anything, because all people are basically just waiting to die, and there's no escaping that fate.

Notice that this is more formal than a freewriting exercise. It always uses complete sentences and correct grammar, and it follows a logical train of thought. However, it's still not nearly as formal as a paper that you would hand in to your professor. It uses casual, colloquial language, and it doesn't state ideas as strongly as it might (because as you write a discovery draft, you're often still trying to figure out what, exactly, those ideas are). Also notice that the discovery draft uses some of the thoughts that showed up in the freewrite. Freewriting helps you find ideas that might be useful in your paper; the discovery draft helps you figure out how they're useful and what you might say about them. A student who writes this freewriting exercise and this discovery draft about *Endgame* is now well on the way to a solid, working thesis.

FIVE Ws AND AN H

Journalism has provided us with perhaps the simplest and most familiar way of coming up with a topic: simply ask questions such as *who, what, when, where, why,* and *how.* Answering these questions initially doesn't seem very hard—at least until one gets to the *why* and *how.* Then it gets tricky.

Let's use this method to try to generate ideas for a paper on Chinua Achebe's *Things Fall Apart.* Maybe when you were reading the novel you got interested in the use of Igbo proverbs and aphorisms in the text, so you have a topic you want to explore. Now begin your interrogation:

Where in the novel do you find aphorisms? Mark the sections.

What are the aphorisms? Write down each specific proverb and what you think it means.

Who is reciting the proverbs, and who is listening to them? Consider not only who might be listening within the text but who is listening *beyond* the text. Who are the book's various audiences?

When in the novel do the aphorisms appear? What is happening in those moments? What purpose do the aphorisms serve at this particular moment?

How is the proverb presented? Is it spoken by a character? Is it part of the narration? How does it comment on the rest of the scene, or on the novel as a whole?

After thinking about the answers to the aforementioned

questions, ask yourself: *Why do aphorisms and proverbs play such a prominent role in* Things Fall Apart?

The last question is a tough one. But it's precisely when you have difficulty answering a *why* question that a real paper is beginning to emerge. When the answer comes too easily, you're on familiar ground, so you're probably not saying anything interesting. Cultivate a taste for confusion. Then cultivate a strategy for clearing up confusion. Only when you ask a question that initially confuses you can real thinking and real writing begin.

TAGMEMICS

Tagmemics is a system that allows you to look at a single object from three different perspectives. One of these perspectives (or even all three) can help you determine a subject for writing. By extending an analogy regarding the different ways physicists think about light, tagmemics involves seeing your topic

as a particle (as a thing in itself);
as a wave (as a thing changing over time);
as part of a field (as a thing in its context).

Suppose you want to write a paper on Bertolt Brecht's *The Good Woman of Szechwan*. If you use tagmemics as a system of invention, you will begin by looking at the play as a thing in itself. In other words, you will do a close textual reading, paying attention to the words on the page and the implications those words have for a staged production.

Next you might consider how the play has changed over time. How was the play received in its day? How does this reception compare to current assessments of the play? Research notable productions of the play. Which elements of the play have been emphasized in each production? How has the approach to the play changed over time?

Finally, consider *The Good Woman of Szechwan* as a thing in context. Relate it to its culture, to its moment in time. Work on *The Good Woman* was begun in 1938, while Brecht was in exile from his native Germany in Finland. The play was finally finished and staged in 1943, by which time Brecht was in the United States, where he would remain until 1947. What was happening in the world between 1938 and 1943? Most significantly, Nazi Germany during this period finally launched what would become known as World War II. Germany was also perpetrating the mass killing of Jews and other "undesirables" within its sphere of influence. By early 1943 the Soviet Union had defeated the Germans at Stalingrad—a victory that turned the tide of Hitler's campaign on the Eastern Front, and in the war overall. Might these events be reflected in the play in some way? How? And why?

ARISTOTLE'S TOPOI

As one of the fathers of rhetoric, Aristotle worked to formalize a system for conceiving, organizing, and expressing ideas. We're concerned here with what Aristotle called the "topoi"—a system of specific strategies for invention. Think of the topoi as a series of questions that you might ask of a work of literature— questions that might lead you to interesting paper topics. The topoi are especially helpful when you're asked to explore a topic that seems very broad. Consider, for instance, how using the topoi can help you write a paper on the importance of Aimé Césaire's *Notebook of a Return to the Native Land* to late twentieth-century understandings of postcolonial literature.

Use definition

You can use definition in two ways to come up with or develop a topic. First you might look at "genus," which Aristotle explains as defining a general idea within specific limits. For example, you could define "postcolonial" with the intent of showing how *Notebook* epitomizes a postcolonial mentality or how the book illustrates the postcolonial condition.

The second way to use definition is to think in terms of division. In other words, try to think of your subject in terms of its parts. For example, identify the aspects of *Notebook* that are most significant with regard to postcolonial politics, or with regard to other well-known works of literature by post- colonial authors.

Use comparison

You can generate ideas by making comparisons in two ways. The first is to look for similarities and/or differences. For example, you might determine how *Notebook* stands apart from other important works of postcolonial poetry, such as Derek Walcott's *Omeros*.

The second method is to compare degree. In other words, you might consider how something is more or less than something else in some particular regard, or perhaps better or worse. For example, is *Notebook* a better representation of Caribbean postcolonial thought than *Omeros*, or works by Jamaica Kincaid? Why or why not? What if you expand that comparison beyond the Caribbean to other parts of the world?

Explore relationships

Aristotle determined four ways of exploring relationships as a strategy for coming up with ideas for writing. The first is to consider either the cause of your subject or its effects. For example, you might research the effects that *Notebook* has had on subsequent poetry, postcolonial or otherwise.

Second, you might consider a subject's antecedent and consequences. In other words, you might ask this question of your subject: If this, then what? For example, if *Notebook* hadn't been written, would poetry or postcolonial literature today look any different?

Third, you might examine contraries, or make an argument

by proving its opposite. An example is to say that war is bad in order to convey the idea that peace is good. Along these lines, you might argue that *Notebook* is a significant work of postcolonial poetry by showing how others miss the mark.

Finally, you might look for contradictions, incompatible statements, or controversy. For example, some critics feel that *Notebook* is one of the greatest poems of the twentieth century; others feel that it's overrated, too confusing and abstract, and deliberately provocative. You can explore the controversy and stake a claim of your own.

Examine circumstances

In seeking an idea for a paper, you can examine circumstances in two ways. The first is to consider the possible and the impossible. Sometimes you can construct an interesting argument by considering what's possible and what's not. For example, imagine if it is possible for Césaire to have written *Notebook* if he had not lived for several years in France. How might his perspective and his art be different if he never left Martinique?

The second strategy is to consider the past or to look to the future. For example, in what ways does *Notebook* influence poets (or other writers) today? In what ways was it influenced by the long history of poetry, or the relatively shorter history of postcolonial literature, and in what ways does it diverge from that history?

Rely on testimony

The opinions of others can be a source for your paper. Look to authorities, testimonials, statistics, maxims, laws, and precedents. For example, you might read what critics have to say about *Notebook* with regard to Césaire's relationship to his friend Leopold Sedar Senghor, or you might think about what the poem's continued success says about it.

Developing Your Ideas

You've done some preliminary brainstorming. Perhaps you've even completed a discovery draft. The problem sitting before you now is that you have too many ideas and you don't know what to do with them, or the ideas you've come up with don't seem to be adequately academic. What do you try next?

NUTSHELLING

Nutshelling is the simple process of trying to explain the main point of your observations in a few sentences—in a nutshell. When you put your thoughts in a nutshell, you come to see just how those thoughts fit together. You see how each thought is relevant to the others, and what the overall point is. In short, nutshelling helps you transform your observations or information into something meaningful, focused, and coherent. For instance, if we return to the ideas about

Beckett's *Endgame* from the sections on freewriting and writing a discovery draft, we can nutshell the main points:

> The fact that nothing ever seems to happen in *Endgame* isn't a flaw that makes the play boring—it's actually the main point of the play. The characters are basically just waiting around to die, both unwilling and unable to prevent or delay their deaths, or even to take any meaningful action whatsoever. From Beckett's perspective, that is the fundamental condition of all humans.

BROADENING YOUR TOPIC

What happens when you've put your thoughts in a nutshell and they seem too "small"? You may have come up with a topic that's too narrow, too particular to support a sustained conversation.

Suppose your assignment is to write a paper on Tayeb Salih's "The Doum Tree of Wad Hamid." As you read, you notice a repeating pattern in which various government officials come to the village with a plan to help modernize life there, always at the expense of the sacred tree, and you decide this is a good topic to explore further for your paper.

You take notes about three keys parts of the story: the colonial official who wants to cut down the tree because its location is perfect for the water pump he wants to construct; the post-independence civil servant who wants to build a dock for the river steamer right where the tree is located; and the official, now accompanied by soldiers, from the new Sudanese government, who wants to revive the plan to have the steamer stop in the village. You've made a great observation.

Still, though this observation is a promising one, it still isn't "big" enough. Why not? Because it remains an observation, not an argument. You've listed three incidents that illustrate that none of the three government officials are successful, but you haven't said why these scenes are significant. How do you broaden your topic, from observation to idea, so that you feel you have something important to say?

First, try to make connections. Are there other people—besides these three government officials—who come to the village and leave? Are there other references to modern technology and transportation infrastructure? Is modernization an important theme in the story, and if it is, how do these three incidents relate to the way modernization is portrayed in the rest of the story?

Next, consider the other side of the issue. Is there anything in the story that seems to favor modernization? How does the story present the interplay between those incidents and the repeated failures of government officials?

Third, consider the context. There are, of course, at least two contexts to consider: the context of modern technology within the story, and the larger social and historical context in which the story takes place. Within the story, you might look for the context in which modernization or new technology is presented. Who attempts to bring new technologies? Why do they fail? Is modernization always set in direct opposition to valued village traditions? Might the struggle between modernization and tradition serve as an overarching theme for the story? How do the incidents with the government officials fit into that theme?

Outside the text of the story are other contexts. For instance, the storyteller refers to rule by a foreign government and at least two other Sudanese governments. What was happening in Sudan during this time period? How might those events affect its citizens or its literature?

All of these questions might help you broaden your topic so that you can tie your observations to bigger questions and make your paper more substantial and interesting.

NARROWING/FOCUSING YOUR TOPIC

What if your topic seems too big to handle? What do you do then?

Let's continue thinking about the hypothetical paper on Tayeb Salih's "The Doum Tree of Wad Hamid" that we were just discussing. Perhaps after brainstorming and freewriting, you've concluded that the villagers, despite continually expelling the government officials, are actually not in any way opposed to modernization. This observation is a good start, but you should resist the temptation to be satisfied with it. Simply stating that an opposition to new technologies is not the reason for rejecting the government officials' proposals is not enough. What you need to do now is focus your topic so that your observation can be extended to an interesting conclusion. How do you focus your topic?

First, test your claim. Broad statements are probably not always true, even if they hold true most of the time. Therefore, you need to address any parts of the text that might challenge your claim. Can you find evidence that indicates that villagers are, in fact, opposed to modernization or new technologies? If so, how do you account for that evidence while still defending your claim? In this case, the fact that the villagers repeatedly refuse attempts to introduce new technologies might suggest that they are opposed to modernization. But if you can find a reasonable alternative explanation for their actions, then your claim may still be valid and defensible.

Then look for examples. Find parts of the text that support your claim, and then keep looking and find more. These examples will often make up the majority of your paper, so it's important to be thorough. It's also important to be detailed. Specific examples, rather than broad information, will make your topic clearer and will help you present your argument. For instance, when the storyteller speaks about the inevitability of change, how does he portray the village of the future, with its water pump and steamer stopping place? If you can successfully argue that he presents the future in a positive light, then you have an important part of the text that supports your claim.

Finally, consider the context. Just as a consideration of context can help you broaden an idea, it can also help you focus it. What does modernization mean for these villagers in the context of the historical period? Does the historical and political context provide other reasons the villagers might expel the government officials, or other reasons they may wish to protect their tree?

Essentially, you are looking for details that support your specific claim while simultaneously weeding out other parts of the text because they're not important to your argument. If you fail to go through that process, you may end up including extraneous information in your essay, and your instructor will likely tell you that the paper seems disorganized. If you do a good job of narrowing your focus, that won't be a problem.

Thinking Beyond the Page

So far, we've been advising you to consider the formal aspects of the literature you're writing about—the literature as it is on the page. Sometimes, however, you will want to "think beyond the page" and consider questions about how the work was originally composed, its historical context, and so on. For example, ask yourself the following questions:

What do you know about the author? Learn more about the life and career of the author. If you have some sense of his or her other works, you'll have a better understanding of the themes and genres that interest the author.

What is the history of this work's composition? See if you can discover anything about the conditions under which the work was written. You might find multiple manuscript versions with significant differences, and there may be fascinating reasons for the changes from one version to the next. Molière's play *Tartuffe*, for instance, was first performed in 1664 and was almost immediately banned because the archbishop of Paris threatened to excommunicate anyone who performed in the play, watched a performance, or even read it. A revised version in 1667 didn't fare any better. It wasn't until the third version in 1669 that the play was deemed suitable for public consumption. Even in this last incarnation, the play was rather controversial, and the earlier, censored versions serve to emphasize the elements of the play that caused the controversy.

You might also discover that a text was published in a periodical before being sold in book form. This was quite common for poems and short stories, and novels were often first published serially in magazines or journals. If there are significant differences between the periodical publication and the book publication, you might want to investigate what led to those changes. Was there a *Tartuffe*-style controversy? Or perhaps the changes were due to demands of the marketplace?

In any case, examining multiple versions of the same work can potentially provide you with a lot of interesting information that you can use for a paper. The same may also be true of different translations (see the section "Writing about Adaptation" in Chapter 2 in this guide).

What do the critics and scholars say? Reading what others have said about the work before you read it may help you focus your observations. If (for example) a work is particularly well known for its innovative approach to rendering characters' inner lives, you'll want to pay close attention to this aspect of the work as you read it.

Does the work reflect an interesting cultural phenomenon? Sometimes a professor will ask you to read certain literary works because she wants you to examine a cultural phenomenon. Readers of *Tartuffe*, for instance, often fixate on the role of women in the play. Dorine, a lowly housemaid, is perhaps the most levelheaded character in the play, and she often speaks above her station, arguing with the master of the household. This is behavior that could be frowned upon both because she is a servant and because she is a woman. However, because she is so sensible, her actions are portrayed in a positive light. This aspect of Dorine's character, combined with other aspects of the play, can be read as social criticism, providing commentary on the role of women in seventeenth-century France.

If asking these questions leads you to a promising topic but you find that you don't know enough to write about the topic without reading other sources, then you will need to conduct research in order to write your paper. The next chapter provides some guidance on the research process.

4

Researching World Literature

Doing research in a world literature class is in many ways similar to doing research for other classes: you'll visit the library, find books and journals, get a clear sense of the scholarly conversation, and then offer a perspective of your own. One important difference, though, is that when you write about a work of literature, the literary text itself is typically the primary source, with literary criticism (books, journal articles, and so on) serving as secondary sources.

Understanding Primary and Secondary Sources

Primary sources are defined as any text, object, photograph, film, or other medium that is the object of scholarly investigation. A *secondary source*, on the other hand, is a work that analyzes, comments on, or otherwise sheds light on the primary text, historical event, object, or phenomenon in question.

A source can be primary or secondary, depending on the purpose of your research. For instance, you might write a paper in which the primary text is something other than a literary work (e.g., an author's journal). Or you might write a paper in which a secondary source consists of fictional elements (e.g., a scene that was removed from a novel in an early manuscript stage).

For example, say you are writing a paper on Joseph Conrad's *Heart of Darkness*. You might read what other people have written about the novel, such as Chinua Achebe's famous essay, "An Image of Africa: Racism in Conrad's *Heart of Darkness*." In this situation, *Heart of Darkness* is the primary text, and "An Image of Africa" is a secondary text. However, your professor might assign a paper that is mainly about Achebe's essay. In this situation "An Image of Africa" is the primary text, and other sources you find in your research may act as secondary texts. In fact, one of those secondary texts can be *Heart of Darkness*, if you are using it to help you examine the primary text ("An Image of Africa").

Using Sources

Having a strategy for collecting and employing sources is a good idea. No one wants to wander from source to source trying to remember what, precisely, that source argued, or why it mattered in the first place. We therefore offer the following research tips, which we think will help you become a more effective and efficient researcher.

64

It may seem at first that these steps take time. "Why should I stop to summarize a source when I can simply go back to the original?" you might wonder. However, the strategies outlined here will save you time in the long run. The work you do to digest and classify your sources as you do your research will make the writing process much more focused, much more efficient, and much less painful in the end.

SUMMARIZE YOUR SOURCES

Before attempting to use any source in your paper, make sure you understand it. The best way to do this is to summarize the source. In summarizing, you accomplish a few things. First, summarizing a source requires you to put the argument in your own language. Some of your secondary sources might use language that puzzles you. When you summarize, you are, in a sense, translating an argument into language that you understand and can work with. Summarizing also helps you see whether there's any aspect of the argument that you aren't getting. If you find yourself stumbling as you attempt to summarize, go back to the original source for clarity.

Summarizing also allows you to restate an argument in terms that are relevant to your paper. Most literary criticism that you will encounter is very complex and offers several ideas for consideration. Some of these ideas will be relevant to your topic, while others will not. When you summarize, you can restate the part of the argument that seems most relevant to the paper you want to write.

Summarizing can also help you organize your source material. If you've used ten sources in a research project, you've probably taken a lot of notes and have gathered several quotations for your paper. This work can amount to pages and pages of text. Summaries can help you organize these notes by telling you almost at a glance which idea comes from which source. You can also include in your summaries a few of the best quotations from each source.

Finally, summarizing is helpful to the entire research process. It's not something that you should do once at the beginning of the research process and then forget about. Every time your understanding of the topic shifts or evolves, take the time to write a brief summary. You'll find that putting your thoughts into writing helps you solidify one stage of understanding before progressing to the next.

CATEGORIZE YOUR SOURCES

Once you've summarized your sources, try to place them into various categories. Remember, writing an academic essay is like taking part in a large, ongoing conversation. Although everyone has a particular point of view, it's safe to say that no one is entering the conversation as a lone wolf. Everyone is speaking from a certain critical perspective. These perspectives might be classified into different groups.

Categorizing your sources might be as simple as looking for similarities among them. Which sources seem to share a point of view? Which seem to arrive at similar conclusions? You will also discover differences among your sources. Try to define these differences and see if they seem to fall into different categories. For example, side A seems to believe X, while side B seems to believe Y. Or, side A attempts to understand the literary work from a feminist perspective, while side B is interested in interpreting the work from a socioeconomic perspective.

Once you've categorized your sources, try to understand what these differences and similarities mean to your argument. Are these categories relevant to the issues you intend to discuss? Where does your own argument fit in? Does the reader need to know about these categories for your argument to make sense? Try to articulate these matters clearly. Write a summary of what you think at this point.

INTERROGATE YOUR SOURCES

In most of the papers that you'll write in college, you'll have to do more than review what other people have said about a topic. You will be asked to present your own point of view. To do this, you'll need to interrogate your sources.

Interrogating your sources does not mean that you have to be contentious. You don't have to search like a bloodhound for the weak spot in an argument. You're not required to "take on" your source. Instead, you'll want to ask questions of your sources. Initiate a conversation: challenge, interrogate, rebut, and confirm. Some good questions to ask are the following:

Is the writer offering evidence for her claims? Is this evidence sufficient? Why or why not?

Is there something that the writer is overlooking? Omitting? If so, is the omission a matter of carelessness, or does it seem purposeful? Why?

Does the writer's argument seem reasonable? If not, can you locate places where the reasoning seems to break down? Can you locate and identify any logical fallacies?

Is the writer's language appropriate? Does she sometimes rely on a pretty phrase or a passionate claim to cover up a lack of evidence?

What can you determine about the writer's perspective? Does she seem to have any important biases? Does she seem to belong to a particular critical school of thought? Does the writer's perspective help or hinder the argument she's trying to make? Why?

Where do you stand in relation to the writer? Do you give her a round of applause? Do you feel like booing her off the stage? Are you sitting with your arms crossed, feeling skeptical?

Keep notes of your personal responses to the writer, and try to translate those responses into comments or questions.

ANNOTATE YOUR SOURCES

Most scholars find it useful whenever possible to mark their texts as they read them. Marking your text enables you to enter into conversations with the author. No longer are you reading passively. Instead, you are reading actively, filling the margins with comments and questions that could blossom into a paper topic down the road. Annotating your texts also ensures that your questions and inspirations won't get lost. Entire books and dissertations have evolved from notes made in the margins. The ideas for these books and dissertations might have been lost had the writer not taken the time to write them down.

You can annotate in various ways. Let's again suppose you are writing a paper on *Heart of Darkness*, and as part of your research you are reading Chinua Achebe's essay "An Image of Africa: Racism in Conrad's *Heart of Darkness*." As Achebe presents each piece of his argument—such as the idea that Conrad is worried about "the lurking hint of kinship"[1] between the Congo and the Thames—you can write in the margin whether you agree with him or not. And, more importantly, you should write why. Perhaps you find a section that you

1 *Massachusetts Review* 18 (1977): 782–794.

believe shows that Achebe's views are biased. This is a key piece of information—underline it, note the bias, and, in the margin, interrogate the bias. It may also be helpful to take quick notes that are purely pragmatic and functional. Where Achebe quotes Conrad, you could write down the page number from your version of *Heart of Darkness* where the quoted passage appears. It will help you cross-reference the text later. Sometimes it may even be helpful to write down any immediate gut reaction you have. In the margin next to the first paragraph of "An Image of Africa," as Achebe relates an incident in which a student told him that "he never had thought of Africa as having [literature and history]," you might write, "Wow, how could a person be this clueless?" Your margin note may not seem especially substantive at first glance, but when you look closer, it's actually a pretty good question: "What is at work in this student's life to perpetuate such a huge error in his worldview?" This question could be the start of an interesting paper.

MAKE YOUR SOURCES WORK FOR YOU

Students often make a grave mistake when they write their first academic papers: overwhelmed by what their sources have to say, they permit their papers to crumble under the weight of scholarly opinion. They end up not writing an informed argument of their own but rehashing what has already been said on a topic. Such a paper might be informative. It might also be competently written. But it does not fulfill the requirements of a good academic paper.

Remember, a good academic paper must be analytical, it must be critical, and it must present a well-crafted, persuasive, informed argument.

Consider the phrase "informed argument." The word with the power in this phrase is the noun "argument." The word "informed" is merely a descriptor. It serves the noun, qualifying it, shading it. The information that you gather should serve your argument in much the same way. Make your sources work for *you*.

You can take some steps to ensure that your sources do indeed work for you without overwhelming your argument. First, don't go to the library or go online before you've thought about your topic on your own. Certainly your research will have an impact on what you think. Sometimes you might even find that you reverse your opinion. But if you go to the library before you've given your topic some thought, you risk jumping on the bandwagon of the first persuasive argument you encounter.

Second, limit your sources to those that are relevant to your topic. It's easy to be swept up in the broader scholarly conversation about your subject and to go off on tangents that don't, in the end, serve your argument.

Finally, keep track of your evolving understanding of the topic by periodically stopping to summarize. As we said earlier, summarizing your sources makes them more manageable.

If you manage your sources as you go along, you will reduce the risk that they'll overwhelm you later.

Keeping Track of Your Sources

During the research process it's very important to keep track of your sources. Nothing is more frustrating than having a great quotation and not knowing where it came from. Develop a good, consistent system for keeping notes.

Every academic discipline requires that you submit with your paper a bibliography or list of works cited. A bibliography should include every work you looked at in your research, even if you didn't quote that source directly. A list of works cited, on the other hand, is just that: a list of works that you quoted, paraphrased, or alluded to in the text of your paper. Both bibliographies and lists of works cited require you to provide information that will make it easier for your reader to find these sources for herself. Consult the MLA (Modern Language Association) Handbook for information about how to construct a proper bibliography and/or list of works cited.

Citing Sources

When you write an academic paper, you must cite all the sources that you've used, even if you don't quote them directly. If you fail to cite these sources, you will be charged with plagiarism. Plagiarism (passing off as your own the words and ideas of others, whether an entire article or just one phrase) is an academic offense for which there are serious consequences.

We can offer several good reasons not to plagiarize. First, it's very easy to get caught. Your instructors—who have spent years teaching students to write and so have read countless student essays—are keenly aware of the difference between professional and student writing. They notice when sophisticated, highly polished academic writing appears out of the blue, with seemingly no development or context. In addition, although the Internet makes plagiarism easy, it also empowers teachers, who can utilize sophisticated search programs to scan literally millions of documents for suspect phrases and sentences.

Second, plagiarism cheats both the reader and the writer. At a fundamental level, citing a source is an academic courtesy. Because scholarship is an ongoing conversation, you should always presume that other students or scholars could want to use your work to develop their own. If you've taken an idea from another scholar but haven't cited it (or have cited it improperly), your reader will have no easy way of finding the source of the ideas that have found their way into your work.

Perhaps the most serious problem raised when you plagiarize or fail to cite your sources is that you're cheating yourself. When you rely on the ideas of others to meet a course requirement, you're denying yourself the opportunity to have the best experience that college can offer: the opportunity to think for yourself. Writing papers can be difficult, and when deadlines loom it can be tempting to look for a shortcut and to lift ideas from scholars who clearly know more about your topic than you do. But it's *your* opinion that your instructor wants to hear. Take each writing assignment as an opportunity to explore and express your ideas. You're paying a lot for this education; you might as well get your money's worth.

5

Developing Your Thesis

Writing a Thesis Sentence

No sentence in your paper will vex you as much as the thesis sentence, and with good reason: the thesis sentence is very often the one sentence in the paper that asserts, controls, and structures the entire argument. Without a strong, persuasive, thoughtful thesis—explicit or implied—a paper might seem unfocused, weak, and not worth the reader's time.

What makes a good thesis sentence? A good thesis sentence generally has the following characteristics:

A good thesis sentence makes a claim. This doesn't mean that you have to reduce an idea to an either-or proposition and then take a stand. Rather, you need to develop an interesting perspective that you can support and defend. This perspective must be more than an observation. "Learning to read and write is important for Frederick Douglass" is merely an observation. Douglass himself comments on that fact on several occasions in his *Narrative*. "Learning to read and write is the most important factor leading to Douglass's escape from slavery" is an argument. Why? Because it posits a perspective. It makes a claim that engages competing claims. Put another way, a good thesis sentence inspires (rather than silences) other points of view. Someone else might argue that the incident in which Douglass fights Mr. Covey is the most important incident in Douglass's life. Another might point to a third factor. In short, if your thesis is positing something that no one can (or would bother to) argue with, then it's not a very good thesis.

A good thesis sentence determines the scope of the argument. The thesis sentence determines what you're required to say in a paper. It also determines what you cannot say. Every paragraph in your paper exists to support or elaborate on your thesis. Accordingly, if one paragraph you've written seems irrelevant to your thesis, you have three choices: get rid of that paragraph, rewrite the thesis sentence, or work to make the paragraph more clearly relevant. Understand that you don't have a fourth option: you can't simply include the idea without making clear its connection to your thesis. The thesis is like a contract between you and your reader. If you introduce ideas that the reader isn't prepared for or doesn't find relevant, you've violated that contract.

A good thesis sentence provides a structure for the argument. The thesis sentence signals to the reader not only what your argument is but how it will be presented. In other words your thesis sentence should either directly or indirectly suggest the structure of your argument to the reader. Say, for example, that you're going to argue the following idea: "That learning to read and write is the most important factor leading to Douglass's escape from slavery is demonstrated in two incidents: A and B." In this case the reader understands that you're going to cover two important points, and that these points will appear in a certain order. If you suggest a particular ordering principle and then abandon it, the reader could feel irritated and confused.

Alternatives to the Thesis Sentence

Sometimes the purpose of a piece of writing is not to make a claim but to raise questions. Other times a writer wants to leave a matter unresolved, inspiring readers to create their own positions. In these cases the thesis sentence might take other forms: the thesis question or the implied thesis.

As we've said, not every piece of writing sets out to make a claim. If your purpose as a writer is to explore, for instance, the reasons for the initial success of *Don Quixote* (a topic for which you're not prepared to make a claim), your thesis question might read, "What cultural forces conspired to make *Don Quixote* a popular success?"

Note that this question, while provocative, does not offer a sense of the argument's structure. It permits the writer to pursue all ideas, without committing to any. Although this freedom might seem appealing, in fact you will find that the lack of a declarative thesis statement requires more work: you need to tighten your internal structure and your transitions from paragraph to paragraph so that the essay is clear and the reader can easily follow your line of inquiry.

But let's suppose, for the sake of illustration, you want to use the thesis question "What cultural forces conspired to make *Don Quixote* a popular success?" You might start by discussing the Spanish Golden Age, and what society looked like in Habsburg Spain. You might follow up by expanding your discussion to look at international contexts, such as the defeat of the Spanish Armada less than two decades prior to the publication of *Don Quixote* (Part I). That discussion of international contexts might include colonial enterprises in the so-called New World, where Spain had a presence. At some point you'll certainly want to touch on the fact that the first part was popular enough to motivate Cervantes to write Part II.

You can see that there's a lot of material to cover here—perhaps too much. If you don't know where the paper will lead or what your conclusions will be, you might find it difficult to avoid digressing into irrelevant tangents. Therefore, if you're going to use a thesis question, make sure that it's a clearly articulated question and that you can structure a well-ordered investigation in response. If the paper starts to feel unwieldy, you might decide instead to use the question as the beginning of a discovery draft. Your findings in the discovery draft can then lead to a declarative thesis for the essay.

One of the most fascinating things about a thesis sentence is that it is the most important sentence in a paper—even when it's not there.

Some of the best writers never explicitly declare a thesis. In some essays you'll find it difficult to point to a single sentence that declares the argument. Still, the essay is coherent and makes a point. In these cases the writers have used an implied thesis.

Writers use an implied thesis when they want readers to come to their own conclusions about the matter at hand. However, just because the writer doesn't declare the thesis doesn't mean that she is working without one. Good writers will clearly state a thesis—either in their own minds or in their notes for the paper. They may elect not to put the thesis in the paper, but each paragraph, each sentence that they write, is controlled by the thesis all the same.

If you decide to write a paper with an implied thesis, be sure that you have a strong grasp of your argument and its structure. Also be sure that you supply adequate transitions so that the reader can follow your argument with ease.

When you begin writing, you should have a solid, well-articulated thesis. The thesis will tell your readers the purpose of your essay, and as you write it will help guide you.

However, it's also important to keep in mind that the thesis you have when you begin is not set in stone; you can still modify it. Often you'll find that as you write, your thoughts about the issue will evolve, and you'll refine your conclusions. Sometimes it will be necessary to change your thesis to reflect those changes in your thinking. Therefore, when you begin writing, what you really have is a *working thesis*. It can change and adapt and develop as you write the paper. A working thesis doesn't necessarily become a final thesis until the paper is finished.

Turning Your Ideas into a Thesis

Now that we've looked at what you want in a thesis, let's take a moment to look at creating one based on work you've already done. Let's say you've done some brainstorming, a little freewriting, and maybe written a discovery draft, and you've come up with some interesting thoughts. After that, you spent a little time nutshelling, trying to focus your ideas. Now you just need to convert one of those focused ideas into a working thesis.

Composing a working thesis is challenging. After all, the thesis is arguably your paper's most important sentence. It cannot be crafted formulaically but must reflect the complexities of the argument that you are hoping to write. But even while no formula exists for writing a successful thesis, we can offer some advice to get you off on the right foot.

First you'll want to determine what you want to write about. Since you've already created some ideas through brainstorming, freewriting, and other exercises, you should have some options. Let's return to the example about Beckett's *Endgame* that we used in Chapter 3, "Generating Ideas." You'll recall that there were plenty of good observations in the accompanying freewriting and discovery draft exercises: repeated words and phrases, humor (or dark humor), Clov's constant threat to leave, waiting for nothing/waiting to die, the condition of humanity, and so on.

From this list of observations, you'll want to find an observation that interests you. You might choose a single observation from your list and focus on it, or you might look for an idea that ties together two or three of these observations, and focus on that. Whatever you decide, don't try to squeeze everything you've observed into a single essay. To do so would require a book—and you simply don't have time to write a book before the paper is due. Determining which idea or set of ideas you want to work with will enable you to stay focused and to do justice to your ideas in the limited time that you have.

Sometimes writers are torn between two or three very good observations. If the ideas can't be synthesized into a single idea or claim, the best strategy is to pick whichever observation looks most interesting. In other words, choose the observation you can have the most fun with. For the sake of this discussion, let's say you decide to write about the repetition you've noticed in *Endgame*. This is a promising topic that offers a lot to talk about—the painkillers, Clov threatening to leave, and so on. It's also a topic that will help you stay focused: you now know not only what you'll want to discuss but what you can leave alone.

You'll also notice something interesting at this point: even though you don't yet have a thesis, the observation you've chosen to write about will help dictate which type of paper you're writing. In this case, since you're writing primarily about repeated words and phrases, you're obviously going to write a textual analysis paper. Again, you now have a strategy that helps you understand not only what you're going to do but what you're not going to do: papers about context, comparison, or adaptation won't really work here.

So now you have your plan: you're going to write a textual analysis paper about repeated words and phrases in Samuel Beckett's *Endgame*. As we noted earlier in this guide, your goal in writing a textual analysis paper is to choose a small textual element and examine in detail how that element contributes to the major themes, underlying message, or overall effect of the text. At this point you need to compose a question, using this goal to guide you. After some doodling you come up with this question: How does Beckett's use of repetition contribute to the overall effect of *Endgame*? Give yourself the opportunity to explore that question. Brainstorm or free-write a response. Then try to shape your response so that you can answer the question in a couple of sentences, then a single sentence. When you can answer that question in one sentence, you'll have your working thesis.

Of course if you were writing a contextual analysis paper, you'd ask yourself a different question, based on the goals of that type of paper. The same is true for an adaptation paper. The strategy is clear: instead of trying to create a thesis out of thin air, pick an element of the literary work that interests you, then ask yourself a relevant question based on the goals of the type of paper you're going to write. When you answer your own question, you'll have a working thesis.

The Thesis Sentence Checklist

In the end you may have spent a good deal of time writing your working thesis and still not know if it's a good one. As we've indicated earlier, a good thesis typically evolves as the writer writes. As you write, you'll want to interrogate your thesis in order to determine how well it's holding up. Some questions to ask yourself follow:

Does the thesis sentence attempt to answer or to explore a challenging intellectual question? If your thesis doesn't challenge you, it likely won't challenge your reader either. If you find yourself bored as you write, or if you are haunted by the sense that you aren't talking about anything important, stop writing. Return to your list of observations. See if you can find some connection between the observations that might raise the intellectual stakes.

Will the point I'm making generate discussion and argument, or will it leave people asking "So what?"? If your thesis doesn't generate discussion, perhaps the point you made is too obvious. Return to your list of observations. Ask of each one, "Why is this important?" The answer to that question should help you refine your thesis.

Is the thesis too vague? Too general? Should you focus on a more specific aspect of the topic? If a thesis is too broad, it's unlikely to hold the reader's interest. Take your more general idea and link it to specific observations about the text. Perhaps in that linkage you'll find the focus for your paper.

Does the thesis deal directly with the topic at hand, or is it a declaration of my personal feelings? Be careful about personal opinions: to make a claim is different from declaring an opinion. An academic paper does the former but eschews the latter.

Does the thesis indicate the direction of my argument? Does it suggest a structure for my paper? If a thesis is well constructed, it will suggest to you and to your reader where the paper is going. Look at your thesis, then look at your outline. Does your thesis reflect or suggest that outline? Can you rewrite the thesis so that the outline/structure is suggested?

Does the introductory paragraph define terms important to my thesis? Don't make your thesis do all the work. Rely on your introduction to help your thesis, especially when it comes to necessary but cumbersome tasks, such as defining terms.

Does the introduction, when writing a research paper, place my thesis within the larger, ongoing scholarly discussion about the topic? Consider again the dinner party metaphor. What do the scholars at the table have to say about the topic? What do you have to say in response to their ideas? Is the relationship between your perspective and theirs clear to the reader? If not, how might it be made clear?

6

Considering Structure and Organization

Once you've figured out what you want to say, you're left with the problem of how to say it. How should you begin the paper? Should you address the opinions of other thinkers? And what should you do with that stubborn contradiction you've uncovered in your own thinking?

Writing papers in college requires you to come up with sophisticated, complex, and even creative ways of structuring your ideas. Accordingly, we can't offer simple formulas that will work for every paper, every time. We can, however, give you some things to think about that will help you as you consider how to structure your paper.

Let Your Thesis Direct You

Begin by listening to your thesis. If it's well written, it will tell you which way to go with your paper. Suppose, for example, that in responding to Bertolt Brecht's play *The Good Woman of*

Szechwan, and after researching Brecht's other plays, you have written a thesis that says this:

> While Brecht used his theater to promote Marxist ideology, his primary artistic goal was to create a completely new type of theater audience.

This thesis provides the writer with several clues about how best to structure the paper, and it prepares readers for what they will encounter therein. First, the thesis promises readers that the paper will argue that Brecht was interested in more than ideology. The paper will therefore begin by acknowledging that although the promotion of Marxist values was important to him, it was not his only goal. The rest of the paper will concern the (more important) creation of a completely new theater experience—and, by extension, a new type of theater spectator.

We say that this idea of a new theater audience is more important than ideology not necessarily because Brecht himself said so but because the writer seems to say so in her thesis. Reread the thesis sentence. Note that the emphasis falls on the last clause: "his primary artistic goal was to create a completely new type of theater audience." We know that this clause is the emphatic clause because it's the grammatically independent clause. In other words, of the two clauses, this is the one that can stand alone. We also know it's emphatic because of the author's word choice: the phrase "primary artistic goal" underscores the significance of the idea in the second clause. Either way, the emphasis tells us that we will be given not simply a description of how Brecht's plays propagate Marxist ideology but, rather, a description of how his methods of propagating this ideology were used to create a new theater experience that would in turn create a new audience. We understand all of this because the writer took the time to make sure that the thesis was written emphatically.

Sketching Your Argument

Although your thesis will identify your paper's general direction, it will not necessarily provide you with a plan for how to organize all of your points, large and small. Here it might be helpful to diagram or sketch your argument.

In sketching your argument, the goal is to fill the page with your ideas. Begin by writing your thesis. Put it where your instincts tell you to: at the top of the page, in the center, at the bottom. Around the thesis, cluster the points you want to make. Under each of these points, note the observations you've made and the evidence you'll use. Don't get nervous when your sketch starts to look messy. Use arrows. Draw circles. Take up colored pens. Any of these methods can help you find connections between your ideas that otherwise might go unnoticed. Working from your sketch, try to see the line of reasoning that is evolving.

Sketching is an important step in the writing process because it allows you to explore visually the connections between your ideas. If you outline a paper too early in the process, you risk missing these connections. You might line up your points—A, B, C—without fully understanding why. Sketching your argument helps you see, for example, that points A and C really overlap and need to be thought through more carefully.

Outlining Your Argument

When you've finished the sketch, you're ready to make an outline. The task of the outline is to identify the paper's best structure. By "best structure" we mean the structure that best supports the argument you intend to make.

When you're outlining a paper, you'll have many options for organization. Understand, however, that each choice you make eliminates dozens of other options. Your goal is to come up with an outline in which all your choices support your thesis.

Treat the outline as if it were a puzzle that you are putting together. In a puzzle, each piece has only one appropriate place. The same should be true of your paper. If it's easy to shift around your ideas—if several of your paragraphs could be switched around and no one would be the wiser—then you haven't yet found the best structure for your paper. Each paragraph should present a single, well-supported idea that is the logical successor to the ideas that preceded it, all of them building inexorably toward your paper's overall point—the thesis. Keep working until your outline fits your ideas like a glove.

When you think you have an outline that works, challenge it. The first outline rarely holds up to a good interrogation. When you start asking questions of your outline, you will begin to see where the plan holds and where it falls apart. Here are some questions you might ask:

Does my thesis control the direction of the outline?

Are all of my main points relevant to the thesis?

Can any of these points be moved around without changing something important about the thesis?

Does the outline seem logical?

Does the argument progress, or does it stall?

If the argument seems to take a turn midstream, does the thesis anticipate that turn?

Do I have sufficient support for each of my points?

Have I made room in the outline for other points of view about the topic?

Does this outline reflect a thorough, thoughtful argument? Have I covered the ground?

Constructing Paragraphs

Imagine that you've written the thesis. You've interrogated the outline. You know which modes of arrangement you intend to use. You've settled on a plan that you think will work. Now you have to go about the serious business of constructing paragraphs.

You were probably told in high school that paragraphs are the workhorses of a paper. Indeed they are. If a single paragraph is incoherent or weak, the entire argument might fail. It's important that you consider carefully the "job" of each paragraph. Know what you want that paragraph to do. Make sure it pulls its weight.

WHAT IS A PARAGRAPH?

A paragraph is generally understood as a single "unit" of a paper. What your readers expect when they encounter a new paragraph is that you're going to declare a point and then offer support for that point. If you violate this expectation—if your paragraphs wander aimlessly among a half dozen points, or if they declare points without offering any evidence to support them—readers will become confused or irritated by your argument. They won't want to read any further.

WHAT SHOULD A PARAGRAPH DO?

At the risk of sounding silly, we suggest that you consider this: what you look for in a boyfriend or girlfriend, a reader looks for in a paragraph. You want a partner who is supportive, strong, and considerate to others. Similarly, a good paragraph is:

- **Supportive.** Even in the most trying of times a good paragraph finds a way to support the thesis. It declares its relationship to the thesis clearly, so that the whole world knows what the paragraph intends to do. In other words, a supportive paragraph's main idea clearly develops the argument of the thesis.
- **Strong.** A good paragraph isn't bloated with irrelevant evidence or redundant sentences. Nor is it a scrawny thing, begging to be fed. It's strong and buff. You know that it's been worked on. In other words, a strong paragraph develops its main idea, using sufficient evidence.
- **Considerate.** Good paragraphs consider their relationship to other paragraphs. A good paragraph never interrupts its fellow paragraphs to babble on about its own irrelevant problems. A good paragraph waits its turn. It shows up when and where it's supposed to. It doesn't make a mess for other paragraphs to clean up. In other words, a considerate paragraph is a coherent paragraph. It makes sense within the text as a whole.

WRITING THE TOPIC SENTENCE
OR GUIDING CLAIM

Just as every paper requires a thesis sentence to assert and control its argument, so also every paragraph requires a topic sentence to assert and control its main idea. Without a topic sentence, your paragraphs will seem jumbled, aimless. Your reader will become confused. Because the topic sentence plays an important role in your paragraph, it must be crafted with care. When you've written a topic sentence, ask yourself the following questions:

Does the topic sentence declare a single point of the argument? Because the reader expects that a paragraph will explore only one idea in your paper, it's important that your topic sentence not be too ambitious. If it points to two or three ideas, perhaps you need to consider developing more paragraphs.

Does the topic sentence further the argument? Give your topic sentences the same "so what?" test that you gave your thesis sentence. If your topic sentence isn't interesting, your paragraph probably won't further the argument. Your paper could stall.

Is the topic sentence relevant to the thesis? It might seem so to you, but the relevance may not be so clear to your reader. If you find that your topic sentence is taking you into brand-new territory, stop writing and consider your options.

If the new territory isn't relevant to the existing thesis, either you'll have to rewrite your thesis to accommodate this new direction, or you'll have to consider excluding this paragraph from your final paper.

Is there a clear relationship between this topic sentence and the paragraph that came before? Make sure that you haven't left out any steps in the process of composing your argument. If you take a sudden turn in your reasoning, signify that turn to the reader by using the proper transitional phrase—"on the other hand," "however," or the like.

Does the topic sentence control the paragraph? If your paragraph seems to unravel, take a second look. Perhaps the topic sentence isn't adequately controlling the paragraph and needs to be rewritten. Or, maybe the paragraph is moving on to a new idea that needs to be developed in a paragraph of its own.

Where have I placed my topic sentence? Readers often look for topic sentences at or near the beginning of a paragraph. Consider this: If you are skimming something quickly, which sentence do you look to in each paragraph? Likely it's the first sentence. But that doesn't mean all of your topic sentences need to be situated at the beginning of your paragraphs. Nevertheless, if you're going to place your topic sentence elsewhere, you'll need to craft your paragraph with care. You might justify putting the topic sentence in the middle of the paragraph, for example, if you have information that needs to precede it. You might also justify putting the topic sentence at the end of the paragraph, if you want the reader to consider your line of reasoning before you declare your main point. Let the argument and what it needs dictate where you place your topic sentence. Wherever you place it, be strategic. Make sure that your decision facilitates your argument.

Developing Your Paragraphs

EVIDENCE

Students often ask how long a paragraph should be. To this we respond, "As long as it takes."

It's possible to make a point quickly. Sometimes it's desirable to keep it short. Notice the preceding paragraph, for example. We might have hemmed and hawed, talked about short paragraphs and long paragraphs. We might have said that the average paragraph is one-half to two-thirds of a page in length. We might have spent time explaining why the too-short paragraph is too short, and the too-long paragraph too long. Instead, we cut to the chase. After huffing and puffing through this paragraph (which is getting longer and longer all the time), we'll give you the same advice: a good paragraph is as long as it needs to be in order to illustrate, explore, and/or prove its main idea.

However, length isn't all that matters in paragraph development. What's important is that a paragraph develops its idea fully, and in a manner that readers can follow with ease.

Let's consider these two issues carefully. First, how do we know when an idea is fully developed? If your topic sentence is well written, it should tell you what the paragraph needs to do. If the topic sentence declares, for example, that there are two conflicting impulses at work in a particular fictional character, then the reader will expect the two impulses to be defined and illustrated. It might take two paragraphs to do this; it might take one. The decision will depend on how important this matter is to the discussion. If the point is important, you'll take your time, and (more likely than not) you'll use at least two paragraphs. In this case a topic sentence might be understood as controlling not only a paragraph but an entire section of text.

When you've written a paragraph, ask yourself the following questions:

Do I have enough evidence to support this paragraph's idea?

Do I have too much evidence? In other words, will the reader be lost in a morass of details, unable to see the argument as a whole?

Does this evidence clearly support the assertion that I'm making in this paragraph, or am I stretching it?

If I'm stretching it, what can I do to persuade the reader that this stretch is worth making?

Am I repeating myself in this paragraph?

Have I defined all of the paragraph's important terms?

Can I say, in a nutshell, what the purpose of this paragraph is? Has the paragraph fulfilled that purpose?

ARRANGEMENT

Equally important to the idea of a paragraph's development is the matter of the paragraph's arrangement. Paragraphs are arranged differently for different purposes. For example, if you're writing a paper about an oral epic's history and wish to summarize a sequence of events, you'll likely want to arrange the information chronologically. If you're writing a paper in which you want to describe the appearance of slave narratives in different cultures during roughly the same time, perhaps you'll choose to arrange the information spatially. You could start with African American narratives, followed by West African narratives, followed by Caribbean narratives. If you're writing a paper about the elements of a novel that make it stand out from other novels of a similar type, you might want to arrange your ideas by working from the specific to the general—and so on.

COHERENCE

So you have your thesis, your topic sentences, and truckloads of evidence to support the whole lot. You've spent three days writing your paragraphs, making sure that each paragraph argues one point and that this point is well supported with textual evidence. But when you read the essay back to yourself, you feel a profound sense of disappointment. Though you've followed your outline, the essay just doesn't seem to hold together. It could be that you have a problem with coherence.

A lack of coherence is easy to diagnose but not so easy to cure. An incoherent essay doesn't seem to flow. Its arguments are hard to understand. The reader has to double back again and again in order to follow the gist of the argument. Something has gone wrong. What?

Look for the following issues in your paper:

Make sure the grammatical subjects of your sentences reflect the real subject of your paragraph. Underline the subjects of all the sentences in the paragraph. Do these subjects match the paragraph's subject in most cases? Or, have you put the paragraph's subject into another, less important part of the sentence? Remember that the reader understands an idea's importance according to where you place it. If your main idea is hidden as an object of a preposition in a subordinate clause, do you really think your reader is going to follow what you're trying to say? For instance, consider the following

paragraph about the way Frederick Douglass discusses religion in *The Narrative of the Life of Frederick Douglass.* The grammatical subject of each sentence is underlined.

> Many <u>situations</u> occur throughout Douglass's *Narrative* in
> which Douglass witnesses slaveholders using the Bible to
> justify their actions. An excellent <u>example</u> is Master Thom-
> as's conversion. Beforehand, <u>Thomas</u> had "relied upon his
> own depravity to shield and sustain him in his savage bar-
> barity, but after his conversion, he found religious sanc-
> tion and support for his slaveholding cruelty." This <u>idea</u>
> appears most clearly when he whips a woman while quot-
> ing scripture: "He that knoweth his master's will, and doeth
> it not, shall be beaten with many stripes."

Look at the four subjects: "situations," "example," "Thomas,"
and "idea." Of these, only "Thomas" is clearly related to the
topic of the paragraph. Now consider this revised paragraph:

> Throughout his *Narrative*, <u>Douglass</u> offers several instances
> of slaveholders who use the Bible to justify their actions.
> <u>He</u> recounts in particular the story of Master Thomas, who
> "relied upon his own depravity to shield and sustain him
> in his savage barbarity, but who, after his conversion . . .
> found religious sanction and support for his slaveholding
> cruelty." <u>Douglass</u> elaborates by relating an incident in
> which Master Thomas, while whipping a naked woman
> with a heavy cow skin, justifies his actions by quoting

scripture: "He that knoweth his master's will, and doeth it not, shall be beaten with many stripes."

Look at the subjects here. All refer to "Douglass." The paragraph's similar string of subjects keeps the reader focused on the topic and creates a paragraph that flows more naturally and seems much more coherent than the first one.

Make sure the grammatical subjects are consistent. Again, look at the grammatical subjects of all your sentences. How many different subjects do you find? If you have too many different sentence subjects, your paragraph will be hard to follow.

Make sure your sentences look backward as well as forward. For a paragraph to be coherent, each sentence should begin by linking itself firmly to the sentence that preceded it. If the link between sentences does not seem firm, use an introductory clause or phrase to connect one idea to the other.

Follow the principle of moving from old to new. If you put the old information at the beginning of the sentence and the new information at the end, you accomplish two things: first, you ensure that your readers are on solid ground, moving from the familiar to the unknown, and, second, because we tend to give emphasis to what comes at the end of a sentence, readers rightfully perceive that the new information is more important than the old.

Use repetition to create a sense of unity. Repeating key words and phrases at appropriate moments will give your readers a sense of coherence in your work. But don't overdo it; you'll risk sounding redundant.

Use transition markers wisely. Sometimes you'll need to announce to your readers a turn in your argument, or you'll want to emphasize one point, or you'll want to make clear a particular relationship in time. In all these cases you'll want to use transition markers. Some examples follow:

- **To give an example:** *for example, for instance*
- **To present a list:** *first, second, third, next, then*
- **To show that you have more to say:** *in addition, furthermore, moreover*
- **To indicate similarity:** *also, likewise, similarly*
- **To show an exception:** *but, however, nevertheless, on the other hand*
- **To show cause and effect:** *accordingly, consequently, therefore, because*
- **To emphasize:** *indeed, in fact, of course*
- **To conclude:** *finally, in conclusion, in the end*

Introductions and Conclusions

Introductions and conclusions are among the most challenging of all paragraphs. Why? Because they must do more than state a topic sentence and offer support. Introductions and conclusions must synthesize and provide context for your entire argument, and they must also make the proper impression on your readers.

The introduction is your chance to get readers interested in your subject. Accordingly, the tone of the paragraph has to be just right. You want to inform, but not to the point of being dull; you want to intrigue, but not to the point of being vague; you want to take a strong stance, but not to the point of alienating readers. Pay attention to the nuances of your tone. Seek out a second reader if you're not sure that you've managed to get the tone the way you want it.

Equally important to the tone of the introduction is that it needs to "place" your argument into a larger context. Some strategies follow:

Announce your topic broadly; then declare your particular take. For example, if you're interested in talking about the symbolism in Henrik Ibsen's *Hedda Gabler*, you might (1) begin by saying that Ibsen's symbolism has posed a problem for many of his critics, (2) provide a quick definition of the problem as others have defined it, and (3) declare your thesis (which states your own position on the matter).

Provide any background material important to your argument. If you're interested in exploring how writers of the modernist movement influenced the work of Samuel Beckett, in your introduction you'll want to provide, in broad strokes, a description of modernism. Don't include irrelevant details in your description; instead, emphasize those aspects of the movement that might have most influenced Beckett.

Define key terms as you intend to make use of them in your argument. If, for example, you're writing a paper on Noh, it is absolutely essential that you define the term for your reader. Begin with a definition of terms, and from there work toward the declaration of your argument.

Use an anecdote or a quotation. Sometimes you'll find a terrific story or quotation that seems to reflect the main point of your paper. Don't be afraid to begin with it. Be sure, however, that you tie that story or quotation clearly and immediately to your main argument.

Acknowledge your opponents. When you're writing a paper about a controversial matter, you might wish to begin by summarizing the point of view of your adversaries. Then state your own position in opposition to theirs. In this way you place yourself clearly in the ongoing conversation.

Remember, the introduction is the first impression that your argument will make on the reader. Take special care with your sentences so that they'll be interesting. Also take the time to consider who your readers are and what background they will bring with them to their reading. If your readers are very knowledgeable about the subject, you will not need to provide a lot of background information. If your readers are less knowledgeable, you will need to be more careful about defining terms.

Finally, you might want to consider writing the introduction after you've written the rest of the paper. Many writers find that they have a better grip on their subject once they've done a first draft. This "better grip" helps them craft an introduction that is sure-footed, persuasive, interesting, and clear. But be careful. Any changes that you make to an introduction and/or a thesis statement will affect the paper that follows. Simply adding the new introductory paragraph will not produce a "completed" paper.

Conclusions are also difficult to write. How do you manage to make the reader feel persuaded by what you've said? Even if the points of your paper are strong, the overall effect of your argument might fall to pieces if the paper as a whole is badly concluded.

Many students end their papers by simply summarizing what has come before. A summary of what the reader has just read is important to the conclusion—particularly if your argument has been complicated or has covered a lot of ground. But a good conclusion will do more. Just as the introduction sought to place the paper in the larger, ongoing conversation about the topic, so should the conclusion insist on returning readers to that ongoing conversation, but with the feeling that they've learned something more. You don't want readers to finish your paper and say "So what?" Admittedly, writing a conclusion isn't easy.

Many of the strategies we've listed for improving introductions can help you improve your conclusions as well. In the conclusion you might do the following:

Return to the ongoing conversation, emphasizing the importance of your own contribution to it.

Consider again the background information with which you began, and illustrate how your argument has shed new light on that information.

Return to the key terms and point out how your essay has added new dimension to their meanings.

Use an anecdote or a quotation that summarizes or reflects your main idea.

Acknowledge your opponents—if only to emphasize that you've countered their positions successfully.

Remember, language is especially important to a conclusion. Your goal in the final sentences is to leave your ideas resounding in the reader's mind. Give the reader something to think about. Make your language ring.

7

Attending to Style

Most of us know good style when we see it—and *hear* it in the mind's ear. We also know when a sentence seems cumbersome to read. However, though we can easily spot beastly sentences, it is not as easy to say why a sentence—especially one that is grammatically correct—isn't working. We look at the sentence; we see that the commas are in the right places; and we find no error to speak of. So why is the sentence so awful? What's gone wrong?

When thinking about what makes a good sentence, be sure to put yourself in the reader's place. What is a reader hoping to find in your sentences? Information, yes. Eloquence, surely. But, most important, a reader is looking for clarity. Your reader does not want to wrestle with sentences. She wants to read with ease. She wants to see one idea build on another. She wants to experience, without struggling, the emphasis of your language and the importance of your idea. Above all, she wants to feel that you, the writer, are doing the bulk of the work. In short, she wants to read sentences that are persuasive, straightforward, and clear.[2]

Basic Principles of the Sentence

FOCUS ON ACTORS AND ACTIONS

To understand what makes a good sentence, it's important to understand one principle: a sentence, at its very basic level, is about actors and actions. As such, the subject of a sentence should point clearly to the actor, and the verb of the sentence should describe the important action.

This principle might seem so obvious to you that you don't think it warrants further discussion. But think again. Look at the following sentence, and then try to determine, in a nutshell, what's wrong with it:

> There is a question in the mind of some critics over whether the employment of extensive dialogue is a sign of weakness in a novel.

This sentence has no grammatical errors. But certainly it lumbers along, without any force. What are the actors? What are the actions?

2 The way of teaching style that is represented here has been greatly influenced by Joseph Williams and his work. For a thorough examination of the fundamental principles of style, see Williams's *Style: Lessons in Clarity and Grace*, 10th ed. (New York: Pearson Longman, 2010).

Now consider the following sentence:

Some critics question whether extensive dialogue signi-
fies a weak novel.

What changes does this sentence make? We can point to the more obvious changes: omitting the empty *there is* phrase; replacing the abstract noun *sign* with the stronger verb *signify*; replacing a second abstract noun *weakness* with the adjective *weak*; omitting all of the prepositions that the abstract nouns require. What principle governs these many changes? Precisely the one mentioned earlier: that the *actors* in a sentence should serve as the sentence's grammatical subjects, and the *actions* should be illustrated forcefully in the sentence's verbs.

Whenever you feel that your prose is confusing or hard to follow, find the actors and the actions of your sentences. Is the actor the subject of your sentence? Is the action related, vividly, in a verb? If not, rewrite your sentences accordingly.

BE CONCRETE

Student writers tend to rely too heavily on abstract nouns: they use *expectation* when the verb *expect* is stronger; they write *evaluation* when *evaluate* is more vivid. So why use an abstract noun when a verb will do better? Many students believe that abstract nouns permit them to sound more "academic." When you write with a lot of abstract nouns, however, you risk confusing your reader. You also end up cornering yourself syntactically. Consider the following:

Nouns often require prepositions. Too many prepositional phrases in a sentence are hard to follow. Verbs, on the other hand, can stand on their own. They're cleaner; they don't box you in. If you need some proof of this claim, consider the following sentence:

> Oral performances of the work by griots occurred long before the work was put into writing by poets.

Notice all of the prepositional phrases that these nouns require. Now look at the following sentence, which uses verbs:

> Griots performed the work long before poets wrote it down.

This sentence has fewer nouns and prepositions and is therefore much easier to read—yet it still conveys all the information found in the prior sentence.

Abstract nouns often invite the *there is* construction. Consider the following sentence:

> There is a method of narration that James Joyce pioneered called "stream of consciousness" in which the inner

thoughts of characters are rendered in dissociated and convoluted form.

We might rewrite this sentence as follows:

James Joyce pioneered a method of narration called "stream of consciousness" that renders characters' thoughts in dissociated and convoluted form.

The result, again, is a sentence that is more direct and easier to read.

Abstract nouns are, well, abstract. Using too many abstract nouns will leave your prose seeming ungrounded. Words such as *falsification, beauteousness,* and *insubstantiality* sound pompous and vague—which may be exactly what you want, if you're striving for a slightly comic, self-mocking effect. But, by and large, people simply don't talk this way. Instead, use concrete nouns, as well as strong verbs, to convey your ideas. *Lying, beauty,* and *flimsiness* reflect the way people really speak; these words point directly to their meanings without drawing undue attention to themselves.

Abstract nouns can obscure your logic. Note how hard it is to follow the line of reasoning in the following sentence (the nouns that might be rewritten as verbs or as adjectives are in boldface):

Decisions with regard to **the elimination** of characters from a novel on the basis of **their insignificance** to the developing narrative rest with the author.

Now consider this sentence:

When characters are no longer significant to a narrative, the author can decide to eliminate them from his novel.

The Exception: When to Use Abstract Nouns

In some instances an abstract noun will be essential to the sentence. Sometimes abstract nouns refer to a previous sentence (*these arguments, this decision,* etc.). Other times they allow you to be more concise (e.g., *her argument* versus *what she argued*). And, in other cases, the abstract noun is a concept important to your argument: freedom, love, revolution, and so on. Still, if you examine your prose, you'll probably find that you overuse abstract nouns. Omitting from your writing those abstract nouns that aren't really necessary makes for leaner, "fitter" prose.

BE CONCISE

One of the most exasperating aspects of reading student texts is that most students don't know how to write concisely. Students use phrases when a single word will do, offer pairs of adjectives and verbs where one is enough, or overwrite, saying the same thing two or three times with the hope that the reader will be impressed by a point worth rephrasing and then rephrasing again.

Stop the madness! It's easy to delete words and phrases from your prose once you've learned to be ruthless about it.

Do you really need words such as *actually, basically, generally,* and so on? If you don't need them, why are they there? Are you using two words where one will do? Isn't the phrase *first and foremost* redundant? What's the point of *future* in *future plans?* And why do you keep saying, *"In my opinion"?* Doesn't the reader understand that this is your paper, based on your point of view? Does drawing attention to yourself in this way make your points any stronger—or does it have the opposite effect, coming across as insecurity or as hedging?

Sometimes you won't be able to fix a wordy sentence by simply deleting a few words or phrases. You'll have to rewrite the whole sentence. Take the following sentence, for example:

> Plagiarism is a serious academic offense resulting in punishments that might include suspension or dismissal, profoundly affecting your academic career.

The idea here is simple: *Plagiarism is a serious offense with serious consequences.* Why not simply say so? Don't be afraid to let your reader connect your ideas to the context—at its most pleasurable, good writing gives the reader a sense of collaboration, of being trusted to connect the dots.

BE COHERENT

At this point in discussing style, we move from the sentence as a discrete unit to the way that sentences fit together. Coherence (or the lack of it) is a common problem in student papers. Sometimes a professor encounters a paper in which all the ideas seem to be there, but they're hard to follow. The prose seems jumbled. The line of reasoning is anything but linear. Couldn't the student have made this paper a bit more readable?

Although coherence is a complicated and difficult matter to address, we can offer a couple of tricks that will help your sentences "flow." Silly as it sounds, you should "dress" your sentences the way a bride might—wear, as the saying goes, something old and something new. In other words most of the sentences you write should begin with the old—with something that looks back to the previous sentence. Then your sentence should move on to telling the reader something new. If you do this, your line of reasoning will be easier for readers to follow.

Though this advice sounds simple enough, it is not always easy to follow. Let's dissect the practice so that we can better understand how our sentences might be "well dressed."

Consider, first, the beginnings of sentences. The coherence of your paper depends largely on how well you begin sentences. "Well begun is half done" says Mary Poppins, and in this case (as in all cases, really) she's right.

Beginning a sentence is hard work. When you begin a sentence, you have three important matters to consider:

114

Basic Principles of the Sentence

1. **Is your topic also the subject of the sentence?** When a sentence lacks coherence, usually it's because the writer has not been careful to ensure that the topic of the sentence is also the grammatical subject of the sentence. If, for instance, you're writing a paper about Zeami's Noh drama *Atsumori*, and at one point you include a sentence whose topic is the importance of traditional Noh masks in staging the play, then the grammatical subject of the sentence should reflect that idea:

> **The actors' masks** are a crucial element of any performance of *Atsumori*; they are just as important as the dialogue.

If, on the other hand, you bury your topic in a subordinate clause, look what happens:

> *An important part of performing* Atsumori *is the staging, such as* **the use of masks for the actors,** *which is just as important as the actors' dialogue.*

The emphasis and focus of the sentence are obscured.

2. **Are the topics/subjects of your sentences consistent?** For a paragraph to be coherent, most of the sentence subjects should be the same. To check for consistency, pick out a paragraph and make a list of its sentence subjects. See if any of the subjects seem out of place. For example, suppose

you're writing a paragraph comparing ancient Greek drama, Japanese Noh drama, and Indian classical drama (such as *Sakuntala and the Ring of Recollection*) in terms of their intended effect on audiences. Do most of your sentence subjects reflect that paragraph topic? Or, do some of your sentences have other, tangential topics as the grammatical subject? Although the full extent of the influence of this topic may indeed have a place in your paper, you will confuse readers if your paragraph's sentence subjects point to too many competing ideas. Revise the sentences (perhaps the entire paragraph) for coherence.

3. **Have you marked, when appropriate, the transitions between ideas?** Coherence depends on how well you connect a sentence to the one that came before it. You'll want to make solid transitions between your sentences, using words such as *however* or *therefore*. You'll also want to signal to readers whenever, for example, something important or disappointing comes up. In these cases you'll want to use expressions such as *note that* or *unfortunately*. You might also want to indicate time or place in your argument. If so, you'll use transitions such as *then, later, earlier*, or *in the previous paragraph*. Be careful not to overuse transition phrases. Some writers think transition phrases can, all by themselves, direct a reader through an argument. Indeed, sometimes all a paragraph needs is a *however* in order for its argument suddenly to make sense. More often, though,

the problem with coherence does not stem from a lack of transition phrases but from the fact that the writer has not articulated, for himself, the connections between his ideas. Don't rely on transition phrases alone to bring sense to muddled prose.

BE EMPHATIC

We've been talking about how sentences begin, but what about how they end?

If the beginnings of sentences must look over their shoulders at what came before, the ends of sentences must forge ahead into new ground. It's the end of a sentence, then, that must be courageous and emphatic. You must construct sentences so that the ends pack the punch.

To write emphatically, follow these principles:

Declare important ideas at the end of a sentence. Shift less important ideas to the front.

Tighten the ends of sentences. Don't trail off into nonsense, don't repeat yourself, and don't qualify what you've just said if you don't have to. Simply make your point and move on.

Use subordinate clauses to house subordinate ideas. Put all the important ideas in main clauses and the less important ideas in subordinate clauses. If you have two ideas of equal importance that you want to express in the same sentence, use parallel constructions or semicolons. These two tricks of the trade are perhaps more useful than any others in balancing equally significant ideas.

BE IN CONTROL

When sentences run on and on, readers know that a writer has lost control. Take command of your sentences. When you read over your paper, look for sentences that never seem to end. Your first impulse might be to take these long sentences and divide them into two (or three or four). This simple solution often works. But sometimes this strategy isn't the most desirable one; it might lead to short, choppy sentences. Moreover, if you always cut your sentences in two, you'll never learn how a sentence can be long and complex without violating the boundaries of good prose.

What do you do when you encounter an overly long sentence? First consider the point of your sentence. Usually it will have more than one point, and sorting out the points helps sort out the grammar. Consider carefully the points that you're trying to make and the connections between those points. Then try to determine which grammatical structure best serves your purpose.

Are the points of equal importance? Use a coordinating conjunction (*and, but, or*) or a semicolon to join the ideas. Try to use parallel constructions when appropriate.

Are the points of unequal importance? Use subordinate clauses (*although, while, because,* and so on) or relative clauses (*that, which*) to join the ideas, putting the less important idea in the subordinate clause.

Does one point make for an interesting aside? Insert that point between commas, dashes, or even parentheses at the appropriate juncture in the sentence.

Do these ideas belong in the same sentence? If not, create two sentences.

WRITE BEAUTIFULLY

In your career as a writer you will sometimes produce a paper that is well written but could be written better. On this happy occasion, you might wish to turn your attention to such matters as balance, parallel structure, emphasis, rhythm, and word choice. If you're interested in exploring these rhetorical tools, consult one of several excellent style books, such as Joe Williams's *Style: The Basics of Clarity and Grace,* William Strunk Jr. and E. B. White's *The Elements of Style,* or John Trimble's *Writing with Style.* You will find plenty of valuable advice in any one of these sources.

8

Revising Your Work

Why and How to Revise

Most of us who compose on a computer understand revision as an ongoing—even constant—process. Every time you hit the delete key, every time you cut and paste, and every time you take out a comma or exchange one word for another, you're revising.

Real revision, however, is more than making a few changes here and there. Real revision, just as the word implies, calls for *seeing again*; it requires that you open yourself up to the possibility that parts of your paper—even your entire paper— might need to be rethought, and rewritten.

Achieving this state of mind is difficult. First, you might be very attached to what you've written. You might be unwilling to change a word, let alone three or four paragraphs. Second, there's the matter of time: you might sense that the paper needs major work, but it's due tomorrow, or you have an exam in physics, or you're coming down with a cold and know that you need to sleep. Third, you might have difficulty understanding what, exactly, is wrong with your paper. Finally, you might simply be sick and tired of the paper. How can you make another pass through it when exhaustion has you in its grip? Why should you be bothered with (or let yourself be overwhelmed by) the process of revising?

Of course we might convince you that revision is worth the extra effort simply by saying that revising a paper will help you achieve a better grade. A good reader can sense when a piece of writing has been thoroughly considered and reconsidered. This consideration (and here we mean the word in both of its meanings) is not lost on your professor and will be rewarded.

More important than grades, however, is the fact that revising your papers teaches you to be a better writer. Professional writers know that to write is to rewrite. In the revision process you improve your reading skills and your analytical skills. You learn to challenge your own ideas, thus deepening and strengthening your argument. You learn to find the weaknesses in your writing. You may even discover patterns of error or habits of organization that are undermining your papers.

Though revising takes time and energy, it also will help you become a more efficient writer down the road. If, for example, you have discovered through the revision process that you tend to bury your topic sentences in the middle of your paragraphs, you can take this discovery with you as you draft your next paper. You may then be less likely to make that particular mistake again.

Perhaps we've answered the question "Why should I revise?" The next question, of course, is "How?" There are many different kinds of revising, including the following:

Large-scale revision. Large-scale revision means looking at the entire paper for places where your thinking seems to go awry. You might need to provide evidence, define terms, or add an entirely new step to your reasoning. You might even decide to restructure or rewrite your paper completely if you discover a new idea that intrigues you, or a structure that seems to be more effective than the one you've been using.

Small-scale revision. Small-scale revision needs to happen when you know that a certain part of your paper isn't working. Maybe the introduction needs work. Maybe one part of the argument seems weak. Once you've located the problem, you'll focus on revising that one section of your paper. When you're finished you'll want to reconsider your paper as a whole to make sure that your revisions work in the context of the entire paper.

Editing. Too often students confuse editing with revision. They are not the same processes. Editing is the process of finding minor problems with a text—problems that might easily be fixed by deleting a word or sentence, cutting and pasting a paragraph, and so on. When you edit, you're considering your reader. You might be happy with how you've written your paper, but will your reader find your paper clear, readable, and interesting? How can you rewrite the paper so that it's clearer, more concise, and, most important of all, a pleasure to read?

The very best writers revise their writing in all the ways listed here. To manage these various levels of revision, it's very important that you get an early start on your papers so that you have time to make any substantive, large-scale revisions that might be needed. Good writers also understand that revision is an ongoing process, not necessarily something that you do only after your first draft is complete. You might find, for example, that you're stuck halfway through the first draft of your paper. You decide to take a look at what you have so far. As you read, you find that you've neglected to make a point that is essential to the success of your argument. You revise what you've written, making that point clear. In the end you find that your block, your "stuckness," is gone. Why? Maybe it's gone because what was blocking you in the first place was a hole in your argument. Or, maybe it's gone because you gave your brain a break. In any case, stopping to revise in the middle of the drafting process often proves wise.

Developing a Critical Eye

We have yet to address the matter of how a writer knows what she should revise. Developing a critical eye is perhaps the most difficult part of the revision process. But having a critical eye makes you a better writer, reader, and thinker. So it's worth considering carefully how you might learn to see your own work with the objectivity that is essential to successful self-criticism.

The first step in developing a critical eye is to get some distance from your work. If you've planned your writing process well, you'll have left yourself a day or two to take a break. If you don't have this luxury, even an hour of video games or a walk over to the printing center to pick up a hard copy of your draft might be enough to clear your head. Many writers find that their mind keeps working on their papers even while their attention is turned elsewhere. When they return to their work, they bring with them a fresh perspective. They also bring a more open mind.

When you return to your paper, the first thing you'll want to do is consider whether or not the paper as a whole meets your (and your professor's) expectations. Read the paper through without stopping (don't get hung up on one troublesome paragraph). Then ask yourself the following questions:

Did I fulfill the assignment? If the professor gave you instructions for this assignment, reread them and then ask yourself whether or not you've addressed all of the matters you're expected to address. Does your paper stray from the assignment? If it does, have you worked to make your argument relevant, or are you coming out of left field? If the professor hasn't given you explicit instructions for this paper, you'll still want to take a moment to consider what she or he expects. What books has the professor asked you to read? What position does he or she take toward your topic? Has the professor emphasized a certain method of scholarship (feminism, Marxism, etc.)? Has she or he said anything to you about research methods in his or her discipline? Does your paper seem to fit into the conversation that the professor has been carrying on in class? Have you written something that other students would find relevant and interesting?

Did I say what I intended to say? This question is perhaps the most difficult question you will ask yourself in the revision process. Many of us think that we have indeed said what we intended to say. When we read our papers, we're able to fill in any holes that might exist in our arguments with the information that we have in our minds. The problem is that our readers sometimes don't have this same information in mind. Your challenge in revising your own writing, therefore, is to forget about what you *meant* and see only what you actually *wrote*—the meaning has to be right there in the words on the page. It's very important to think carefully about what you've said—and to think just as carefully about what you haven't said. Ask yourself the following questions: Was I clear? Do I need to define my terms? Has every stage of the argument been articulated clearly? Have I made adequate transitions between my ideas? Is my logic solid—is it there for all to see? If the answer to any of these questions is no, you will want to revise your draft.

What are the strengths of my paper? In order to develop a critical eye it's just as important to know when you've written well as it is to know when you've written poorly. It helps, therefore, to make a list of what you think you've done well in your draft. It's also helpful to pick out your favorite or strongest paragraph. When you find a good paragraph, sentence, or idea, think about why it's good. You'll not only be gaining an understanding of what it means to write well, but you'll also be giving yourself a pat on the back—something that's very important to do in the revision process.

What are the weaknesses of my paper? Looking for weaknesses isn't as fun as looking for strengths, but it's necessary to the revision process. Again, try to make a list of what you haven't done well in this paper. Your list should be as specific as you can make it. Instead of writing "problems with paragraphs," you might say, "problems with unity in my paragraphs," or, even more specific, "problems with the transitions between paragraphs 3 and 4, and 12 and 13." Also force your-self to determine which paragraph (or sentence) you like least in the paper. Figure out why you don't like it, and work to make it better. Then go back through your paper and look for others like it.

Analyzing Your Work

If you've been considering the strengths and weaknesses of your paper, you've already begun to analyze your work. The process of analysis involves breaking down an idea or an argument into its parts and evaluating those parts on their merits. When you analyze your own paper, then, you're break-ing down that paper into its parts and asking yourself whether or not these parts support the paper as you envision it.

The following checklist reiterates our earlier advice. Use it to analyze your whole paper, or use it to help you figure out what has gone wrong with a particular part of your work.

Consider your introduction:

If you're writing a research paper, does the introduction place your argument in an ongoing conversation?

If you're not writing a research paper, does the introduc-tion establish context?

Does the introduction define all of your key terms?

Does the introduction draw the reader in?

Does the introduction lead the reader clearly to your thesis?

Consider your thesis:

Does the thesis say what you want it to say?

Does the thesis make a point worth considering? Does it answer the question "So what?"

Does the thesis provide the reader with some sense of the paper's structure?

Does the paper deliver what your thesis promises to deliver?

Consider your structure:

Make an outline of the paper you've just written. Does this outline reflect your intentions?

Does this outline make sense, or are there gaps in the logic—places where you've asked your readers to make leaps for which they haven't been prepared?

Is each point in the outline adequately developed?

Is each point equally developed? (That is, does your paper seem balanced overall?)

Is each point relevant? Interesting?

Underline the thesis sentence and all of the topic sentences. Then cut and paste them together to form a paragraph. Does this paragraph make sense?

Consider your paragraphs:

Does each paragraph have a topic sentence that clearly controls it?

Are the paragraphs internally coherent?

Are the paragraphs externally coherent? (That is, have you made adequate transitions between paragraphs? Is each paragraph clearly related to the thesis?)

Consider your argument and its logic:

Have you really presented an argument, an assertion worth making, or is your paper merely a series of observations, a summary?

Do you see any holes in your argument, or do you find it convincing?

Have you dealt fairly with the opposition, or have you neglected to mention other possible arguments concerning your topic for fear that they might undermine your own argument?

Have you supplied ample evidence for your arguments?

Consider your conclusion:

Does the conclusion sum up the main point of the paper?

Is the conclusion appropriate, or does it introduce a completely new idea?

Does the language resonate, or does it fall flat?

Have you inflated the language in order to pad a conclusion that is empty and ineffective?

Does the conclusion leave the reader with something to think about?

The final step that you'll want to take before submitting your paper is to make sure that the grammar, spelling, and punctuation throughout the paper are correct and that you've formatted it appropriately. These details may seem frustratingly minor, but errors often cause readers to grow impatient with otherwise well-written essays. So be sure to take the time to carefully proofread your essay.

When you proofread, you need to slow down your reading, allowing your eye to focus on every word, every phrase of your paper. Reading aloud is the most effective way to make yourself see and hear what you actually *wrote*, not just what you *meant*. Remember, a computer spellchecker is not an editor; for example, the word "form" will be spelled correctly, even if you meant "from." As you read, look for common errors—spelling errors, faulty subject-verb agreement, unclear pronoun antecedents, *its/it's* confusion, *their/there* confusion, and so on. If you have time, get the opinion of a second reader. Treat the proofreading stage as you would a word search or sudoku puzzle—that is, as a puzzle to be solved. No doubt, some errors are lurking in your prose (even professional writers find errors when they proofread their own work). Make it your mission to find them and root them out.

You'll also want to format the paper correctly. Some instructors provide explicit directions about constructing a title page, choosing a font, setting margins, paginating, footnoting, and so on. Be sure to follow these instructions carefully. If the instructor does not provide directions, consult the *MLA Handbook*—the standard reference for writers in the humanities—for specific advice. Instructors appreciate papers that are not only well written but also beautifully presented. In academic writing, "beauty" equals simplicity: no needless ornamentation, no fancy fonts, and nothing to distract the reader from the sound of your writer's voice and the clarity of your thoughts.

THE THOUSAND AND ONE NIGHTS
fourteenth century

[The Story of the Porter and the Three Ladies][†]

THE TWENTY-EIGHTH NIGHT

Dinarzad said to her sister Shahrazad, "Sister, if you are not sleepy, tell us one of your lovely little tales." Shahrazad replied, "With the greatest pleasure":

I heard, O happy King, that once there lived in the city of Baghdad a bachelor who worked as a porter. One day he was standing in the market, leaning on his basket, when a woman approached him. She wore a Mosul cloak, a silk veil, a fine kerchief embroidered with gold, and a pair of leggings tied with fluttering laces. When she lifted her veil, she revealed a pair of beautiful dark eyes graced with long lashes and a tender expression, like those celebrated by the poets. Then with a soft voice and a sweet tone, she said to him, "Porter, take your basket and follow me." Hardly believing his ears, the porter took his basket and hurried behind her, saying, "O lucky day, O happy day." She walked before him until she stopped at the door of a house, and when she knocked, an old Christian came down, received a dinar from her and handed her an olive green jug of wine. She placed the jug in the basket and said, "Porter, take your basket and follow me." Saying, "Very well, O auspicious day, O lucky day, O happy day," the porter lifted the basket and followed her until she stopped at the fruit vendor's, where she bought yellow and red apples, Hebron peaches and Turkish quinces, and seacoast lemons and royal oranges, as well as baby cucumbers. She also bought Aleppo jasmine and Damascus lilies, myrtle berries and mignonettes, daisies and gillyflowers, lilies of the valley and irises, narcissus

† Translated by Husain Haddawy.

and daffodils, violets and anemones, as well as pomegranate blossoms. She placed everything in the porter's basket and asked him to follow her.

Then she stopped at the butcher's and said, "Cut me off ten pounds of fresh mutton." She paid him, and he cut off the pieces she desired, wrapped them, and handed them to her. She placed them in the basket, together with some charcoal, and said, "Porter, take your basket and follow me." The porter, wondering at all these purchases, placed his basket on his head and followed her until she came to the grocer's, where she bought whatever she needed of condiments, such as olives of all kinds, pitted, salted, and pickled, tarragon, cream cheese, Syrian cheese, and sweet as well as sour pickles. She placed the container in the basket and said, "Porter, take your basket and follow me." The porter carried his basket and followed her until she came to the dry grocer's, where she bought all sorts of dry fruits and nuts: Aleppo raisins, Iraqi sugar canes, pressed Ba'albak figs, roasted chick-peas, as well as shelled pistachios, almonds, and hazelnuts. She placed everything in the porter's basket, turned to him, and said, "Porter take your basket and follow me."

The porter carried the basket and followed her until she came to the confectioner's, where she bought a whole tray full of every kind of pastry and sweet in the shop, such as sour barley rolls, sweet rolls, date rolls, Cairo rolls, Turkish rolls, and open-worked Balkan rolls, as well as cookies, stuffed and musk-scented kataifs, amber combs, ladyfingers, widows' bread, Kadi's tidbits, eat-and-thanks, and almond pudding. When she placed the tray in the basket, the porter said to her, "Mistress, if you had let me know, I would have brought with me a nag or a camel to carry all these purchases." She smiled and walked ahead until she came to the druggist's, where she bought ten bottles of scented waters, lilywater, rosewater scented with musk, and the like, as well as ambergris, musk, aloewood, and rosemary. She also bought two loaves of sugar and candles and torches. Then she put everything in the basket, turned to the porter, and said, "Porter, take your basket and follow me." The porter carried the basket and walked behind her until she came to a spacious courtyard facing a tall, stately mansion with massive pillars and a double door inlaid with ivory and shining gold. The girl stopped at the door and knocked gently.

But morning overtook Shahrazad, and she lapsed into silence. Then her sister said, "Sister, what a lovely and entertaining story!" Shahrazad replied, "What is this compared with what I shall tell you tomorrow night if the king spares me and lets me live! May God grant him long life."

THE TWENTY-NINTH NIGHT

The following night Dinarzad said to her sister Shahrazad, "Sister, if you are not sleepy, tell us one of your little tales to while away the night." Shahrazad replied, "I hear and obey":

I heard, O wise and happy King, that as the porter stood with the basket, at the door, behind the girl, marveling at her beauty, her charm, and her elegant, eloquent, and liberal ways, the door was unlocked, and the two leaves swung open. The porter, looking to see who opened the door, saw a full-bosomed girl, about five feet tall. She was all charm, beauty, and perfect grace, with a fore-head like the new moon, eyes like those of a deer or wild heifer, eyebrows like the crescent in the month of Sha'ban, cheeks like red anemones, mouth like the seal of Solomon, lips like red carnelian, teeth like a row of pearls set in coral, neck like a cake for a king, bosom like a fountain, breasts like a pair of big pomegranates resembling a rabbit with uplifted ears, and belly with a navel like a cup that holds a pound of benzoin ointment. She was like her of whom the poet aptly said:

> On stately sun and full moon cast your sight;
> Savor the flowers and lavender's delight.
> Your eyes have never seen such white in black,
> Such radiant face with hair so deeply dark.
> With rosy cheeks, Beauty proclaimed her name,
> To those who had not yet received her fame.
> Her swaying heavy hips I joyed to see,
> But her sweet, slender waist brought tears to me.

When the porter saw her, he lost his senses and his wits, and the basket nearly fell from his head, as he exclaimed, "Never in my life have I seen a more blessed day than this!" Then the girl who had opened the door said to the girl who had done the shopping, "Sister, what are you waiting for? Come in and relieve this poor man of his heavy burden." The shopper and the porter went in, and the doorkeeper locked the door and followed them until they came to a spacious, well-appointed, and splendid hall. It had arched compartments and niches with carved woodwork; it had a booth hung with drapes; and it had closets and cupboards covered with curtains. In the middle stood a large pool full of water, with a fountain in the center, and at the far end stood a couch of black juniper wood, covered with white silk and set with gems and pearls, with a canopylike mosquito net of red silk, fastened with pearls as big as hazelnuts or bigger. The curtain was unfastened, and a dazzling girl emerged, with genial charm, wise mien, and features as radiant as the moon. She had an elegant figure, the scent of ambergris, sugared lips, Babylonian eyes, with eyebrows as arched as a pair of bent bows, and a face whose radiance put the shining sun to shame, for she was like a great star soaring in the heavens, or a dome of gold, or an unveiled bride, or a splendid fish swimming in a fountain, or a morsel of luscious fat in a bowl of milk soup. She was like her of whom the poet said:

> Her smile reveals twin rows of pearls
> Or white daisies or pearly hail.
> Her forelock like the night unfurls;
> Before her light the sun is pale.

The third girl rose from the couch and strutted slowly until she joined her sisters in the middle of the hall, saying, "Why are you standing? Lift the load off this poor man." The doorkeeper stood in front of the porter, and the shop-per stood behind him, and with the help of the third girl, they lifted the basket down and emptied its contents, stacking up the fruits and pickles on one side and the flowers and fresh herbs on the other. When everything was arranged, they gave the porter one dinar and said . . .

But morning overtook Shahrazad, and she lapsed into silence. Then Dinarzad said to her sister Shahrazad, "What an amazing and entertaining story!" Shahrazad replied, "If I am alive tomorrow night, I shall tell you something stranger and more amazing than this."

THE THIRTIETH NIGHT

The following night Dinarzad said to her sister Shahrazad, "Sister, tell us the rest of the story of the three girls." Shahrazad replied, "With the greatest pleasure":

I heard, O King, that when the porter saw how charming and beautiful the girls were and saw how much they had stacked of wine, meat, fruits, nuts, sweets, fresh herbs, candles, charcoal, and the like for drinking and carousing, without seeing any man around, he was very astonished and stood there, hesitant to leave. One of the girls asked him, "Why don't you go? Do you find your pay too little?" and, turning to her sister, said, "Give him another dinar." The porter replied, "By God, ladies, my pay is not little, for I deserve not even two dirhams, but I have been wondering about your situation and the absence of anyone to entertain you. For as a table needs four legs to stand on, you being three, likewise need a fourth, for the pleasure of men is not complete without women, and the pleasure of women is not complete without men. The poet says:

> For our delight four things we need, the lute,
> The harp, the zither, and the double flute,
> Blending with the scent of four lovely flowers,
> Roses, myrtles, anemones, and gillyflowers.
> Only in four such things join together,
> Money, and wine, and youth, and a lover.

You are three and you need a fourth, a man." His words pleased the girls, who laughed and said, "How can we manage that, being girls who keep our business to ourselves, for we fear to entrust our secrets where they may not be kept. We have read in some book what ibn al-Tammam has said:

> Your own secret to none reveal;
> It will be lost when it is told.
> If your own breast cannot conceal,
> How can another better hold?"

When the porter heard their words, he replied, "Trust me; I am a sensible and wise man. I have studied the sciences and attained knowledge; I have read and learned, and presented my knowledge and cited my authorities. I reveal the good and conceal the bad, and I am well-behaved. I am like the man of whom the poet said:

> Only the faithful does a secret keep;
> None but the best can hold it unrevealed.
> I keep a secret in a well-shut house
> Of which the key is lost and the lock sealed."

When the girls heard what he said, they replied, "You know very well that this table has cost us a lot and that we have spent a great deal of money to get all these provisions. Do you have anything to pay in return for the entertainment? For we shall not let you stay unless we see your share; otherwise you will drink and enjoy yourself with us at our expense." The mistress of the house said, "'Without gain, love is not worth a grain.'" The doorkeeper added, "Have you got anything, my dear? If you are emptyhanded, go emptyhanded." But the shopper said, "Sisters, stop teasing him, for by God, he served me well today; no one else would have been as patient with me. Whatever his share will come to, I shall pay for him myself." The porter, overjoyed, kissed the ground before her and thanked her, saying, "By God, it was you who brought me my first business today and I still have the dinar you gave me; take it back and take me, not as a companion but as a servant." The girls replied, "You are very welcome to join us."

Then the shopper, girding herself, began to arrange this and that. She first tidied up, strained the wine, stacked up the flasks, and arranged the bowls, goblets, cups, decanters, plates, and serving spoons, as well as various utensils in silver and gold. Having prepared all the requisites, she set the table by the pool and laid it with all kinds of food and drink. Then she invited them to the banquet and sat down to serve. Her sisters joined her, as did the porter, who thought that he was in a dream. She filled the first cup and drank it, filled the second and offered it to one of her sisters, who drank it, filled a third and gave it to the other sister to drink, and filled a fourth and gave it to the porter, who held it in his hand and, saluting with a bow, thanked her and recited the following verses:

> Drink not the cup, save with a friend you trust,
> One whose blood to noble forefathers owes.
> Wine, like the wind, is sweet if o'er the sweet,
> And foul if o'er the foul it haply blows.

Then he emptied his cup, and the doorkeeper returned his salute and recited the following verses:

> Cheers, and drink it in good health;
> This wine is good for your health.

The porter thanked her and kissed her hand. After the girls had drunk again and had given the porter more to drink, he turned to his companion, the shopper, saying, "My lady, your servant is calling on you," and recited the following verses:

> One of your slaves is waiting at your door,
> With ample thanks for your ample favor.

She replied "By God, you are welcome. Drink the wine and enjoy it in good health, for it relieves pain, hastens the cure, and restores health." The porter emptied his cup and, pouring out another, kissed her hand, offered it to her, and proceeded to recite the following verses:

> I gave her pure old wine, red as her cheeks,
> Which with red fire did like a furnace glow.
> She kissed the brim and with a smile she asked,
> "How can you cheeks with cheeks pay what you owe?"
> I said, "Drink! This wine is my blood and tears,

And my soul is the fragrance in the cup."
She said, "If for me you have shed your blood,
Most gladly will I on this red wine sup."

The girl took the cup, drank it off, then sat by her sister.

Thus receiving the full and returning the empty, they went on drinking cup after cup until the porter began to feel tipsy, lost his inhibitions, and was aroused. He danced and sang lyrics and ballads and carried on with the girls, toying, kissing, biting, groping, rubbing, fingering, and playing jokes on them, while one girl thrust a morsel in his mouth, another flirted with him, another served him with some fresh herbs, and another fed him sweets until he was in utter bliss. They carried on until they got drunk and the wine turned their heads. When the wine got the better of them, the doorkeeper went to the pool, took off her clothes, and stood stark naked, save for what was covered of her body by her loosened hair. Then she said, "Whee," went into the pool, and immersed herself in the water.

But morning overtook Shahrazad, and she lapsed into silence. Then Dinarzad said, "What an amazing and entertaining story!" Shahrazad replied, "What is this compared with what I shall tell you tomorrow night!"

THE THIRTY-FIRST NIGHT

The following night Dinarzad said, "Sister, if you are not sleepy, tell us one of your lovely little tales to while away the night." Shahrazad replied, "With the greatest pleasure":

I heard that the doorkeeper went into the pool, threw water on herself, and, after immersing herself completely, began to sport, taking water in her mouth and squirting it all over her sisters and the porter. Then she washed herself under her breasts, between her thighs, and inside her navel. Then she rushed out of the pool, sat naked in the porter's lap and, pointing to her slit, asked, "My lord and my love, what is this?" "Your womb," said he, and she replied, "Pooh, pooh, you have no shame," and slapped him on the neck. "Your vulva," said he, and the other sister pinched him, shouting, "Bah, this is an ugly word." "Your cunt," said he, and the third sister boxed him on the chest and knocked him over, saying, "Fie, have some shame." "Your clitoris," said he, and again the naked girl slapped him, saying, "No." "Your pudenda, your pussy, your sex tool," said he, and she kept replying, "No, no." He kept giving various other names, but every time he uttered a name, one of the girls hit him and asked, "What do you call this?" And they went on, this one boxing him, that one slapping him, another hitting him. At last, he turned to them and asked, "All right, what is its name?" The naked girl replied, "The basil of the bridges." The porter cried, "The basil of the bridges! You should have told me this from the beginning, oh, oh!" Then they passed the cup around and went on drinking for a while.

Then the shopper, like her sister, took off all her clothes, saying, "Whee," went into the pool, and immersed herself completely in the water. Then she washed herself under the belly, around the breasts, and between the thighs.

Then she rushed out, threw herself in the porter's lap, and asked, "My little lord, what is this?" "Your vulva," said he, and she gave him a blow with which the hall resounded, saying, "Fie, you have no shame." "Your womb," said he, and her sister hit him, saying, "Fie, what an ugly word!" "Your clitoris," said he, and the other sister boxed him, saying, "Fie, fie, you are shameless." They kept at it, this one boxing him, that one slapping him, another hitting him, another jabbing him, repeating, "No, no," while he kept shouting, "Your womb, your cunt, your pussy." Finally he cried, "The basil of the bridges," and all three burst out laughing till they fell on their backs. But again all three slapped him on the neck and said, "No, this is not its name." He cried, "All right, what is its name?" One of them replied, "Why don't you say 'the husked sesame'?" He cried out, "The husked sesame! Thank God, we are finally there." Then the girl put on her clothes and they sat, passing the cup around, while the porter moaned with sore neck and shoulders.

They drank for a while, and then the eldest and fairest of the three stood up and began to undress. The porter touched his neck and began to rub it with his hand, saying, "For God's sake, spare my neck and shoulders," while the girl stripped naked, threw herself into the pool, and immersed herself. The porter looked at her naked body, which looked like a slice of the moon, and at her face, which shone like the full moon or the rising sun, and admired her figure, her breasts, and her swaying heavy hips, for she was naked as God had created her. Moaning "Oh, oh," he addressed her with the following verses:

> If I compare your figure to the bough,
> When green, I err and a sore burden bear.
> The bough is fairest when covered with leaves,
> And you are fairest when completely bare.

When the girl heard his verses, she came quickly out of the pool, sat in his lap and, pointing to her slit, asked, "O light of my eyes, O sweetheart, what is the name of this?" "The basil of the bridges," said he, but she replied, "Bah!" "The husked sesame," said he, and she replied, "Pooh!" "Your womb," said he, and she replied, "Fie, you have no shame," and slapped him on the neck. To make a long story short, O King, the porter kept declaring, "Its name is so," and she kept saying "No, no, no, no." When he had had his fill of blows, pinches, and bites until his neck swelled and he choked and felt miserable, he cried out, "All right, what is its name?" She replied, "Why don't you say the Inn of Abu Masrur?" "Ha, ha, the Inn of Abu Masrur," said the porter. Then she got up, and after she put on her clothes, they resumed their drinking and passed the cup around for a while.

Then the porter stood up, took off his clothes, and, revealing something dangling between his legs, he leapt and plunged into the middle of the pool.

But morning overtook Shahrazad, and she lapsed into silence. Then Dinarzad said to her sister Shahrazad, "Sister, what a lovely and entertaining story!" Shahrazad replied, "What is this compared with what I shall tell you tomorrow night if the king spares me and lets me live!" The king said to himself, "By God, I will not have her put to death until I hear the rest of the story. Then I shall do to her what I did to the others."

THE THIRTY-SECOND NIGHT

The following night Dinarzad said to her sister Shahrazad, "Sister, if you are not sleepy, tell us one of your lovely little tales." Shahrazad replied, "With the greatest pleasure":

I heard, O King, that when the porter went down into the pool, he bathed and washed himself under the beard and under the arms; then he rushed out of the pool, planted himself in the lap of the fairest girl, put his arms on the lap of the doorkeeper, rested his legs in the lap of the shopper and, pointing to his penis, asked, "Ladies, what is this?" They were pleased with his antics and laughed, for his disposition agreed with theirs, and they found him entertaining. One of them said, "Your cock," and he replied, "You have no shame; this is an ugly word." The other said, "Your penis," and he replied, "You should be ashamed; may God put you to shame." The third said, "Your dick," and he replied, "No." Another said, "Your stick," and he replied "No." Another said, "Your thing, your testicles, your prick," and he kept saying, "No, no, no." They asked, "What is the name of this?" He hugged this and kissed that, pinched the one, bit the other, and nibbled on the third, as he took satisfaction, while they laughed until they fell on their backs. At last they asked, "Friend, what is its name?" The porter replied, "Don't you know its name? It is the smashing mule." They asked, "What is the meaning of the name the smashing mule?" He replied, "It is the one who grazes in the basil of the bridges, eats the husked sesame, and gallops in the Inn of Abu Masrur." Again they laughed until they fell on their backs and almost fainted with laughter. Then they resumed their carousing and drinking and carried on until nightfall.

When it was dark, they said to the porter, "Sir, it is time that you get up, put on your slippers, and show us your back." The porter replied, "Where do I go from here? The departure of my soul from my body is easier for me than my departure from your company. Let us join the night with the day and let each of us go his way early tomorrow morning." The shopper said, "By God, sisters, he is right. For God's sake and for my sake, let him stay tonight, so that we may laugh at him and amuse ourselves with him, for who will live to meet with one like him again? He is a clever and witty rogue." They said, "You cannot spend the night with us unless you agree to abide by our condition, that whatever we do and whatever happens to us, you shall refrain from asking for any explanation, for 'speak not of what concerns you not, lest you hear what pleases you not.' This is our condition; don't be too curious about any action of ours." He replied, "Yes, yes, yes, I am dumb and blind." They said, "Rise, then, go to the entrance, and read what is inscribed on the door and the entrance." He got up, went to the door, and found on the door and the entrance the following inscription written in letters of gold, "Whoever speaks of what concerns him not hears what pleases him not." The porter came back and said, "I pledge to you that I will not speak of what concerns me not."

Then the shopper went and prepared supper, and after they had something to eat, they lighted the lamps, and, sticking the aloewood and ambergris into the wax, they lighted the candles, and the incense burned, rose, and filled the hall. Then they changed the plates, laid the table with wine and fresh fruits, and sat to drink. They sat for a long time, eating, drinking, engaging in refined conversation, bantering, and laughing, and joking, when suddenly they heard a knocking at the door. Without showing much concern, one of the girls rose, went to the door, and returned after a while, saying, "Sisters, if you listen to me, you will spend a delightful night, a night to remember." They asked, "How so?" She replied, "At this very moment, three one-eyed dervishes are standing at the door, each with a shaven head, shaven beard, and shaven eyebrows, and each blind in the right eye. It is a most amazing coincidence. They have just arrived in Baghdad from their travel, as one can see from their condition, and this is their first time in our city. Night overtook them and, being strangers with no one to go to and unable to find a place to sleep, they knocked at our door, hoping that someone would give them the key to the stable or offer them a room for the night. Sisters, each one of them is a sight, with a face that would make a mourner laugh. Would you agree to let them in for this one time, so that we may amuse ourselves with them tonight and let them go early tomorrow morning?" She continued to persuade her sisters until they consented, saying, "Let them in, but make it a condition that they 'speak not of what concerns them not, lest they hear what pleases them not.'"

Pleased, she disappeared for a while and returned, followed by three one-eyed dervishes, who greeted them, bowed, and stood back. The three girls rose to greet them, extended welcomes, expressed delight at their visit, and congratulated them on their safe arrival. The three dervishes thanked them and again saluted with bows, and when they saw the beautiful hall, the well-set table laden with wine, nuts, and dried fruits, the burning candles, the smoking incense, and the three girls, who had thrown off all restraint, they exclaimed with one voice, "By God, this is fine." When they turned and looked at the porter, who, sore from the beating and slapping and intoxicated with the wine, lay almost unconscious, they said, "Whether an Arab or a foreigner, he is a brother dervish." The porter sat up and, fixing his eyes on them, said, "Sit here without meddling. Haven't you read the inscription on the door, which is quite clearly written, 'Speak not of what concerns you not, lest you hear what pleases you not'? Yet as soon as you come in you wag your tongues at us." They replied, "O mendicant, we ask for God's forgiveness. Our heads are in your hands." The girls laughed and made peace between the dervishes and the porter; then the shopper offered the dervishes something to eat, and after they ate, they all sat down to carouse and drink, with the doorkeeper replenishing the cups as they passed them around. Then the porter asked, "Friends, can you entertain us with something?"

But morning overtook Shahrazad, and she lapsed into silence. Then her sister Dinarzad said, "Sister, what a lovely and entertaining story!" Shahrazad replied, "What is this compared with what I shall tell you tomorrow night if I live!"

THE THIRTY-THIRD NIGHT

The following night Dinarzad said to her sister Shahrazad, "Sister, if you are not sleepy, tell us one of your lovely little tales to while away the night." Shahrazad replied, "With the greatest pleasure":

I heard, O King, that the dervishes, heated with the wine, called for musical instruments, and the doorkeeper brought them a tambourine, a flute, and a Persian harp. The dervishes rose, and one took the tambourine, another the flute, another the Persian harp, tuned their instruments, and began to play and sing, and the girls began to sing with them until it got very loud. While they were thus playing and singing, they heard a knocking at the door and the doorkeeper went to see what was the matter.

Now the cause of that knocking, O King, was that it happened on that very night that the Caliph Harun al-Rashid and Ja'far came into the city, as they used to do every now and then, and as they walked through, they passed by the door and heard the music of the flute, the harp, and the tambourine, the singing of the girls, and the sounds of people partying and laughing. The caliph said, "Ja'far, I would like to enter this house and visit the people inside." Ja'far replied, "O Prince of the Faithful, these are people who are intoxicated and who do not know who we are, and I fear that they may insult us and abuse us." The caliph said, "Don't argue; I must go in and I want you to find a pretext to get us in." Ja'far replied, "I hear and obey." Then Ja'far knocked at the door, and when the doorkeeper came and opened the door, he stepped forward, kissed the ground before her, and said, "O my lady, we are merchants from the city of Mosul, and we have been in Baghdad for ten days. We have brought with us our merchandise and have taken lodgings at an inn. Tonight a merchant of your city invited us to his home and offered us food and drink. We drank and enjoyed ourselves and sent for a troop of musicians and singing women and invited the rest of our companions to join us. They all came and we had a good time, listening to the girls blow on the flutes, beat the tambourines, and sing, but while we were enjoying ourselves, the prefect of the police raided the place, and we tried to escape by jumping from walls. Some of us broke our limbs and were arrested, while some escaped safely. We have come now to seek refuge in your house, for, being strangers in your city, we are afraid that if we continue to walk the streets, the prefect of the police will stop us, discover that we are intoxicated, and arrest us. If we go to the inn, we shall find the door locked for, as is the rule, it is not to be opened till sunrise. As we passed by your house, we heard the sounds of music and the noise of a lovely party and hoped that you would be kind enough to let us join you to enjoy the rest of the night, giving us the chance to pay you for our share. If you refuse our company, let us sleep in the hallway till the morning, and God will reward you. The matter is in your magnanimous hands and the decision is yours, but we will not depart from your door."

After the doorkeeper had listened to Ja'far's speech, looked at their dress, and seen that they were respectable, she went back to her sisters and repeated Ja'far's story. The girls felt sorry for them and said, "Let them in," and she invited them to come in. When the caliph, together with Ja'far and Masrur, entered the hall, the entire group, the girls, the dervishes, and the porter, rose to greet them, and then everyone sat down.

But morning overtook Shahrazad, and she lapsed into silence. Then Dinarzad said, "What a lovely and entertaining story!" Shahrazad replied, "What is this compared with what I shall tell you tomorrow night if I stay alive!"

THE THIRTY-FOURTH NIGHT

The following night Dinarzad said to her sister Shahrazad, "Please, if you are not sleepy, tell us the rest of the story of the three girls." Shahrazad replied, "Very well":

It is related, O King, that when the caliph, together with Ja'far and Masrur, entered and sat down, the girls turned to them and said, "You are welcome, and we are delighted to have you as our guests, but on one condition." They asked, "What is your condition?" The girls replied, "That you will be eyes without tongues and will not inquire about whatever you see. You will 'speak not of what concerns you not, lest you hear what pleases you not.'" They replied, "Yes, as you wish, for we have no need to meddle." Pleased with them, the girls sat to entertain them, drinking and conversing with them. The caliph was astonished to see three dervishes, all blind in the right eye, and he was especially astonished to see girls with such beauty, charm, eloquence, and generosity, in such a lovely place, with a music band consisting of three one-eyed dervishes. But he felt that at that moment he could not ask any questions. They continued to converse and drink, and then the dervishes rose, bowed, and played another round of music; then they sat down and passed the cup around.

When the wine had taken hold, the mistress of the house rose, bowed, and, taking the shopper by the hand, said, "Sister, let us do our duty." Both sisters replied, "Very well." The doorkeeper got up, cleared the table, got rid of the peels and shells, replenished the incense, and cleared the middle of the hall. Then she made the dervishes sit on a sofa at one side of the hall and seated the caliph, Ja'far, and Masrur on another sofa at the other side of the hall. Then she shouted at the porter, saying, "You are very lazy. Get up and lend us a hand, for you are a member of the household." The porter got up and, girding himself, asked, "What is up?" She replied, "Stand where you are." Then the shopper placed a chair in the middle of the hall, opened a cupboard, and said to the porter, "Come and help me." When the porter approached, he saw two black female hounds with chains around their necks. He took them and led them to the middle of the hall. Saying, "It is time to perform our duty," the mistress of the house came forward, rolled up her sleeves, took a braided whip, and called to the porter, "Bring me one of the bitches." The porter dragged one of the bitches by the chain and brought her forward, while she wept and shook her head at the girl. As the porter stood holding the chain, the girl came down on the bitch with hard blows on the sides, while the bitch howled and wept. The girl kept beating the bitch until her arm got weary. Then she stopped, threw the whip away, and, taking the chain from the porter, embraced the bitch and began to cry. The bitch too began to cry, and the two cried together for a long time. Then the girl wiped the bitch's tears with her handkerchief, kissed her on the head, and said to the porter, "Take her back to her place, and bring me the other." The porter took the bitch to the cupboard and brought the other bitch to the girl, who did to her as she had done to the first, beating her until she fainted. Then she took the bitch, cried with her, kissed her on the head, and asked the porter to take her back to her sister, and he took her back. When those who were present saw what happened, how the girl beat the bitch until the bitch fainted, and how she cried with the bitch and kissed her on the head, they were completely amazed and began to speak under their breath. The caliph himself felt troubled and lost all patience as he burned with curiosity to know the story of these two bitches. He winked to Ja'far, but Ja'far, turning to him, said with a sign, "This is not the time to inquire."

O happy King, when the girl finished punishing the two bitches, the doorkeeper said to her, "My lady, go and sit on your couch, so that I in turn may fulfill my desire." Saying, "Very well," the girl went to the far end of the hall and seated herself on the couch, with the caliph, Ja'far, and Masrur seated in a row to her right and the dervishes and the porter, to her left, and although the lamps glowed, the candles burned, and the incense filled the place, these men were depressed and felt that their evening was spoiled. Then the doorkeeper sat on the chair.

But morning overtook Shahrazad, and she lapsed into silence. Then Dinarzad said to her sister, "Sister, what an amazing and entertaining story!" Shahrazad replied, "What is this compared with what I shall tell you tomorrow night if I live!"

THE THIRTY-FIFTH NIGHT

The following night, Dinarzad said to her sister Shahrazad, "Sister, if you are not sleepy, tell us one of your lovely little tales to while away the night." Shahrazad replied, "Very well":

I heard, O happy King, that the doorkeeper sat on the chair and said to her sister the shopper, "Get up and pay me my due." The shopper rose, entered a chamber, and soon brought back a bag of yellow satin with two green silk tassels ornamented with red gold and two beads of pure ambergris. She sat in front of the doorkeeper, drew a lute out of the bag, and with its side resting on her knee, held it in her lap. Then she tuned the lute and, plucking the strings with her fingertips, began to play and sing the following verses of the *Kan wa Kan* variety:

> My love, you are my aim,
> And you are my desire.
> Your company is constant joy,
> Your absence, hellish fire.
> You are the madness of my life,
> My one infatuation,
> A love in which there is no shame,
> A blameless adoration.
> The shirt of agony I wore
> Revealed my secret passion,
> Betrayed my agitated heart
> And left me in confusion.
> My tears to all declared my love,
> As o'er my cheeks they flowed,
> My treacherous tears betrayed me
> And all my secrets showed.
> O, cure me from my dire disease;
> You are the sickness and the cure,
> But he whose remedy you are

Will suffer evermore.
Your brilliant eyes have wasted me,
Your jet-black hair has me in thrall,
Your rosy cheeks have vanquished me
And told my tale to all.
My hardship is my martyrdom,
The sword of love, my death.
How often have the best of men
This way ended their breath?
I will not cease from loving you,
Nor unlock what is sealed.
Love is my law and remedy,
Whether hid or revealed.
Blessed my eyes that gazed on you,
O treasured revelation;
Which has left me confused, alone,
In helpless adoration.

When the girl finished the poem, her sister let out a loud cry and moaned, "Oh, oh, oh!" Then she grabbed her dress by the collar and tore it down to the hem, baring her entire body, and fell down in a swoon. When the caliph looked at her, he saw that her whole body, from her head to her toe, bore the marks of the whip, which left it black and blue. Seeing the girl's condition and not knowing the cause, he and his companions were troubled, and he said to Ja'far, "By God, I will not wait a moment until I get to the bottom of this and ask for an explanation for what has happened, the flogging of the girl, the whipping of the two bitches, then the crying and the kissing." Ja'far replied, "My lord, this is not the time to ask for an explanation, especially since they have imposed on us the condition that we speak not of what concerns us not, for 'he who speaks of what concerns him not hears what pleases him not.'"

Then the shopper rose and, entering the chamber, came out with a fine dress that she put on her sister, replacing the one her sister had torn, and sat down. The sister said to the shopper, "For God's sake, give me some more to drink," and the shopper took the cup, filled it, and handed it to her. Then the shopper held the lute in her lap, improvised a number of measures, and sang the following verses:

If I bemoan your absence, what will you say?
If I pine with longing, what is the way?
If I dispatch someone to tell my tale,
The lover's complaint no one can convey.
If I with patience try to bear my pain,
After the loss of love, I can't endure the blow.
Nothing remains but longing and regret
And tears that over the cheeks profusely flow.
You, who have long been absent from my eyes,
Will in my loving heart forever stay.
Was it you who have taught me how to love,
And from the pledge of love never to stray?

When the sister finished her song, the girl cried out, "Oh, oh, oh!" and, over-come by passion, again grabbed her dress by the collar and tore it to the hem. Then she shrieked and fell down in a swoon. Again the shopper entered the chamber and came out with a dress even better than the first. Then she sprin-kled her sister's face with rosewater, and when her sister came to herself, she put the dress on her. Then the sister said, "For God's sake, sister, pay me and finish off, for there remains only this one song." "With the greatest pleasure," replied the shopper, and she took the lute and began to play and sing the follow-ing verses:

> How long shall I endure this cruel disdain?
> Have I not paid enough with tears of woe?
> For how long suffer your willful neglect,
> As if it were a vengeful, envious foe?
> Be kind! Your cruel ways inflict a cruel pain,
> Master, 'tis time to me you pity show.
> O gentlemen, avenge this thrall of love,
> Who neither sleep nor patience does now know.
> Is it the law of love that one my love enjoys,
> While I alone do empty-handed go?
> My lord, let him my unjust tyrant be;
> Many the toils and trials I undergo.

When she finished her song . . .

But morning overtook Shahrazad, and she lapsed into silence. Then Dinarzad said, "Sister, what an amazing and entertaining story!" Shahrazad replied, "Tomorrow night I shall tell you something stranger, more amazing, and more entertaining if the king spares me and lets me live!"

THE THIRTY-SIXTH NIGHT

The following night Dinarzad said to her sister Shahrazad, "Sister, tell us the rest of the girls' story." Shahrazad said:

It is related, O King, that when the girl heard the third song, she cried out, "By God, this is good." Then she grabbed her dress and tore it, and, as she fell down in a swoon, she revealed on her chest marks like welts from a whip. The dervishes muttered. "We wish that we had never entered this house, but had rather spent the night on the rubbish mounds outside the city, for our visit has been spoiled by such heartrending sights." The caliph turned to them and asked, "How so?" and they replied, "O distinguished gentleman, our minds are troubled by this matter." The caliph asked, "But you are members of the household; perhaps you can explain to me the story of these two black bitches and this girl." They replied, "By God, we know nothing and we have never laid eyes on this place until tonight." Surprised, the caliph said, "Then this man who sits beside you should know the explanation." They winked at the porter, questioning him, but he replied, "By the Almighty God, 'In love all are alike,' for even though I have been raised in Baghdad, never in my life have I entered this house until today. I did spend an amazing day with them. Still, I kept wondering that they were all women without men." They said to him, "By God, we took you to be one of them, but now we find that you are in the same predicament as we are."

Then the caliph said, "Adding Ja'far and Masrur, we are seven men, and they are only three women, without even a single man. Let us ask them for an explanation; if they don't answer by choice, they will answer by force." They agreed to proceed with this plan, but Ja'far said, "This is not right; let them be, for we are their guests and, as you know, they made a condition that we promised to keep. It is better to keep silent about this matter, for little remains of the night, and soon each of us will go his own way." Then he winked at the caliph and whispered to him, "O Commander of the Faithful, be patient for this one last hour of the night, and tomorrow morning I will come back and bring them before you to tell us their story." But the caliph yelled at him, saying, "Damn it, I can no longer wait for an explanation. Let the dervishes question them." Ja'far replied, "This is not a good idea." Then they talked at length and disputed as to who should first put the question, and at last all agreed on the porter.

When the girls heard their clamor, one of them asked, "Men, what is the matter?" The porter approached her and said, "My lady, these men express the wish that you acquaint them with the story of the two black bitches and why you punish them and then weep over them, and they wish to know the story of your sister and how it was that she got flogged with the whip, like a man. That is all; that is what they want to know." Turning to them, the girl asked, "Is it true what he says about you?" They all replied, "Yes," except Ja'far, who remained silent. When the girl heard their reply, she said, "O guests, you have wronged us. Have we not told you of our condition, that 'he who speaks of what concerns him not will hear what pleases him not'? We took you into our home and fed you with our food, but after all this you meddled and did us wrong. Yet the fault is not so much yours as hers who let you in and brought you to us." Then she rolled up her sleeves and struck the floor three times, crying out, "Come at once," and a door opened and out came seven black men, with drawn swords in their hands. Then with the palm of the sword, each man dealt one of the men a blow that threw him on his face to the ground, and in no time they had the seven guests tied by the hands and bound each to each. Then they led them in a single file to the center of the hall, and each black man stood with his sword drawn above the head of his man. Then they said to the girl, "O most honorable and most virtuous lady, permit us to strike off their heads." She replied, "Wait a while until I question them, before you strike off their heads." The porter cried, "God protect me. O lady, slay me not for another's sin. All these men have sinned and offended, except me. By God, we had a delightful day. If only we could have escaped these one-eyed dervishes, whose entrance into any city blights it, destroys it, and lays it waste!" Then he began to weep and recite the following verses:

> Fair is the forgiveness of mighty men,
> And fairest when to weakest men 'tis shown.
> Break off not the first friendship for the last,
> By the bond of the love that has between us grown.

The girl, despite her anger, laughed, and, coming up to the group, said, "Tell me who you are, for you have only one hour to live. Were you not men of rank or eminent among your people or powerful rulers, you would not have dared to offend us." The caliph said to Ja'far, "Damn it, tell her who we are, lest we be slain by mistake." Ja'far replied, "This is part of what we deserve." The caliph yelled at him, saying, "This is no time for your witticisms." Then the lady approached the dervishes and asked, "Are you brothers?" They replied, "No, by God, mistress, we are not, nor are we mendicants." Then she asked one of them, "Were you born blind in one eye?" and he replied, "No, by God my lady. It was an amazing event and a strange mischance that caused me to lose my eye, shave off my beard, and become a dervish. Mine is a tale that, if it were engraved with needles at the corner of the eye, would be a warning to those who wish to consider." Then she questioned the second dervish, and he said the same, and questioned the third, and again he replied like the other two. Then they added, "By God, lady, each one of us comes from a different city, and each one of us is the son of a king, a prince sovereign over land and people." The girl turned to the black men and said, "Whoever tells us his tale and explains what has happened to him and what has brought him to our place, let him stroke his head and go, but whoever refuses, strike off his head."

But morning overtook Shahrazad, and she lapsed into silence. Then Dinarzad said to her sister, "What an amazing and entertaining story!" Shahrazad replied, "What is this compared with what I shall tell you tomorrow night if I stay alive!"

THE THIRTY-SEVENTH NIGHT

The following night Dinarzad said to her sister Shahrazad, "Sister, if you are not sleepy, tell us one of your lovely little tales to while away the night." Shahrazad replied, "With the greatest pleasure":

I heard, O King, that after the girl spoke, the first to come forth was the porter, who said, "Mistress, you know that the reason I came to this place was that I was hired as a porter by this shopper, who led me from the vintner to the butcher, and from the butcher to the greengrocer, and from the greengrocer to the fruit vendor, and from the fruit vendor to the dry grocer, then to the confectioner, to the druggist, and finally to this house. This is my tale." The girl replied, "Stroke your head and go." But he replied, "By God, I will not go until I hear the tales of the others."

THE OLD TESTAMENT†
ca. 1000–300 B.C.E.

From Exodus

[The Story of Moses]

1. Now these are the names of the children of Israel, which came into Egypt; every man and his household came with Jacob. Reuben, Simeon, Levi, and Judah, Issachar, Zebulun, and Benjamin, Dan, and Naphtali, Gad, and Asher. And all the souls that came out of the loins of Jacob were seventy souls: for Joseph was in Egypt already. And Joseph died, and all his brethren, and all that generation. And the children of Isreael were fruitful, and increased abundantly, and multiplied, and waxed exceeding mighty; and the land was filled with them.

Now there arose up a new king over Egypt, which knew not Joseph. And he said unto his people, Behold, the people of the children of Israel are more and mightier than we: come on, let us deal wisely with them; lest they multiply, and it come to pass, that, when there falleth out any war, they join also unto our enemies, and fight against us, and so get them up out of the land. Therefore they did set over them taskmasters to afflict them with their burdens. And they built for Pharaoh treasure cities, Pithom and Raamses. But the more they afflicted them, the more they multiplied and grew. And they were grieved because of the children of Israel. And the Egyptians made the children of Israel to serve with rigour: and they made their lives bitter with hard bondage, in morter, and in brick, and in all manner of service in the field: all their service, wherein they made them serve, was with rigour.

And the king of Egypt spake to the Hebrew midwives, of which the name of the one was Shiphrah, and the name of the other Puah: and he said, when ye do the office of a midwife to the Hebrew women, and see them upon the stools; if it be a son, then ye shall kill him: but if it be a daughter, then she shall live. But the midwives feared God, and did not as the king of Egypt commanded them, but saved the men children alive. And the king of Egypt called for the midwives, and said unto them, Why have ye done this thing, and have saved the men children alive? And the midwives said unto Pharaoh, Because the Hebrew women are not as the Egyptian women; for they are lively, and are delivered ere the midwives come in unto them. Therefore God dealt well with the midwives: and the people multiplied, and waxed very mighty. And it came to pass, because the midwives feared God, that he made them houses. And Pharaoh charged all his people, saying, Every son that is born ye shall cast into the river, and every daughter ye shall save alive.

2. And there went a man of the house of Levi, and took to wife a daughter of Levi. And the woman conceived, and bare a son: and when she saw him that

† The King James Version.

he was a goodly child, she hid him three months. And when she could not longer hide him, she took for him an ark of bulrushes, and daubed it with slime and with pitch, and put the child therein; and she laid it in the flags by the river's brink. And his sister stood afar off, to wit what would be done to him. And the daughter of Pharaoh came down to wash herself at the river; and her maidens walked along by the river's side; and when she saw the ark among the flags, she sent her maid to fetch it. And when she had opened it, she saw the child: and, behold, the babe wept. And she had compassion on him, and said, This is one of the Hebrews' children. Then said his sister to Pharaoh's daughter, Shall I go and call to thee a nurse of the Hebrew women, that she may nurse the child for thee? And Pharaoh's daughter said to her, Go. And the maid went and called the child's mother. And Pharaoh's daughter said unto her, Take this child away, and nurse it for me, and I will give thee thy wages. And the woman took the child, and nursed it. And the child grew, and she brought him unto Pharaoh's daughter, and he became her son. And she called his name Moses: and she said, Because I drew him out of the water.

And it came to pass in those days, when Moses was grown, that he went out unto his brethren, and looked on their burdens: and he spied an Egyptian smiting an Hebrew, one of his brethren. And he looked this way and that way, and when he saw that there was no man, he slew the Egyptian, and hid him in the sand. And when he went out the second day, behold, two men of the Hebrews strove together: and he said to him that did the wrong, Wherefore smitest thou thy fellow? And he said, Who made thee a prince and judge over us? intendest thou to kill me, as thou killedst the Egyptian? And Moses feared, and said, Surely this thing is known.

Now when Pharaoh heard this thing, he sought to slay Moses. But Moses fled from the face of Pharaoh, and dwelt in the land of Midian: and he sat down by a well. Now the priest of Midian had seven daughters: and they came and drew water, and filled the troughs to water their father's flock. And the shepherds came and drove them away: but Moses stood up and helped them, and watered their flock. And when they came to Reuel their father, he said, How is it that ye are come so soon to day? And they said, An Egyptian delivered us out of the hand of the shepherds, and also drew water enough for us, and watered the flock. And he said unto his daughters, And where is he? why is it that ye have left the man? call him, that he may eat bread. And Moses was content to dwell with the man: and he gave Moses Zipporah his daughter. And she bare him a son, and he called his name Gershom: for he said, I have been a stranger in a strange land.

And it came to pass in process of time, that the king of Egypt died: and the children of Israel sighed by reason of the bondage, and they cried, and their cry came up unto God by reason of the bondage. And God heard their groaning, and God remembered his covenant with Abraham, with Isaac, and with Jacob. And God looked upon the children of Israel, and God had respect unto them.

3. Now Moses kept the flock of Jethro his father in law, the priest of Midian: and he led the flock to the backside of the desert, and came to the mountain of God, even to Horeb. And the angel of the LORD appeared unto him in a flame of fire out of the midst of a bush: and he looked, and, behold, the bush

burned with fire, and the bush was not consumed. And Moses said, I will now turn aside, and see this great sight, why the bush is not burnt. And when the LORD saw that he turned aside to see, God called unto him out of the midst of the bush, and said, Moses, Moses. And he said, Here am I. And he said, Draw not nigh hither: put off thy shoes from off thy feet, for the place whereon thou standest is holy ground. Moreover he said, I am the God of thy father, the God of Abraham, the God of Isaac, and the God of Jacob. And Moses hid his face; for he was afraid to look upon God.

And the LORD said, I have surely seen the affliction of my people which are in Egypt, and have heard their cry by reason of their taskmasters; for I know their sorrows; and I am come down to deliver them out of the hand of the Egyptians, and to bring them up out of that land unto a good land and a large, unto a land flowing with milk and honey; unto the place of the Canaanites, and the Hittites, and the Amorites, and the Perizzites, and the Hivites, and the Jebusites. Now therefore, behold, the cry of the children of Israel is come unto me: and I have also seen the oppression wherewith the Egyptians oppress them. Come now therefore, and I will send thee unto Pharaoh, that thou mayest bring forth my people the children of Israel out of Egypt. And Moses said unto God, Who am I, that I should go unto Pharaoh, and that I should bring forth the children of Israel out of Egypt? And he said, Certainly I will be with thee; and this shall be a token unto thee, that I have sent thee: When thou hast brought forth the people out of Egypt, ye shall serve God upon this mountain.

And Moses said unto God, Behold, when I come unto the children of Israel, and shall say unto them, The God of your fathers hath sent me unto you; and they shall say to me, What is his name? what shall I say unto them? And God said unto Moses, I AM THAT I AM: and he said, Thus shalt thou say unto the children of Israel, I AM hath sent me unto you. And God said moreover unto Moses, Thus shalt thou say unto the children of Israel, The LORD God of your fathers, the God of Abraham, the God of Isaac, and the God of Jacob, hath sent me unto you: this is my name for ever, and this is my memorial unto all generations. Go, and gather the elders of Israel together, and say unto them, The LORD God of your fathers, the God of Abraham, of Isaac, and of Jacob, appeared unto me, saying, I have surely visited you, and seen that which is done to you in Egypt: and I have said, I will bring you up out of the affliction of Egypt unto the land of the Canaanites, and the Hittites, and the Amorites, and the Perizzites, and the Hivites, and the Jebusites, unto a land flowing with milk and honey. And they shall hearken to thy voice: and thou shalt come, thou and the elders of Israel, unto the king of Egypt, and ye shall say unto him, The LORD God of the Hebrews hath met with us: and now let us go, we beseech thee, three days' journey into the wilderness, that we may sacrifice to the LORD our God. And I am sure that the king of Egypt will not let you go, no, not by a mighty hand. And I will stretch out my hand, and smite Egypt with all my wonders which I will do in the midst thereof: and after that he will let you go. And I will give this people favour in the sight of the Egyptians: and it shall come to pass, that, when ye go, ye shall not go empty: but every woman shall borrow of her neighbour, and of her that sojourneth in her house, jewels of silver, and jewels of gold, and raiment: and ye shall put them upon your sons, and upon your daughters; and ye shall spoil the Egyptians.

4. And Moses answered and said, But, behold, they will not believe me, nor hearken unto my voice: for they will say, The Lord hath not appeared unto thee. And the Lord said unto him, What is that in thine hand? And he said, A rod. And he said, Cast it on the ground. And he cast it on the ground, and it became a serpent; and Moses fled from before it. And the Lord said unto Moses, Put forth thine hand, and take it by the tail. And he put forth his hand, and caught it, and it became a rod in his hand: that they may believe that the Lord God of their fathers, the God of Abraham, the God of Isaac, and the God of Jacob, hath appeared unto thee. And the Lord said furthermore unto him, Put now thine hand into thy bosom. And he put his hand into his bosom: and when he took it out, behold, his hand was leprous as snow. And he said, Put thine hand into thy bosom again. And he put his hand into his bosom again; and plucked it out of his bosom, and, behold, it was turned again as his other flesh. And it shall come to pass, if they will not believe thee, neither hearken to the voice of the first sign, that they will believe the voice of the latter sign. And it shall come to pass, if they will not believe also these two signs, neither hearken unto thy voice, that thou shalt take of the water of the river, and pour it upon the dry land: and the water which thou takest out of the river shall become blood upon the dry land.

And Moses said unto the Lord, O my Lord, I am not eloquent, neither heretofore, nor since thou hast spoken unto thy servant: but I am slow of speech, and of a slow tongue. And the Lord said unto him, Who hath made man's mouth? or who maketh the dumb, or deaf, or the seeing, or the blind? have not I the Lord? Now therefore go, and I will be with thy mouth, and teach thee what thou shalt say. And he said, O my Lord, send, I pray thee, by the hand of him whom thou wilt send. And the anger of the Lord was kindled against Moses, and he said, Is not Aaron the Levite thy brother? I know that he can speak well. And also, behold, he cometh forth to meet thee: and when he seeth thee, he will be glad in his heart. And thou shalt speak unto him, and put words in his mouth: and I will be with thy mouth, and with his mouth, and will teach you what ye shall do. And he shall be thy spokesman unto the people: and he shall be, even he shall be to thee instead of a mouth, and thou shalt be to him instead of God. And thou shalt take this rod in thine hand, wherewith thou shalt do signs. And Moses went and returned to Jethro his father in law, and said unto him, Let me go, I pray thee, and return unto my brethren which are in Egypt, and see whether they be yet alive. And Jethro said to Moses, Go in peace.

And the Lord said unto Moses in Midian, Go, return into Egypt: for all the men are dead which sought thy life. And Moses took his wife and his sons, and set them upon an ass, and he returned to the land of Egypt: and Moses took the rod of God in his hand. And the Lord said unto Moses, When thou goest to return into Egypt, see that thou do all those wonders before Pharaoh, which I have put in thine hand: but I will harden his heart, that he shall not let the people go. And thou shalt say unto Pharaoh, Thus saith the Lord, Israel is my son, even my firstborn: and I say unto thee, Let my son go, that he may serve me: and if thou refuse to let him go, behold, I will slay thy son, even thy firstborn.

And it came to pass by the way in the inn, that the Lord met him, and sought to kill him. Then Zipporah took a sharp stone, and cut off the foreskin of her son, and cast it at his feet, and said, Surely a bloody husband art thou to me. So he let him go: then she said, A bloody husband thou art, because of the circumcision.

And the LORD said to Aaron, Go into the wilderness to meet Moses. And he went, and met him in the mount of God, and kissed him. And Moses told Aaron all the words of the LORD who had sent him, and all the signs which he had commanded him. And Moses and Aaron went and gathered together all the elders of the children of Israel: and Aaron spake all the words which the LORD had spoken unto Moses, and did the signs in the sight of the people. And the people believed: and when they heard that the LORD had visited the children of Israel, and that he had looked upon their affliction, then they bowed their heads and worshipped.

5. And afterward Moses and Aaron went in, and told Pharaoh, Thus saith the LORD God of Israel, Let my people go, that they may hold a feast unto me in the wilderness. And Pharaoh said, Who is the LORD, that I should obey his voice to let Israel go? I know not the LORD, neither will I let Israel go. And they said, The God of the Hebrews hath met with us: let us go, we pray thee, three days' journey into the desert, and sacrifice unto the LORD our God; lest he fall upon us with pestilence, or with the sword. And the king of Egypt said unto them, Wherefore do ye, Moses and Aaron, let the people from their works? get you unto your burdens. And Pharaoh said, Behold, the people of the land now are many, and ye make them rest from their burdens. And Pharaoh commanded the same day the taskmasters of the people, and their officers, saying, Ye shall no more give the people straw to make brick, as heretofore: let them go and gather straw for themselves. And the tale of the bricks, which they did make heretofore, ye shall lay upon them; ye shall not diminish ought thereof: for they be idle; therefore they cry, saying, Let us go and sacrifice to our God. Let there more work be laid upon the men, that they may labour therein; and let them not regard vain words.

And the taskmasters of the people went out, and their officers, and they spake to the people, saying, Thus saith Pharaoh, I will not give you straw. Go ye, get you straw where ye can find it: yet not ought of your work shall be diminished. So the people were scattered abroad throughout all the land of Egypt to gather stubble instead of straw. And the taskmasters hasted them, saying, Fulfil your works, your daily tasks, as when there was straw. And the officers of the children of Israel, which Pharaoh's taskmasters had set over them, were beaten, and demanded, Wherefore have ye not fulfilled your task in making brick both yesterday and to day, as heretofore? Then the officers of the children of Israel came and cried unto Pharaoh, saying, Wherefore dealest thou thus with thy servants? There is no straw given unto they servants, and they say to us, Make brick: and, behold, thy servants are beaten; but the fault is in thine own people. But he said, Ye are idle, ye are idle: therefore ye say, Let us go and do sacrifice to the LORD. Go therefore now, and work; for there shall no straw be given you, yet shall ye deliver the tale of bricks. And the officers of the children of Israel did see that they were in evil case, after it was said, Ye shall not minish ought from your bricks of your daily task.

And they met Moses and Aaron, who stood in the way, as they came forth from Pharaoh: and they said unto them, The LORD look upon you, and judge; because ye have made our savour to be abhorred in the eyes of Pharaoh, and in the eyes of his servants, to put a sword in their hand to slay us. And Moses returned unto the LORD, and said, Lord, wherefore hast thou so evil entreated this people? Why is it that thou hast sent me? For since I came to Pharaoh to speak in thy name, he hath done evil to this people; neither hast thou delivered

6. thy people at all. Then the LORD said unto Moses, Now shalt thou see what I will do to Pharaoh: for with a strong hand shall he let them go, and with a strong hand shall he drive them out of his land.

And God spake unto Moses, and said unto him, I am the LORD: and I appeared unto Abraham, unto Isaac, and unto Jacob, by the name of God Almighty, but by my name JEHOVAH was I not known to them. And I have also established my covenant with them, to give them the land of Canaan, the land of their pilgrimage, wherein they were strangers. And I have also heard the groaning of the children of Israel, whom the Egyptians keep in bondage; and I have remembered my covenant. Wherefore say unto the children of Israel, I am the LORD, and I will bring you out from under the burdens of the Egyptians, and I will rid you out of their bondage, and I will redeem you with a stretched out arm, and with great judgments: and I will take you to me for a people, and I will be to you a God: and ye shall know that I am the LORD your God, which bringeth you out from under the burdens of the Egyptians. And I will bring you in unto the land, concerning the which I did swear to give it to Abraham, to Isaac, and to Jacob; and I will give it you for an heritage: I am the LORD.

And Moses spake so unto the children of Israel: but they hearkened not unto Moses for anguish of spirit, and for cruel bondage. And the LORD spake unto Moses, saying, Go in, speak unto Pharaoh king of Egypt, that he let the children of Israel go out of his land. And Moses spake before the LORD, saying, Behold, the children of Israel have not hearkened unto me; how then shall Pharaoh hear me, who am of uncircumcised lips? And the LORD spake unto Moses and unto Aaron, and gave them a charge unto the children of Israel, and unto Pharaoh king of Egypt, to bring the children of Israel out of the land of Egypt.

These be the heads of their fathers' houses: The sons of Reuben the first-born of Israel; Hanoch, and Pallu, Hezron, and Carmi: these be the families of Reuben. And the sons of Simeon; Jemuel, and Jamin, and Ohad, and Jachin, and Zohar, and Shaul the son of a Canaanitish woman: these are the families of Simeon.

And these are the names of the sons of Levi according to their generations; Gershon, and Kohath, and Merari: and the years of the life of Levi were an hundred thirty and seven years. The sons of Gershon; Libni, and Shimi, according to their families. And the sons of Kohath: Amram, and Izhar, and Hebron, and Uzziel: and the years of the life of Kohath were an hundred thirty and three years. And the sons of Merari; Mahali and Mushi: these are the families of Levi according to their generations.

And Amram took him Jochebed his father's sister to wife; and she bare him Aaron and Moses: and the years of the life of Amram were an hundred and thirty and seven years. And the sons of Izhar; Korah, and Nepheg, and Zichri. And the sons of Uzziel; Mishael, and Elzaphan, and Zithri. And Aaron took him Elisheba, daughter of Amminadab, sister of Naashon, to wife; and she bare him Nadab, and Abihu, Eleazar, and Ithamar. And the sons of Korah; Assir, and Elkanah, and Abiasaph: these are the families of the Korhites. And Eleazar

Aaron's son took him one of the daughters of Putiel to wife; and she bare him Phinehas: these are the heads of the fathers of the Levites according to their families. These are that Aaron and Moses, to whom the LORD said, Bring out the children of Israel from the land of Egypt according to their armies. These are they which spake to Pharaoh king of Egypt, to bring out the children of Israel from Egypt: these are that Moses and Aaron.

And it came to pass on the day when the LORD spake unto Moses in the land of Egypt, that the LORD spake unto Moses, saying, I am the LORD: speak thou unto Pharaoh king of Egypt all that I say unto thee. And Moses said before the LORD, Behold, I am of uncircumcised lips, and how shall Pharaoh hearken unto me?

7. And the LORD said unto Moses, See, I have made thee a god to Pharaoh: and Aaron thy brother shall be thy prophet. Thou shalt speak all that I command thee: and Aaron thy brother shall speak unto Pharaoh, that he send the children of Israel out of his land. And I will harden Pharaoh's heart, and multiply my signs and my wonders in the land of Egypt. But Pharaoh shall not hearken unto you, that I may lay my hand upon Egypt, and bring forth mine armies, and my people the children of Israel, out of the land of Egypt by great judgments. And the Egyptians shall know that I am the LORD, when I stretch forth mine hand upon Egypt, and bring out the children of Israel from among them. And Moses and Aaron did as the LORD commanded them, so did they. And Moses was fourscore years old, and Aaron fourscore and three years old, when they spake unto Pharaoh.

And the LORD spake unto Moses and unto Aaron, saying, When Pharaoh shall speak unto you, saying, Shew a miracle for you: then thou shalt say unto Aaron, Take thy rod, and cast it before Pharaoh, and it shall become a serpent.

And Moses and Aaron went in unto Pharaoh, and they did so as the LORD had commanded: and Aaron cast down his rod before Pharaoh, and before his servants, and it became a serpent. Then Pharaoh also called the wise men and the sorcerers: now the magicians of Egypt, they also did in like manner with their enchantments. For they cast down every man his rod, and they became serpents: but Aaron's rod swallowed up their rods. And he hardened Pharaoh's heart, that he hearkened not unto them; as the LORD had said.

And the LORD said unto Moses, Pharaoh's heart is hardened, he refuseth to let the people go. Get thee unto Pharaoh in the morning; lo, he goeth out unto the water; and thou shalt stand by the river's brink against he come; and the rod which was turned to a serpent shalt thou take in thine hand. And thou shalt say unto him, The LORD God of the Hebrews hath sent me unto thee, saying, Let my people go, that they may serve me in the wilderness: and, behold, hitherto thou wouldest not hear. Thus saith the LORD, In this thou shalt know that I am the LORD: behold, I will smite with the rod that is in mine hand upon the waters which are in the river, and they shall be turned to blood. And the fish that is in the river shall die, and the river shall stink; and the Egyptians shall lothe to drink of the water of the river.

And the LORD spake unto Moses, Say unto Aaron, Take thy rod, and stretch out thine hand upon the waters of Egypt, upon their streams, upon their rivers, and upon their ponds, and upon all their pools of water, that they may become blood; and that there may be blood throughout all the land of Egypt, both in vessels of wood, and in vessels of stone. And Moses and Aaron did so, as the LORD commanded; and he lifted up the rod, and smote the waters that were in the river, in the sight of Pharaoh, and in the sight of his servants; and all the waters that were in the river were turned to blood. And the fish that was in the river died; and the river stank, and the Egyptians could not drink of the water of the river; and there was blood throughout all the land of Egypt. And the magicians of Egypt did so with their enchantments: and Pharaoh's heart was hardened, neither did he hearken unto them; as the LORD had said. And Pharaoh turned and went into his house, neither did he set his heart to this also. And all the Egyptians digged round about the river for water to drink; for they could not drink of the water of the river. And seven days were fulfilled, after that the LORD had smitten the river.

8. And the LORD spake unto Moses, Go unto Pharaoh, and say unto him, Thus saith the LORD, Let my people go, that they may serve me. And if thou refuse to let them go, behold, I will smite all thy borders with frogs: and the river shall bring forth frogs abundantly, which shall go up and come into thine house, and into thy bedchamber, and upon thy bed, and into the house of thy servants, and upon thy people, and into thine ovens, and into thy kneading troughs: and the frogs shall come up both on thee, and upon thy people, and upon all thy servants.

And the LORD spake unto Moses, Say unto Aaron, Stretch forth thine hand with thy rod over the streams, over the rivers, and over the ponds, and cause frogs to come up upon the land of Egypt. And Aaron stretched out his hand over the waters of Egypt; and the frogs came up, and covered the land of Egypt. And the magicians did so with their enchantments, and brought up frogs upon the land of Egypt.

Then Pharaoh called for Moses and Aaron, and said, Intreat the LORD, that he may take away the frogs from me, and from my people; and I will let the people go, that they may do sacrifice unto the LORD. And Moses said unto Pharaoh, Glory over me: when shall I intreat for thee, and for thy servants, and for thy people, to destroy the frogs from thee and thy houses, that they may remain in the river only? And he said, To morrow. And he said, Be it according to thy word: that thou mayest know that there is none like unto the LORD our God. And the frogs shall depart from thee, and from thy houses, and from thy servants, and from thy people; they shall remain in the river only. And Moses and Aaron went out from Pharaoh: and Moses cried unto the LORD because of the frogs which he had brought against Pharaoh. And the LORD did according to the word of Moses; and the frogs died out of the houses, out of the villages, and out of the fields. And they gathered them together upon heaps: and the land stank. But when Pharaoh saw that there was respite, he hardened his heart, and hearkened not unto them; as the LORD had said.

And the LORD said unto Moses, Say unto Aaron, Stretch out thy rod, and smite the dust of the land, that it may become lice throughout all the land of Egypt. And they did so; for Aaron stretched out his hand with his rod, and smote the dust of the earth, and it became lice in man, and in beast; all the dust of the land became lice throughout all the land of Egypt. And the magicians did so with their enchantments to bring forth lice, but they could not: so there were lice upon man, and upon beast. Then the magicians said unto Pharaoh, This is the finger of God: and Pharaoh's heart was hardened, and he hearkened not unto them; as the LORD had said.

And the LORD said unto Moses, Rise up early in the morning, and stand before Pharaoh; lo, he cometh forth to the water; and say unto him, Thus saith the LORD, Let my people go, that they may serve me. Else, if thou wilt not let my people go, behold, I will send swarms of flies upon thee, and upon thy servants, and upon thy people, and into thy houses: and the houses of the Egyptians shall be full of swarms of flies, and also the ground whereon they are. And I will sever in that day the land of Goshen, in which my people dwell, that no swarms of flies shall be there; to the end thou mayest know that I am the LORD in the midst of the earth. And I will put a division between my people and thy people: to morrow shall this sign be. And the LORD did so; and there came a grievous swarm of flies into the house of Pharaoh, and into his servants' houses, and into all the land of Egypt: the land was corrupted by reason of the swarm of flies.

And Pharaoh called for Moses and for Aaron, and said, Go ye, sacrifice to your God in the land. And Moses said, It is not meet so to do; for we shall sacrifice the abomination of the Egyptians to the LORD our God: lo, shall we sacrifice the abomination of the Egyptians before their eyes, and will they not stone us? We will go three days' journey into the wilderness, and sacrifice to the LORD our God, as he shall command us. And Pharaoh said, I will let you go, that ye may sacrifice to the LORD your God in the wilderness; only ye shall not go very far away: intreat for me. And Moses said, Behold, I go out from thee, and I will intreat the LORD that the swarms of flies may depart from Pharaoh, from his servants, and from his people, to morrow: but let not Pharaoh deal deceitfully any more in not letting the people go to sacrifice to the LORD. And Moses went out from Pharaoh, and intreated the LORD. And the LORD did according to the word of Moses; and he removed the swarms of flies from Pharaoh, from his servants, and from his people; there remained not one. And Pharaoh hardened his heart at this time also, neither would he let the people go.

9. Then the LORD said unto Moses, Go in unto Pharaoh, and tell him, Thus saith the LORD God of the Hebrews, Let my people go, that they may serve me. For if thou refuse to let them go, and wilt hold them still, behold, the hand of the LORD is upon thy cattle which is in the field, upon the horses, upon the asses, upon the camels, upon the oxen, and upon the sheep: there shall be a very grievous murrain. And the LORD shall sever between the cattle of Israel and the cattle of Egypt: and there shall nothing die of all that is the children's of Israel. And the LORD appointed a set time, saying, To morrow the LORD shall do this thing in the land. And the LORD did that thing on the morrow, and all the cattle of Egypt died: but of the cattle of the children of Israel died not one. And Pharaoh sent, and, behold, there was not one of the cattle of the Israelites dead. And the heart of Pharaoh was hardened, and he did not let the people go.

And the LORD said unto Moses and unto Aaron, Take to you handfuls of ashes of the furnace, and let Moses sprinkle it toward the heaven in the sight of Pharaoh. And it shall become small dust in all the land of Egypt, and shall be a boil breaking forth with blains upon man, and upon beast, throughout all the land of Egypt. And they took ashes of the furnace, and stood before Pharaoh; and Moses sprinkled it up toward heaven; and it became a boil breaking forth with blains upon man, and upon beast. And the magicians could not stand before Moses because of the boils; for the boil was upon the magicians, and upon all the Egyptians. And the LORD hardened the heart of Pharaoh, and he hearkened not unto them; as the LORD had spoken unto Moses.

And the LORD said unto Moses, Rise up early in the morning, and stand before Pharaoh, and say unto him, Thus saith the LORD God of the Hebrews, Let my people go, that they may serve me. For I will at this time send all my plagues upon thine heart, and upon thy servants, and upon thy people; that thou mayest know that there is none like me in all the earth. For now I will stretch out my hand, that I may smite thee and thy people with pestilence; and thou shalt be cut off from the earth. And in very deed for this cause have I raised thee up, for to shew in thee my power; and that my name may be declared throughout all the earth. As yet exaltest thou thyself against my people, that thou wilt not let them go? Behold, to morrow about this time I will cause it to rain a very grievous hail, such as hath not been in Egypt since the foundation thereof even until now. Send therefore now, and gather thy cattle, and all that thou hast in the field; for upon every man and beast which shall be found in the field, and shall not be brought home, the hail shall come down upon them, and they shall die. He that feared the word of the LORD among the servants of Pharaoh made his servants and his cattle flee into the houses: and he that regarded not the word of the LORD left his servants and his cattle in the field.

And the LORD said unto Moses, Stretch forth thine hand toward heaven, that there may be hail in all the land of Egypt, upon man, and upon beast, and upon every herb of the field, throughout the land of Egypt. And Moses stretched forth his rod toward heaven: and the LORD sent thunder and hail, and the fire ran along upon the ground; and the LORD rained hail upon the land of Egypt. So there was hail, and fire mingled with the hail, very grievous, such as there was none like it in all the land of Egypt since it became a nation. And the hail smote throughout all the land of Egypt all that was in the field, both man and beast; and the hail smote every herb of the field, and brake every tree of the field. Only in the land of Goshen, where the children of Israel were, was there no hail.

And Pharaoh sent, and called for Moses and Aaron, and said unto them, I have sinned this time: the LORD is righteous, and I and my people are wicked. Intreat the LORD (for it is enough) that there be no more mighty thunderings and hail; and I will let you go, and ye shall stay no longer. And Moses said unto him, As soon as I am gone out of the city, I will spread abroad my hands unto the LORD; and the thunder shall cease, neither shall there be any more hail; that thou mayest know how that the earth is the LORD's. But as for thee and thy servants, I know that ye will not yet fear the LORD God. And the flax and the barley was smitten: for the barley was in the ear, and the flax was bolled. But the wheat and the rie were not smitten: for they were not grown up. And Moses went out of the city from Pharaoh, and spread abroad his hands unto the LORD: and the thunders and hail ceased, and the rain was not poured upon the earth. And when Pharaoh saw that the rain and the hail and the thunders were ceased, he sinned yet more, and hardened his heart, he and his servants. And the heart of Pharaoh was hardened, neither would he let the children of Israel go; as the LORD had spoken by Moses.

10. And the Lord said unto Moses, Go in unto Pharaoh: for I have hardened his heart, and the heart of his servants, that I might shew these my signs before him: and that thou mayest tell in the ears of thy son, and of thy son's son, what things I have wrought in Egypt, and my signs which I have done among them; that ye may know how that I am the Lord. And Moses and Aaron came in unto Pharaoh, and said unto him, Thus saith the Lord God of the Hebrews, How long wilt thou refuse to humble thyself before me? let my people go, that they may serve me. Else, if thou refuse to let my people go, behold, to morrow will I bring the locusts into thy coast: and they shall cover the face of the earth, that one cannot be able to see the earth: and they shall eat the residue of that which is escaped, which remaineth unto you from the hail, and shall eat every tree which groweth for you out of the field: and they shall fill thy houses, and the houses of all thy servants, and the houses of all the Egyptians; which neither thy fathers, nor thy fathers' fathers have seen, since the day that they were upon the earth unto this day. And he turned himself, and went out from Pharaoh. And Pharaoh's servants said unto him, How long shall this man be a snare unto us? let the men go, that they may serve the Lord their God: knowest thou not yet that Egypt is destroyed? And Moses and Aaron were brought again unto Pharaoh: and he said unto them, Go, serve the Lord your God: but who are they that shall go? And Moses said, We will go with our young and with our old, with our sons and with our daughters, with our flocks and with our herds will we go; for we must hold a feast unto the Lord. And he said unto them, Let the Lord be so with you, as I will let you go, and your little ones: look to it; for evil is before you. Not so: go now ye that are men, and serve the Lord; for that ye did desire. And they were driven out from Pharaoh's presence.

And the Lord said unto Moses, Stretch out thine hand over the land of Egypt for the locusts, that they may come up upon the land of Egypt, and eat every herb of the land, even all that the hail hath left. And Moses stretched forth his rod over the land of Egypt, and the Lord brought an east wind upon the land all that day, and all that night; and when it was morning, the east wind brought the locusts. And the locusts went up over all the land of Egypt, and rested in all the coasts of Egypt: very grievous were they; before them there were no such locusts as they, neither after them shall be such. For they covered the face of the whole earth, so that the land was darkened; and they did eat every herb of the land, and all the fruit of the trees which the hail had left: and there remained not any green thing in the trees, or in the herbs of the field, through all the land of Egypt.

Then Pharaoh called for Moses and Aaron in haste; and he said, I have sinned against the Lord your God, and against you. Now therefore forgive, I pray thee, my sin only this once, and intreat the Lord your God, that he may take away from me this death only. And he went out from Pharaoh, and intreated the Lord. And the Lord turned a mighty strong west wind, which took away the locusts, and cast them into the Red sea; there remained not one locust in all the coasts of Egypt. But the Lord hardened Pharaoh's heart, so that he would not let the children of Israel go.

And the Lord said unto Moses, Stretch out thine hand toward heaven, that there may be darkness over the land of Egypt, even darkness which may be felt. And Moses stretched forth his hand toward heaven; and there was a thick darkness in all the land of Egypt three days: they saw not one another, neither rose any from his place for three days: but all the children of Israel had light in their dwellings.

And Pharaoh called unto Moses, and said, Go ye, serve the LORD; only let your flocks and your herds be stayed: let your little ones also go with you. And Moses said, Thou must give us also sacrifices and burnt offerings, that we may sacrifice unto the LORD our God. Our cattle also shall go with us; there shall not an hoof be left behind; for thereof must we take to serve the LORD our God; and we know not with what we must serve the LORD, until we come thither. But the LORD hardened Pharaoh's heart, and he would not let them go. And Pharaoh said unto him, Get thee from me, take heed to thyself, see my face no more; for in that day thou seest my face thou shalt die. And Moses said, Thou hast spoken well, I will see thy face again no more.

11. And the LORD said unto Moses, Yet will I bring one plague more upon Pharaoh, and upon Egypt; afterwards he will let you go hence: when he shall let you go, he shall surely thrust you out hence altogether. Speak now in the ears of the people, and let every man borrow of his neighbour, and every woman of her neighbour, jewels of silver, and jewels of gold. And the LORD gave the people favour in the sight of the Egyptians. Moreover the man Moses was very great in the land of Egypt, in the sight of Pharaoh's servants, and in the sight of the people.

And Moses said, Thus saith the LORD, About midnight will I go out into the midst of Egypt: And all the firstborn in the land of Egypt shall die, from the firstborn of Pharaoh that sitteth upon his throne, even unto the firstborn of the maidservant that is behind the mill; and all the firstborn of beasts. And there shall be a great cry throughout all the land of Egypt, such as there was none like it, nor shall be like it any more. But against any of the children of Israel shall not a dog move his tongue, against man or beast: that ye may know how that the LORD doth put a difference between the Egyptians and Israel. And all these thy servants shall come down unto me, and bow down themselves unto me, saying, Get thee out, and all the people that follow thee: and after that I will go out. And he went out from Pharaoh in a great anger.

And the LORD said unto Moses, Pharaoh shall not hearken unto you; that my wonders may be multiplied in the land of Egypt. And Moses and Aaron did all these wonders before Pharaoh: and the LORD hardened Pharaoh's heart, so that he would not let the children of Israel go out of his land.

12. And the LORD spake unto Moses and Aaron in the land of Egypt, saying, This month shall be unto you the beginning of months: it shall be the first month of the year to you. Speak ye unto all the congregation of Israel, saying, In the tenth day of this month they shall take to them every man a lamb, according to the house of their fathers, a lamb for an house: and if the household be too little for the lamb, let him and his neighbour next unto his house take it according to the number of the souls; every man according to his eating shall make your count for the lamb. Your lamb shall be without blemish, a male of the first year: ye shall take it out from the sheep, or from the goats: and ye shall keep it up until the fourteenth day of the same month: and the whole assembly of the congregation of Israel shall kill it in the evening. And they shall take of the blood, and strike it on the two side posts and on the

upper door post of the houses, wherein they shall eat it. And they shall eat the flesh in that night, roast with fire, and unleavened bread; and with bitter herbs they shall eat it. Eat not of it raw, nor sodden at all with water, but roast with fire; his head with his legs, and with the purtenance thereof. And ye shall let nothing of it remain until the morning; and that which remaineth of it until the morning ye shall burn with fire. And thus shall ye eat it; with your loins girded, your shoes on your feet, and your staff in your hand; and ye shall eat it in haste: it is the LORD's passover. For I will pass through the land of Egypt this night, and will smite all the firstborn in the land of Egypt, both man and beast; and against all the gods of Egypt I will execute judgment: I am the LORD. And the blood shall be to you for a token upon the houses where ye are: and when I see the blood, I will pass over you, and the plague shall not be upon you to destroy you, when I smite the land of Egypt.

And this day shall be unto you for a memorial; and ye shall keep it a feast to the LORD throughout your generations; ye shall keep it a feast by an ordinance for ever. Seven days shall ye eat unleavened bread; even the first day ye shall put away leaven out of your houses: for whosoever eateth leavened bread from the first day until the seventh day, that soul shall be cut off from Israel. And in the first day there shall be an holy convocation, and in the seventh day there shall be an holy convocation to you; no manner of work shall be done in them, save that which every man must eat, that only may be done of you. And ye shall observe the feast of unleavened bread; for in this selfsame day have I brought your armies out of the land of Egypt: therefore shall ye observe this day in your generations by an ordinance for ever. In the first month, on the fourteenth day of the month at even, ye shall eat unleavened bread, until the one and twentieth day of the month at even. Seven days shall there be no leaven found in your houses: for whosoever eateth that which is leavened, even that soul shall be cut off from the congregation of Israel, whether he be a stranger, or born in the land. Ye shall eat nothing leavened; in all your habitations shall ye eat unleavened bread.

Then Moses called for all the elders of Israel, and said unto them, Draw out and take you a lamb according to your families, and kill the passover. And ye shall take a bunch of hyssop, and dip it in the blood that is in the bason, and strike the lintel and the two side posts with the blood that is in the bason; and none of you shall go out at the door of his house until the morning. For the LORD will pass through to smite the Egyptians; and when he seeth the blood upon the lintel, and on the two side posts, the LORD will pass over the door, and will not suffer the destroyer to come in unto your houses to smite you. And ye shall observe this thing for an ordinance to thee and to thy sons for ever. And it shall come to pass, when ye be come to the land which the LORD will give you, according as he hath promised, that ye shall keep this service. And it shall come to pass, when your children shall say unto you, What mean ye by this service? That ye shall say, It is the sacrifice of the LORD's passover, who passed over the houses of the children of Israel in Egypt, when he smote the Egyptians, and delivered our houses. And the people bowed the head and worshipped. And the children of Israel went away, and did as the LORD had commanded Moses and Aaron, so did they.

And it came to pass, that at midnight the LORD smote all the firstborn in the land of Egypt, from the firstborn of Pharaoh that sat on his throne unto the firstborn of the captive that was in the dungeon; and all the firstborn of cattle. And Pharaoh rose up in the night, he, and all his servants, and all the Egyptians; and there was a great cry in Egypt; for there was not a house where there was not one dead. And he called for Moses and Aaron by night, and said, Rise up, and get you forth from among my people, both ye and the children of Israel; and go, serve the LORD, as ye have said. Also take your flocks and your herds, as ye have said, and be gone; and bless me also. And the Egyptians were urgent upon the people, that they might send them out of the land in haste; for they said, We be all dead men. And the people took their dough before it was leavened, their kneadingtroughs being bound up in their clothes upon their shoulders. And the children of Israel did according to the word of Moses; and they borrowed of the Egyptians jewels of silver, and jewels of gold, and raiment: and the LORD gave the people favour in the sight of the Egyptians, so that they lent unto them such things as they required. And they spoiled the Egyptians.

And the children of Israel journeyed from Rameses to Succoth, about six hundred thousand on foot that were men, beside children. And a mixed multitude went up also with them; and flocks, and herds, even very much cattle. And they baked unleavened cakes of the dough which they brought forth out of Egypt, for it was not leavened; because they were thrust out of Egypt, and could not tarry, neither had they prepared for themselves any victual.

Now the sojourning of the children of Israel, who dwelt in Egypt, was four hundred and thirty years. And it came to pass at the end of the four hundred and thirty years, even the selfsame day it came to pass, that all the hosts of the LORD went out from the land of Egypt. It is a night to be much observed unto the LORD for bringing them out from the land of Egypt: this is that night of the LORD to be observed of all the children of Israel in their generations.

And the LORD said unto Moses and Aaron, This is the ordinance of the passover: There shall no stranger eat thereof: but every man's servant that is bought for money, when thou hast circumcised him, then shall he eat thereof. A foreigner and an hired servant shall not eat thereof. In one house shall it be eaten; thou shalt not carry forth ought of the flesh abroad out of the house; neither shall ye break a bone thereof. All the congregation of Israel shall keep it. And when a stranger shall sojourn with thee, and will keep the passover to the LORD, let all his males be circumcised, and then let him come near and keep it; and he shall be as one that is born in the land: for no uncircumcised person shall eat thereof. One law shall be to him that is homeborn, and unto the stranger that sojourneth among you. Thus did all the children of Israel; as the LORD commanded Moses and Aaron, so did they. And it came to pass the selfsame day, that the LORD did bring the children of Israel out of the land of Egypt by their armies.

*   *   *

[Moses in the Desert; The Ten Commandments]

17. And all the congregation of the children of Israel journeyed from the wilderness of Sin, after their journeys, according to the commandment of the LORD, and pitched in Rephidim: and there was no water for the people to drink. Wherefore the people did chide with Moses, and said, Give us water that we

may drink. And Moses said unto them, Why chide ye with me? wherefore do ye tempt the LORD? And the people thirsted there for water; and the people murmured against Moses, and said, Wherefore is this that thou hast brought us up out of Egypt, to kill us and our children and our cattle with thirst? And Moses cried unto the LORD, saying, What shall I do unto this people? they be almost ready to stone me. And the LORD said unto Moses, Go on before the people, and take with thee of the elders of Israel; and thy rod, wherewith thou smotest the river, take in thine hand, and go. Behold, I will stand before thee there upon the rock in Horeb; and thou shalt smite the rock, and there shall come water out of it, that the people may drink. And Moses did so in the sight of the elders of Israel. And he called the name of the place Massah, and Meribah, because of the chiding of the children of Israel, and because they tempted the LORD, saying, Is the LORD among us, or not?

Then came Amalek, and fought with Israel in Rephidim. And Moses said unto Joshua, Choose us out men, and go out, fight with Amalek: to morrow I will stand on the top of the hill with the rod of God in mine hand. So Joshua did as Moses had said to him, and fought with Amalek: and Moses, Aaron, and Hur went up to the top of the hill. And it came to pass, when Moses held up his hand, that Israel prevailed: and when he let down his hand, Amalek prevailed. But Moses' hands were heavy; and they took a stone, and put it under him, and he sat thereon; and Aaron and Hur stayed up his hands, the one on the one side, and the other on the other side; and his hands were steady until the going down of the sun. And Joshua discomfited Amalek and his people with the edge of the sword. And the LORD said unto Moses, Write this for a memorial in a book, and rehearse it in the ears of Joshua: for I will utterly put out the remembrance of Amalek from under heaven. And Moses built an altar, and called the name of it Jehovah-nissi: for he said, Because the LORD hath sworn that the LORD will have war with Amalek from generation to generation.

18. When Jethro, the priest of Midian, Moses' father in law, heard of all that God had done for Moses, and for Israel his people, and that the LORD had brought Israel out of Egypt; then Jethro, Moses' father in law, took Zipporah, Moses' wife, after he had sent her back, and her two sons; of which the name of the one was Gershom; for he said, I have been an alien in a strange land: and the name of the other was Eliezer; for the God of my father, said he, was mine help, and delivered me from the sword of Pharaoh: and Jethro, Moses' father in law, came with his sons and his wife unto Moses into the wilderness, where he encamped at the mount of God: and he said unto Moses, I thy father in law Jethro am come unto thee, and thy wife, and her two sons with her. And Moses went out to meet his father in law, and did obeisance, and kissed him; and they asked each other of their welfare; and they came into the tent. And Moses told his father in law all that the LORD had done unto Pharaoh and to the Egyptians for Israel's sake, and all the travail that had come upon them by the way, and how the LORD delivered them. And Jethro rejoiced for all the goodness which the LORD had done to Israel, whom he had delivered out of the hand of the Egyptians. And Jethro said, Blessed be the LORD, who hath delivered you out of the hand of the Egyptians, and out of the hand of Pharaoh, who hath delivered the people from under the hand of the Egyptians. Now I know that the LORD is greater than all gods: for in the thing wherein they dealt proudly he was above them. And Jethro, Moses' father in law, took a burnt offering and sacrifices for God: and Aaron came, and all the elders of Israel, to eat bread with Moses' father in law before God.

And it came to pass on the morrow, that Moses sat to judge the people: and the people stood by Moses from the morning unto the evening. And when Moses' father in law saw all that he did to the people, he said, What is this thing that thou doest to the people? why sittest thou thyself alone, and all the people stand by thee from morning unto even? And Moses said unto his father in law, Because the people come unto me to inquire of God: when they have a matter, they come unto me; and I judge between one and another, and I do make them know the statutes of God, and his laws. And Moses' father in law said unto him, The thing that thou doest is not good. Thou wilt surely wear away, both thou, and this people that is with thee: for this thing is too heavy for thee; thou art not able to perform it thyself alone. Hearken now unto my voice, I will give thee counsel, and God shall be with thee: Be thou for the people to God-ward, that thou mayest bring the causes unto God: and thou shalt teach them ordinances and laws, and shalt shew them the way wherein they must walk, and the work that they must do. Moreover thou shalt provide out of all the people able men, such as fear God, men of truth, hating covetousness; and place such over them, to be rulers of thousands, and rulers of hundreds, rulers of fifties, and rulers of tens: and let them judge the people at all seasons: and it shall be, that every great matter they shall bring unto thee, but every small matter they shall judge: so shall it be easier for thyself, and they shall bear the burden with thee. If thou shalt do this thing, and God command thee so, then thou shalt be able to endure, and all this people shall also go to their place in peace.

So Moses hearkened to the voice of his father in law, and did all that he had said. And Moses chose able men out of all Israel, and made them heads over the people, rulers of thousands, rulers of hundreds, rulers of fifties, and rulers of tens. And they judged the people at all seasons: the hard causes they brought unto Moses, but every small matter they judged themselves. And Moses let his father in law depart; and he went his way into his own land.

19. In the third month, when the children of Israel were gone forth out of the land of Egypt, the same day came they into the wilderness of Sinai. For they were departed from Rephidim, and were come to the desert of Sinai, and had pitched in the wilderness; and there Israel camped before the mount. And Moses went up unto God, and the Lord called unto him out of the mountain, saying, Thus shalt thou say to the house of Jacob, and tell the children of Israel; Ye have seen what I did unto the Egyptians, and how I bare you on eagles' wings, and brought you unto myself. Now therefore, if ye will obey my voice indeed, and keep my covenant, then ye shall be a peculiar treasure unto me above all people: for all the earth is mine: and ye shall be unto me a kingdom of priests, and an holy nation. These are the words which thou shalt speak unto the children of Israel.

And Moses came and called for the elders of the people, and laid before their faces all these words which the Lord commanded him. And all the people answered together, and said, All that the Lord hath spoken we will do. And

Moses returned the words of the people unto the LORD. And the LORD said unto Moses, Lo, I come unto thee in a thick cloud, that the people may hear when I speak with thee, and believe thee for ever. And Moses told the words of the people unto the LORD.

And the LORD said unto Moses, Go unto the people, and sanctify them to day and to morrow, and let them wash their clothes, and be ready against the third day: for the third day the LORD will come down in the sight of all the people upon mount Sinai. And thou shalt set bounds unto the people round about, saying, Take heed to yourselves, that ye go not up into the mount, or touch the border of it: whosoever toucheth the mount shall be surely put to death: there shall not an hand touch it, but he shall surely be stoned, or shot through; whether it be beast or man, it shall not live: when the trumpet soundeth long, they shall come up to the mount. And Moses went down from the mount unto the people, and sanctified the people; and they washed their clothes. And he said unto the people, Be ready against the third day: come not at your wives.

And it came to pass on the third day in the morning, that there were thunders and lightnings, and a thick cloud upon the mount, and the voice of the trumpet exceeding loud; so that all the people that was in the camp trembled. And Moses brought forth the people out of the camp to meet with God; and they stood at the nether part of the mount. And mount Sinai was altogether on a smoke, because the LORD descended upon it in fire: and the smoke thereof ascended as the smoke of a furnace, and the whole mount quaked greatly. And when the voice of the trumpet sounded long, and waxed louder and louder, Moses spake, and God answered him by a voice.

And the LORD came down upon mount Sinai, on the top of the mount: and the LORD called Moses up to the top of the mount; and Moses went up. And the LORD said unto Moses, Go down, charge the people, lest they break through unto the LORD to gaze, and many of them perish. And let the priests also, which come near to the LORD, sanctify themselves, lest the LORD break forth upon them. And Moses said unto the LORD, The people cannot come up to mount Sinai: for thou chargedst us, saying, Set bounds about the mount, and sanctify it. And the LORD said unto him, Away, get thee down, and thou shalt come up, thou, and Aaron with thee: but let not the priests and the people break through to come up unto the LORD, lest he break forth upon them. So Moses went down unto the people, and spake unto them.

20. And God spake all these words, saying,

I am the LORD thy God, which have brought thee out of the land of Egypt, out of the house of bondage.

Thou shalt have no other gods before me.

Thou shalt not make unto thee any graven image, or any likeness of any thing that is in heaven above, or that is in the earth beneath, or that is in the water under the earth: thou shalt not bow down thyself to them, nor serve them: for I the LORD thy God am a jealous God, visiting the iniquity of the fathers upon the children unto the third and fourth generation of them that hate me; and shewing mercy unto thousands of them that love me, and keep my commandments.

Thou shalt not take the name of the LORD thy God in vain; for the LORD will not hold him guiltless that taketh his name in vain.

Remember the sabbath day, to keep it holy. Six days shalt thou labour, and do all thy work: but the seventh day is the sabbath of the LORD thy God: in it thou shalt not do any work, thou, nor thy son, nor thy daughter, thy manservant, nor thy maidservant, nor thy cattle, nor thy stranger that is within thy gates: for in six days the LORD made heaven and earth, the sea, and all that in them is, and rested the seventh day: wherefore the LORD blessed the sabbath day, and hallowed it.

Honour thy father and thy mother: that thy days may be long upon the land which the LORD thy God giveth thee.

Thou shalt not kill.

Thou shalt not commit adultery.

Thou shalt not steal.

Thou shalt not bear false witness against thy neighbour.

Thou shalt not covet thy neighbour's house, thou shalt not covet thy neighbour's wife, nor his manservant, nor his maidservant, nor his ox, nor his ass, nor any thing that is thy neighbour's.

And all the people saw the thunderings, and the lightnings, and the noise of the trumpet, and the mountain smoking: and when the people saw it, they removed, and stood afar off. And they said unto Moses, Speak thou with us, and we will hear: but let not God speak with us, lest we die. And Moses said unto the people, Fear not: for God is come to prove you, and that his fear may be before your faces, that ye sin not. And the people stood afar off, and Moses drew near unto the thick darkness where God was.

And the LORD said unto Moses, Thus thou shalt say unto the children of Israel, Ye have seen that I have talked with you from heaven. Ye shall not make with me gods of silver, neither shall ye make unto you gods of gold. An altar of earth thou shalt make unto me, and shalt sacrifice thereon thy burnt offerings, and thy peace offerings, thy sheep, and thine oxen: in all places where I record my name I will come unto thee, and I will bless thee. And if thou wilt make me an altar of stone, thou shalt not build it of hewn stone: for if thou lift up thy tool upon it, thou hast polluted it. Neither shalt thou go up by steps unto mine altar, that thy nakedness be not discovered thereon.

*　*　*

[The Golden Calf; Religious Laws]

31. AND the LORD spake unto Moses, saying, See, I have called by name Bezaleel the son of Uri, the son of Hur, of the tribe of Judah: and I have filled him with the spirit of God, in wisdom, and in understanding, and in knowledge, and in all manner of workmanship, to devise cunning works, to work in gold, and in silver, and in brass, and in cutting of stones, to set them, and in carving of timber, to work in all manner of workmanship. And I, behold, I have given with him Aholiab, the son of Ahisamach, of the tribe of Dan: and in the hearts of all that are wise hearted I have put wisdom, that they may make all that I have commanded thee; the tabernacle of the congregation, and the ark of the testimony, and the mercy seat that is thereupon, and all the furniture of the tabernacle, and the table and his furniture, and the pure candlestick with all his furniture, and the altar of incense, and the altar of burnt offering with all his

furniture, and the laver and his foot, and the cloths of service, and the holy garments for Aaron the priest, and the garments of his sons, to minister in the priest's office, and the anointing oil, and sweet incense for the holy place: according to all that I have commanded thee shall they do.

And the LORD spake unto Moses, saying, Speak thou also unto the children of Israel, saying, Verily my sabbaths ye shall keep: for it is a sign between me and you throughout your generations; that ye may know that I am the LORD that doth sanctify you. Ye shall keep the sabbath therefore; for it is holy unto you: every one that defileth it shall surely be put to death: for whosoever doeth any work therein, that soul shall be cut off from among his people. Six days may work be done; but in the seventh is the sabbath of rest, holy to the LORD: whosoever doeth any work in the sabbath day, he shall surely be put to death. Wherefore the children of Israel shall keep the sabbath to observe the sabbath throughout their generations, for a perpetual covenant. It is a sign between me and the children of Israel for ever: for in six days the LORD made heaven and earth, and on the seventh day he rested, and was refreshed.

And he gave unto Moses, when he had made an end of communing with him upon mount Sinai, two tables of testimony, tables of stone, written with the finger of God.

32. AND when the people saw that Moses delayed to come down out of the mount, the people gathered themselves together unto Aaron, and said unto him, Up, make us gods, which shall go before us; for as for this Moses, the man that brought us up out of the land of Egypt, we wot not what is become of him. And Aaron said unto them, Break off the golden earrings, which are in the ears of your wives, of your sons, and of your daughters, and bring them unto me. And all the people brake off the golden earrings which were in their ears, and brought them unto Aaron. And he received them at their hand, and fashioned it with a graving tool, after he had made it a molten calf: and they said, These be thy gods, O Israel, which brought thee up out of the land of Egypt. And when Aaron saw it, he built an altar before it; and Aaron made proclamation, and said, To morrow is a feast to the LORD. And they rose up early on the morrow, and offered burnt offerings, and brought peace offerings; and the people sat down to eat and to drink, and rose up to play.

And the LORD said unto Moses, Go, get thee down; for thy people, which thou broughtest out of the land of Egypt, have corrupted themselves: they have turned aside quickly out of the way which I commanded them: they have made them a molten calf, and have worshipped it, and have sacrificed thereunto, and said, These be thy gods, O Israel, which have brought thee up out of the land of Egypt. And the LORD said unto Moses, I have seen this people, and, behold, it is a stiffnecked people: now therefore let me alone, that my wrath may wax hot against them, and that I may consume them: and I will make of thee a great nation. And Moses besought the LORD his God, and said, LORD, why doth thy wrath wax hot against thy people, which thou hast brought forth out of the land of Egypt with great power, and with a mighty hand? Wherefore should the Egyptians speak, and say, For mischief did he bring them out, to slay them in the mountains, and to consume them from the face of the earth? Turn from thy fierce wrath, and repent of this evil against thy people. Remember Abraham, Isaac, and Israel, thy servants, to whom thou swarest by thine own self, and saidst unto them, I will multiply your seed as the stars of heaven, and all this land that I have spoken of will I give unto your seed, and they shall inherit it for ever. And the LORD repented of the evil which he thought to do unto his people.

And Moses turned, and went down from the mount, and the two tables of the testimony were in his hand: the tables were written on both their sides; on the one side and on the other were they written. And the tables were the work of God, and the writing was the writing of God, graven upon the tables. And when Joshua heard the noise of the people as they shouted, he said unto Moses, There is a noise of war in the camp. And he said, It is not the voice of them that shout for mastery, neither is it the voice of them that cry for being overcome: but the noise of them that sing do I hear. And it came to pass, as soon as he came nigh unto the camp, that he saw the calf, and the dancing: and Moses' anger waxed hot, and he cast the tables out of his hands, and brake them beneath the mount. And he took the calf which they had made, and burnt it in the fire, and ground it to powder, and strawed it upon the water, and made the children of Israel drink of it.

And Moses said unto Aaron, What did this people unto thee, that thou hast brought so great a sin upon them? And Aaron said, Let not the anger of my lord wax hot: thou knowest the people, that they are set on mischief. For they said unto me, Make us gods, which shall go before us: for as for this Moses, the man that brought us up out of the land of Egypt, we wot not what is become of him. And I said unto them, Whosoever hath any gold, let them break it off. So they gave it me: then I cast it into the fire, and there came out this calf.

And when Moses saw that the people were naked; (for Aaron had made them naked unto their shame among their enemies:) then Moses stood in the gate of the camp, and said, Who is on the LORD's side? let him come unto me. And all the sons of Levi gathered themselves together unto him. And he said unto them, Thus saith the LORD God of Israel, Put every man his sword by his side, and go in and out from gate to gate throughout the camp, and slay every man his brother, and every man his companion, and every man his neighbour. And the children of Levi did according to the word of Moses: and there fell of the people that day about three thousand men. For Moses had said, Consecrate yourselves to day to the LORD, even every man upon his son, and upon his brother; that he may bestow upon you a blessing this day.

And it came to pass on the morrow, that Moses said unto the people, Ye have sinned a great sin: and now I will go up unto the LORD; peradventure I shall make an atonement for your sin. And Moses returned unto the LORD, and said, Oh, this people have sinned a great sin, and have made them gods of gold. Yet now, if thou wilt forgive their sin—; and if not, blot me, I pray thee, out of thy book which thou hast written. And the LORD said unto Moses, Whosoever hath sinned against me, him will I blot out of my book. Therefore now go, lead the people unto the place of which I have spoken unto thee: behold, mine Angel shall go before thee: nevertheless in the day when I visit I will visit their sin upon them.

And the LORD plagued the people, because they made the calf, which Aaron made.

33. AND the LORD said unto Moses, Depart, and go up hence, thou and the people which thou hast brought up out of the land of Egypt, unto the land

which I sware unto Abraham, to Isaac, and to Jacob, saying, Unto thy seed will I give it: and I will send an angel before thee; and I will drive out the Canaanite, the Amorite, and the Hittite, and the Perizzite, the Hivite, and the Jebusite: unto a land flowing with milk and honey: for I will not go up in the midst of thee; for thou art a stiffnecked people: lest I consume thee in the way. And when the people heard these evil tidings, they mourned: and no man did put on him his ornaments. For the Lord had said unto Moses, Say unto the children of Israel, Ye are a stiffnecked people: I will come up into the midst of thee in a moment, and consume thee: therefore now put off thy ornaments from thee, that I may know what to do unto thee. And the children of Israel stripped themselves of their ornaments by the mount Horeb.

And Moses took the tabernacle, and pitched it without the camp, afar off from the camp, and called it the Tabernacle of the congregation. And it came to pass, that every one which sought the Lord went out unto the tabernacle of the congregation, which was without the camp. And it came to pass, when Moses went out unto the tabernacle, that all the people rose up, and stood every man at his tent door, and looked after Moses, until he was gone into the tabernacle. And it came to pass, as Moses entered into the tabernacle, the cloudy pillar descended, and stood at the door of the tabernacle, and the Lord talked with Moses. And all the people saw the cloudy pillar stand at the tabernacle door: and all the people rose up and worshipped, every man in his tent door. And the Lord spake unto Moses face to face, as a man speaketh unto his friend. And he turned again into the camp: but his servant Joshua, the son of Nun, a young man, departed not out of the tabernacle.

And Moses said unto the Lord, See, thou sayest unto me, Bring up this people: and thou hast not let me know whom thou wilt send with me. Yet thou hast said, I know thee by name, and thou hast also found grace in my sight. Now therefore, I pray thee, if I have found grace in thy sight, shew me now thy way, that I may know thee, that I may find grace in thy sight: and consider that this nation is thy people. And he said, My presence shall go with thee, and I will give thee rest. And he said unto him, If thy presence go not with me, carry us not up hence. For wherein shall it be known here that I and thy people have found grace in thy sight? is it not in that thou goest with us? so shall we be separated, I and thy people, from all the people that are upon the face of the earth. And the Lord said unto Moses, I will do this thing also that thou hast spoken: for thou hast found grace in my sight, and I know thee by name.

And he said, I beseech thee, shew me thy glory. And he said, I will make all my goodness pass before thee, and I will proclaim the name of the Lord before thee; and will be gracious to whom I will be gracious, and will shew mercy on whom I will shew mercy. And he said, Thou canst not see my face: for there shall no man see me, and live. And the Lord said, Behold, there is a place by me, and thou shalt stand upon a rock: and it shall come to pass, while my glory passeth by, that I will put thee in a clift of the rock, and will cover thee with my hand while I pass by: and I will take away mine hand, and thou shalt see my back parts: but my face shall not be seen.

34. And the Lord said unto Moses, Hew thee two tables of stone like unto the first: and I will write upon these tables the words that were in the first tables, which thou brakest. And be ready in the morning, and come up in the

morning unto mount Sinai, and present thyself there to me in the top of the mount. And no man shall come up with thee, neither let any man be seen throughout all the mount; neither let the flocks nor herds feed before that mount. And he hewed two tables of stone like unto the first; and Moses rose up early in the morning, and went up unto mount Sinai, as the LORD had commanded him, and took in his hand the two tables of stone. And the LORD descended in the cloud, and stood with him there, and proclaimed the name of the LORD. And the LORD passed by before him, and proclaimed, The LORD, The LORD God, merciful and gracious, longsuffering, and abundant in goodness and truth, keeping mercy for thousands, forgiving iniquity and transgression and sin, and that will by no means clear the guilty; visiting the iniquity of the fathers upon the children and upon the children's children, unto the third and to the fourth generation. And Moses made haste, and bowed his head toward the earth, and worshipped. And he said, If now I have found grace in thy sight, O Lord, let my Lord, I pray thee go among us; for it is a stiffnecked people; and pardon our iniquity and our sin, and take us for thine inheritance.

And he said, Behold, I make a covenant: before all thy people I will do marvels, such as have not been done in all the earth, nor in any nation: and all the people among which thou art shall see the work of the LORD: for it is a terrible thing that I will do with thee.

Observe thou that which I command thee this day: behold, I drive out before thee the Amorite, and the Canaanite, and the Hittite, and the Perizzite, and the Hivite, and the Jebusite. Take heed to thyself, lest thou make a covenant with the inhabitants of the land whither thou goest, lest it be for a snare in the midst of thee: but ye shall destroy their altars, break their images, and cut down their groves: for thou shalt worship no other god: for the LORD, whose name is Jealous, is a jealous God: lest thou make a covenant with the inhabitants of the land, and they go a whoring after their gods, and do sacrifice unto their gods, and one call thee, and thou eat of his sacrifice; and thou take of their daughters unto thy sons, and their daughters go a whoring after their gods, and make thy sons go a whoring after their gods.

Thou shalt make thee no molten gods.

The feast of unleavened bread shalt thou keep. Seven days thou shalt eat unleavened bread, as I commanded thee, in the time of the month Abib: for in the month Abib thou camest out from Egypt.

All that openeth the matrix is mine; and every firstling among thy cattle, whether ox or sheep, that is male. But the firstling of an ass thou shalt redeem with a lamb: and if thou redeem him not, then shalt thou break his neck. All the firstborn of thy sons thou shalt redeem. And none shall appear before me empty.

Six days thou shalt work, but on the seventh day thou shalt rest: in earing time and in harvest thou shalt rest.

And thou shalt observe the feast of weeks, of the firstfruits of wheat harvest, and the feast of ingathering at the year's end. Thrice in the year shall all your men children appear before the Lord GOD, the God of Israel. For I will cast out the nations before thee, and enlarge thy borders: neither shall any man desire thy land, when thou shalt go up to appear before the LORD thy God thrice in the year.

Thou shalt not offer the blood of my sacrifice with leaven; neither shall the sacrifice of the feast of the passover be left unto the morning.

The first of the firstfruits of thy land thou shalt bring unto the house of the LORD thy God.

Thou shalt not seethe a kid in his mother's milk.

And the LORD said unto Moses, Write thou these words: for after the tenor of these words I have made a covenant with thee and with Israel. And he was there with the LORD forty days and forty nights; he did neither eat bread, nor drink water. And he wrote upon the tables the words of the covenant, the ten commandments.

And it came to pass, when Moses came down from mount Sinai with the two tables of testimony in Moses' hand, when he came down from the mount, that Moses wist not that the skin of his face shone while he talked with him. And when Aaron and all the children of Israel saw Moses, behold, the skin of his face shone; and they were afraid to come nigh him. And Moses called unto them; and Aaron and all the rulers of the congregation returned unto him: and Moses talked with them. And afterward all the children of Israel came nigh: and he gave them in commandment all that the LORD had spoken with him in mount Sinai. And till Moses had done speaking with them, he put a vail on his face. But when Moses went in before the LORD to speak with him, he took the vail off, until he came out. And he came out, and spake unto the children of Israel that which he was commanded. And the children of Israel saw the face of Moses, that the skin of Moses' face shone: and Moses put the vail upon his face again, until he went in to speak with him.

35. AND Moses gathered all the congregation of the children of Israel together, and said unto them, These are the words which the LORD hath commanded, that ye should do them. Six days shall work be done, but on the seventh day there shall be to you an holy day, a sabbath of rest to the LORD: whosoever doeth work therein shall be put to death. Ye shall kindle no fire throughout your habitations upon the sabbath day.

And Moses spake unto all the congregation of the children of Israel, saying, This is the thing which the LORD commanded, saying, Take ye from among you an offering unto the LORD: whosoever is of a willing heart, let him bring it, an offering of the LORD; gold, and silver, and brass, and blue, and purple, and scarlet, and fine linen, and goats' hair, and rams' skins dyed red and badgers' skins, and shittim wood, and oil for the light, and spices for anointing oil, and for the sweet incense, and onyx stones, and stones to be set for the ephod, and for the breastplate.

And every wise hearted among you shall come, and make all that the LORD hath commanded; the tabernacle, his tent, and his covering, his taches, and his boards, his bars, his pillars, and his sockets, the ark, and the staves thereof, with the mercy seat, and the vail of the covering, the table, and his staves, and all his vessels, and the shewbread, the candlestick also for the light, and his furniture, and his lamps, with the oil for the light, and the incense altar, and his staves, and the anointing oil, and the sweet incense, and the hanging for the door at the entering in of the tabernacle, the altar of burnt offering, with his brasen grate, his staves, and all his vessels, the laver and his foot, the hangings of the court, his pillars, and their sockets, and the hanging for the door of the court, the pins of the tabernacle, and the pins of the court, and their cords, the cloths of service, to do service in the holy place, the holy garments for Aaron the priest, and the garments of his sons, to minister in the priest's office.

And all the congregation of the children of Israel departed from the presence of Moses. And they came, every one whose heart stirred him up, and every one whom his spirit made willing, and they brought the LORD's offering to the work of the tabernacle of the congregation, and for all his service, and for the holy garments. And they came, both men and women, as many as were willing hearted, and brought bracelets, and earrings, and rings, and tablets, all jewels of gold: and every man that offered offered an offering of gold unto the LORD. And every man, with whom was found blue, and purple, and scarlet, and fine linen, and goats' hair, and red skins of rams, and badgers' skins, brought them. Every one that did offer an offering of silver and brass brought the LORD's offering: and every man, with whom was found shittim wood for any work of the service, brought it. And all the women that were wise hearted did spin with their hands, and brought that which they had spun, both of blue, and of purple, and of scarlet, and of fine linen. And all the women whose heart stirred them up in wisdom spun goats' hair. And the rulers brought onyx stones, and stones to be set, for the ephod, and for the breastplate; and spice, and oil for the light, and for the anointing oil, and for the sweet incense. The children of Israel brought a willing offering unto the LORD, every man and woman, whose heart made them willing to bring for all manner of work, which the LORD had commanded to be made by the hand of Moses.

And Moses said unto the children of Israel, See, the LORD hath called by name Bezaleel the son of Uri, the son of Hur, of the tribe of Judah; and he hath filled him with the spirit of God, in wisdom, in understanding, and in knowledge, and in all manner of workmanship; and to devise curious works, to work in gold, and in silver, and in brass, and in the cutting of stones, to set them, and in carving of wood, to make any manner of cunning work. And he hath put in his heart that he may teach, both he, and Aholiab, the son of Ahisamach, of the tribe of Dan. Them hath he filled with wisdom of heart, to work all manner of work, of the engraver, and of the cunning workman, and of the embroiderer, in blue, and in purple, in scarlet, and in fine linen, and of the weaver, even of them that do any work, and of those that devise cunning work.

Ruth

1. Now it came to pass in the days when the judges ruled, that there was a famine in the land. And a certain man of Bethlehem-judah went to sojourn in the country of Moab, he, and his wife, and his two sons. And the name of the man was Elimelech, and the name of his wife Naomi, and the name of his two sons Mahlon and Chilion, Ephrathites of Bethlehem-judah. And they came into the country of Moab, and continued there. And Elimelech Naomi's husband died; and she was left, and her two sons. And they took them wives of the women of Moab; the name of the one was Orpah, and the name of the other Ruth: and they dwelled there about ten years. And Mahlon and Chilion died also both of them; and the woman was left of her two sons and her husband.

Then she arose with her daughters in law, that she might return from the country of Moab: for she had heard in the country of Moab how that the Lord had visited his people in giving them bread. Wherefore she went forth out of the place where she was, and her two daughters in law with her; and they went on the way to return unto the land of Judah. And Naomi said unto her two daughters in law, Go, return each to her mother's house: the Lord deal kindly with you, as ye have dealt with the dead, and with me. The Lord grant you that ye may find rest, each of you in the house of her husband. Then she kissed them; and they lifted up their voice, and wept. And they said unto her, Surely we will return with thee unto thy people. And Naomi said, Turn again, my daughters: why will ye go with me? are there yet any more sons in my womb, that they may be your husbands? Turn again, my daughters, go your way; for I am too old to have an husband. If I should say, I have hope, if I should have an husband also to night, and should also bear sons; would ye tarry for them till they were grown? would ye stay for them from having husbands? nay, my daughters; for it grieveth me much for your sakes that the hand of the Lord is gone out against me. And they lifted up their voice, and wept again: and Orpah kissed her mother in law; but Ruth clave unto her. And she said, Behold, thy sister in law is gone back unto her people, and unto her gods: return thou after thy sister in law. And Ruth said, Intreat me not to leave thee, or to return from following after thee: for whither thou goest, I will go; and where thou lodgest, I will lodge: thy people shall be my people, and thy God my God: where thou diest, will I die, and there will I be buried: the Lord do so to me, and more also, if ought but death part thee and me. When she saw that she was stedfastly minded to go with her, then she left speaking unto her.

So they two went until they came to Bethlehem. And it came to pass, when they were come to Bethlehem, that all the city was moved about them, and they said, Is this Naomi? And she said unto them, Call me not Naomi, call me Mara: for the Almighty hath dealt very bitterly with me. I went out full, and the Lord hath brought me home again empty: why then call ye me Naomi, seeing the Lord hath testified against me, and the Almighty hath afflicted me? So Naomi returned, and Ruth the Moabitess, her daughter in law, with her, which returned out of the country of Moab: and they came to Bethlehem in the beginning of barley harvest.

2. And Naomi had a kinsman of her husband's, a mighty man of wealth, of the family of Elimelech; and his name was Boaz. And Ruth the Moabitess said unto Naomi, Let me now go to the field, and glean ears of corn after him in whose sight I shall find grace. And she said unto her, Go, my daughter. And she went, and came, and gleaned in the field after the reapers: and her hap was to light on a part of the field belonging unto Boaz, who was of the kindred of Elimelech.

And, behold, Boaz came from Bethlehem, and said unto the reapers, The Lord be with you. And they answered him, The Lord bless thee. Then said Boaz unto his servant that was set over the reapers, Whose damsel is this? And the servant that was set over the reapers answered and said, It is the Moabitish damsel that came back with Naomi out of the country of Moab: and she said, I pray you, let me glean and gather after the reapers among the sheaves: so she came, and hath continued even from the morning until now, that she tarried a little in the house. Then said Boaz unto Ruth, Hearest thou not, my daughter? Go not to glean in another field, neither go from hence, but abide here fast by my maidens: let thine eyes be on the field that they do reap, and go thou after them: have I not charged the young men that they shall not touch thee? and when thou art athirst, go unto the vessels, and drink of that which the young men have drawn. Then she fell on her face, and bowed herself to the ground, and said unto him, Why have I found grace in thine eyes, that thou shouldest take knowledge of me, seeing I am a stranger? And Boaz answered and said unto her, It hath fully been shewed me, all that thou hast done unto thy mother in law since the death of thine husband: and how thou hast left thy father and thy mother, and the land of thy nativity, and art come unto a people which thou knewest not heretofore. The LORD recompense thy work, and a full reward be given thee of the LORD God of Israel, under whose wings thou art come to trust. Then she said, Let me find favour in thy sight, my lord; for that thou hast comforted me, and for that thou hast spoken friendly unto thine handmaid, though I be not like unto one of thine handmaidens. And Boaz said unto her, At mealtime come thou hither, and eat of the bread, and dip thy morsel in the vinegar. And she sat beside the reapers: and he reached her parched corn, and she did eat, and was sufficed, and left.

And when she was risen up to glean, Boaz commanded his young men, saying, Let her glean even among the sheaves, and reproach her not: and let fall also some of the handfuls of purpose for her, and leave them, that she may glean them, and rebuke her not. So she gleaned in the field until even, and beat out that she had gleaned: and it was about an ephah of barley. And she took it up, and went into the city: and her mother in law saw what she had gleaned: and she brought forth, and gave to her that she had reserved after she was sufficed. And her mother in law said unto her, Where hast thou gleaned to day? and where wroughtest thou? blessed be he that did take knowledge of thee. And she shewed her mother in law with whom she had wrought, and said, The man's name with whom I wrought to day is Boaz. And Naomi said unto her daughter in law, Blessed be he of the LORD, who hath not left off his kindness to the living and to the dead. And Naomi said unto her, The man is near of kin unto us, one of our next kinsmen. And Ruth the Moabitess said, He said unto me also, Thou shalt keep fast by my young men, until they have ended all my harvest. And Naomi said unto Ruth her daughter in law, It is good, my daughter, that thou go out with his maidens, that they meet thee not in any other field. So she kept fast by the maidens of Boaz to glean unto the end of barley harvest and of wheat harvest; and dwelt with her mother in law.

3. Then Naomi her mother in law said unto her, My daughter, shall I not seek rest for thee, that it may be well with thee? And now is not Boaz of our kindred, with whose maidens thou wast? Behold, he winnoweth barley to night in the threshingfloor. Wash thyself therefore, and anoint thee, and put thy raiment upon thee, and get thee down to the floor: but make not thyself known unto the man, until he shall have done eating and drinking. And it shall be, when he lieth down, that thou shalt mark the place where he shall lie, and thou shalt go in, and uncover his feet, and lay thee down; and he will tell thee what thou shalt do. And she said unto her, All that thou sayest unto me I will

do. And she went down unto the floor, and did according to all that her mother in law bade her. And when Boaz had eaten and drunk, and his heart was merry, he went to lie down at the end of the heap of corn: and she came softly, and uncovered his feet, and laid her down.

And it came to pass at midnight, that the man was afraid, and turned himself: and, behold, a woman lay at his feet. And he said, Who art thou? And she answered, I am Ruth thine handmaid: spread therefore thy skirt over thine handmaid; for thou art a near kinsman. And he said, Blessed be thou of the LORD, my daughter: for thou hast shewed more kindness in the latter end than at the beginning, inasmuch as thou followedst not young men, whether poor or rich. And now, my daughter, fear not; I will do to thee all that thou requirest: for all the city of my people doth know that thou art a virtuous woman. And now it is true that I am thy near kinsman: howbeit there is a kinsman nearer than I. Tarry this night, and it shall be in the morning, that if he will perform unto thee the part of a kinsman, well; let him do the kinsman's part: but if he will not do the part of a kinsman to thee, then will I do the part of a kinsman to thee, as the LORD liveth: lie down until the morning. And she lay at his feet until the morning: and she rose up before one could know another. And he said, Let it not be known that a woman came into the floor. Also he said, Bring the vail that thou hast upon thee, and hold it. And when she held it, he measured six measures of barley, and laid it on her: and she went into the city.

And when she came to her mother in law, she said, Who art thou, my daughter? And she told her all that the man had done to her. And she said, These six measures of barley gave he me; for he said to me, Go not empty unto thy mother in law. Then said she, Sit still, my daughter, until thou know how the matter will fall: for the man will not be in rest, until he have finished the thing this day.

4. Then went Boaz up to the gate, and sat him down there: and, behold, the kinsman of whom Boaz spake came by; unto whom he said, Ho, such a one! turn aside, sit down here. And he turned aside, and sat down. And he took ten men of the elders of the city, and said, Sit ye down here. And they sat down. And he said unto the kinsman, Naomi, that is come again out of the country of Moab, selleth a parcel of land, which was our brother Elimelech's: and I thought to advertise thee, saying, Buy it before the inhabitants, and before the elders of my people. If thou wilt redeem it, redeem it: but if thou wilt not redeem it, then tell me, that I may know: for there is none to redeem it beside thee; and I am after thee. And he said, I will redeem it. Then said Boaz, What day thou buyest the field of the hand of Naomi, thou must buy it also of Ruth the Moabitess, the wife of the dead, to raise up the name of the dead upon his inheritance. And the kinsman said, I cannot redeem it for myself, lest I mar mine own inheritance: redeem thou my right to thyself; for I cannot redeem it.

Now this was the manner in former time in Israel concerning redeeming and concerning changing, for to confirm all things; a man plucked off his shoe, and gave it to his neighbour: and this was a testimony in Israel. Therefore the kinsman said unto Boaz, Buy it for thee. So he drew off his shoe. And Boaz said unto the elders, and unto all the people, Ye are witnesses this day, that I have bought all that was Elimelech's, and all that was Chilion's and Mahlon's, of the hand of Naomi. Moreover Ruth the Moabitess, the wife of Mahlon, have I purchased to be my wife, to raise up the name of the dead upon his inheritance, that the name of the dead be not cut off from among his brethren, and from the gate of his place: ye are witnesses this day. And all the people that were in the gate, and the elders, said, We are witnesses. The LORD make the woman that is come into thine house like Rachel and like Leah, which two did build the house of Israel: and do thou worthily in Ephratah, and be famous in Bethlehem: and let thy house be like the house of Pharez, whom Tamar bare unto Judah, of the seed which the LORD shall give thee of this young woman.

So Boaz took Ruth, and she was his wife: and when he went in unto her, the LORD gave her conception, and she bare a son. And the women said unto Naomi, Blessed be the LORD, which hath not left thee this day without a kinsman, that his name may be famous in Israel. And he shall be unto thee a restorer of thy life, and a nourisher of thine old age: for thy daughter in law, which loveth thee, which is better to thee than seven sons, hath born him. And Naomi took the child, and laid it in her bosom, and became nurse unto it. And the women her neighbours gave it a name, saying, There is a son born to Naomi; and they called his name Obed: he is the father of Jesse, the father of David.

Now these are the generations of Pharez: Pharez begat Hezron, and Hezron begat Ram, and Ram begat Amminadab, and Amminadab begat Nahshon, and Nahshon begat Salmon, and Salmon begat Boaz, and Boaz begat Obed, and Obed begat Jesse, and Jesse begat David.

Jonah

1. Now the word of the LORD came unto Jonah the son of Amittai, saying, Arise, go to Nineveh, that great city, and cry against it; for their wickedness is come up before me. But Jonah rose up to flee unto Tarshish from the presence of the LORD, and went down to Joppa; and he found a ship going to Tarshish: so he paid the fare thereof, and went down into it, to go with them unto Tarshish from the presence of the LORD. But the LORD sent out a great wind into the sea, and there was a mighty tempest in the sea, so that the ship was like to be broken. Then the mariners were afraid, and cried every man unto his god, and cast forth the wares that were in the ship into the sea, to lighten it of them. But Jonah was gone down into the sides of the ship; and he lay, and was fast asleep.

So the shipmaster came to him, and said unto him, What meanest thou, O sleeper? arise, call upon thy God, if so be that God will think upon us, that we perish not. And they said every one to his fellow, Come, and let us cast lots, that we may know for whose cause this evil is upon us. So they cast lots, and the lot fell upon Jonah. Then said they unto him, Tell us, we pray thee, for whose cause this evil is upon us; What is thine occupation? and whence comest thou? what is thy country? and of what people art thou? And he said unto them, I am an Hebrew; and I fear the LORD, the God of heaven, which hath made the sea and the dry land. Then were the men exceedingly afraid, and said unto him, Why hast thou done this? For the men knew that he fled from the presence of the LORD, because he had told them.

Then said they unto him, What shall we do unto thee, that the sea may be calm unto us? for the sea wrought, and was tempestuous. And he said unto them, Take me up, and cast me forth into the sea; so shall the sea be calm unto you: for I know that for my sake this great tempest is upon you. Nevertheless the men rowed hard to bring it to the land; but they could not: for the sea wrought, and was tempestuous against them. Wherefore they cried unto the LORD, and said, We beseech thee, O LORD, we beseech thee, let us not perish for this man's life, and lay not upon us innocent blood: for thou, O LORD, hast done as it pleased thee. So they took up Jonah, and cast him forth into the sea: and the sea ceased from her raging. Then the men feared the LORD exceedingly, and offered a sacrifice unto the LORD, and made vows.

Now the LORD had prepared a great fish to swallow up Jonah. And Jonah was in the belly of the fish three days and three nights.

2. Then Jonah prayed unto the LORD his God out of the fish's belly, and said,
> I cried by reason of mine affliction unto the LORD, and he heard
>   me; out of the belly of hell cried I, and thou heardest my
>   voice.
> For thou hadst cast me into the deep, in the midst of the seas;
>   and the floods compassed me about: all thy billows and thy
>   waves passed over me.
> Then I said, I am cast out of thy sight; yet I will look again
>   toward thy holy temple.
> The waters compassed me about, even to the soul: the depth
>   closed me round about, the weeds were wrapped about my
>   head.
> I went down to the bottoms of the mountains; the earth with
>   her bars was about me for ever: yet hast thou brought up my
>   life from corruption, O LORD my God.
> When my soul fainted within me I remembered the LORD: and
>   my prayer came in unto thee, into thine holy temple.
> They that observe lying vanities forsake their own mercy.
> But I will sacrifice unto thee with the voice of thanksgiving; I
>   will pay that that I have vowed. Salvation is of the LORD.

And the LORD spake unto the fish, and it vomited out Jonah upon the dry land.

3. And the word of the LORD came unto Jonah the second time, saying, Arise, go unto Nineveh, that great city, and preach unto it the preaching that I bid thee. So Jonah arose, and went unto Nineveh, according to the word of the LORD. Now Nineveh was an exceeding great city of three days' journey. And Jonah began to enter into the city a day's journey, and he cried, and said, Yet forty days, and Nineveh shall be overthrown. So the people of Nineveh believed God, and proclaimed a fast, and put on sackcloth, from the greatest of them even to the least of them. For word came unto the king of Nineveh, and he arose from his throne, and he laid his robe from him, and covered him with sackcloth, and sat in ashes. And he caused it to be proclaimed and published through Nineveh by the decree of the king and his nobles, saying, Let neither man nor beast, herd nor flock, taste any thing: let them not feed, nor drink water: But let man

and beast be covered with sackcloth, and cry mightily unto God: yea, let them turn every one from his evil way, and from the violence that is in their hands. Who can tell if God will turn and repent, and turn away from his fierce anger, that we perish not? And God saw their works, that they turned from their evil way; and God repented of the evil, that he had said that he would do unto them; and he did it not.

4. But it displeased Jonah exceedingly, and he was very angry. And he prayed unto the LORD, and said, I pray thee, O LORD, was not this my saying, when I was yet in my country? Therefore I fled before unto Tarshish: for I knew that thou art a gracious God, and merciful, slow to anger, and of great kindness, and repentest thee of the evil. Therefore now, O LORD, take, I beseech thee, my life from me; for it is better for me to die than to live. Then said the LORD, Doest thou well to be angry?

So Jonah went out of the city, and sat on the east side of the city, and there made him a booth, and sat under it in the shadow, till he might see what would become of the city. And the LORD God prepared a gourd, and made it to come up over Jonah, that it might be a shadow over his head, to deliver him from his grief. So Jonah was exceeding glad of the gourd. But God prepared a worm when the morning rose the next day, and it smote the gourd that it withered. And it came to pass, when the sun did arise, that God prepared a vehement east wind; and the sun beat upon the head of Jonah, that he fainted, and wished in himself to die, and said, It is better for me to die than to live. And God said to Jonah, Doest thou well to be angry for the gourd? And he said, I do well to be angry, even unto death. Then said the LORD, Thou hast had pity on the gourd, for the which thou hast not laboured, neither madest it grow; which came up in a night, and perished in a night: and should not I spare Nineveh, that great city, wherein are more than sixscore thousand persons that cannot discern between their right hand and their left hand; and also much cattle?

From Isaiah

[Immanuel Prophecy]

6. In the year that king Uzziah died I saw also the Lord sitting upon a throne, high and lifted up, and his train filled the temple. Above it stood the seraphims: each one had six wings; with twain he covered his face, and with twain he covered his feet, and with twain he did fly. And one cried unto another, and said, Holy, holy, holy, is the LORD of hosts: the whole earth is full of his glory. And the posts of the door moved at the voice of him that cried, and the house was filled with smoke.

Then said I, Woe is me! for I am undone; because I am a man of unclean lips, and I dwell in the midst of a people of unclean lips: for mine eyes have seen the King, the LORD of hosts. Then flew one of the seraphims unto me, having a live coal in his hand, which he had taken with the tongs from off the altar: and he laid it upon my mouth, and said, Lo, this hath touched thy lips; and thine iniquity is taken away, and thy sin purged.

Also I heard the voice of the Lord, saying, Whom shall I send, and who will go for us? Then said I, Here am I; send me. And he said, Go, and tell this people, Hear ye indeed, but understand not; and see ye indeed, but perceive not. Make the heart of this people fat, and make their ears heavy, and shut their eyes; lest they see with their eyes, and hear with their ears, and understand with their heart, and convert, and be healed.

Then said I, Lord, how long? And he answered, Until the cities be wasted without inhabitant, and the houses without man, and the land be utterly desolate, and the LORD have removed men far away, and there be a great forsaking in the midst of the land. But yet in it shall be a tenth, and it shall return, and shall be eaten: as a teil tree, and as an oak, whose substance is in them, when they cast their leaves: so the holy seed shall be the substance thereof.

* * *

[The Servant of the Lord]

49. Listen, O isles, unto me; and hearken, ye people, from far; The
LORD hath called me from the womb; from the bowels of
my mother hath he made mention of my name.
And he hath made my mouth like a sharp sword; in the shadow
of his hand hath he hid me, and made me a polished shaft;
in his quiver hath he hid me;
And said unto me, Thou art my servant, O Israel, in whom I
will be glorified.
Then I said, I have laboured in vain, I have spent my strength
for nought, and in vain: yet surely my judgment is with the
LORD, and my work with my God.
And now, saith the LORD that formed me from the womb to be
his servant, to bring Jacob again to him, Though Israel be
not gathered, yet shall I be glorious in the eyes of the LORD,
and my God shall be my strength.
And he said, It is a light thing that thou shouldest be my
servant to raise up the tribes of Jacob, and to restore the
preserved of Israel: I will also give thee for a light to the
Gentiles, that thou mayest be my salvation unto the end of
the earth.

Thus saith the LORD, the Redeemer of Israel, and his Holy
One, to him whom man despiseth, to him whom the nation
abhorreth, to a servant of rulers, Kings shall see and arise,
princes also shall worship, because of the LORD that is
faithful, and the Holy One of Israel, and he shall choose
thee.
Thus saith the LORD, In an acceptable time have I heard thee,
and in a day of salvation have I helped thee: and I will
preserve thee, and give thee for a covenant of the people, to
establish the earth, to cause to inherit the desolate
heritages;

That thou mayest say to the prisoners, Go forth; to them that
are in darkness, Shew yourselves. They shall feed in the
ways, and their pastures shall be in all high places.
They shall not hunger nor thirst; neither shall the heat nor sun
smite them: for he that hath mercy on them shall lead
them, even by the springs of water shall he guide them.
And I will make all my mountains a way, and my highways
shall be exalted.
Behold, these shall come from far: and, lo, these from the
north and from the west; and these from the land of
Sinim.

Sing, O heavens; and be joyful, O earth; and break forth into
singing, O mountains: for the LORD hath comforted his
people, and will have mercy upon his afflicted.

But Zion said, The LORD hath forsaken me, and my Lord hath
forgotten me.
Can a woman forget her sucking child, that she should not
have compassion on the son of her womb? yea, they may
forget, yet will I not forget thee.
Behold, I have graven thee upon the palms of my hands; thy
walls are continually before me.
Thy children shall make haste; thy destroyers and they that
made thee waste shall go forth of thee.
Lift up thine eyes round about, and behold: all these gather
themselves together, and come to thee. As I live, saith the
LORD, thou shalt surely clothe thee with them all, as with
an ornament, and bind them on thee, as a bride doeth.
For thy waste and thy desolate places, and the land of thy
destruction, shall even now be too narrow by reason of the
inhabitants, and they that swallowed thee up shall be far
away.
The children which thou shalt have, after thou hast lost the
other, shall say again in thine ears, The place is too strait
for me: give place to me that I may dwell.
Then shalt thou say in thine heart, Who hath begotten me
these, seeing I have lost my children, and am desolate, a
captive, and removing to and fro? and who hath brought up
these? Behold, I was left alone; these, where had they been?

Thus saith the Lord GOD, Behold, I will lift up mine hand to
the Gentiles, and set up my standard to the people: and
they shall bring thy sons in their arms, and thy daughters
shall be carried upon their shoulders.
And kings shall be thy nursing fathers, and their queens thy
nursing mothers: they shall bow down to thee with their
face toward the earth, and lick up the dust of thy feet; and

thou shalt know that I am the LORD: for they shall not be
ashamed that wait for me.

Shall the prey be taken from the mighty, or the lawful captive
delivered?
But thus saith the LORD, Even the captives of the mighty shall
be taken away, and the prey of the terrible shall be delivered: for I will contend with him that contendeth with thee,
and I will save thy children.
And I will feed them that oppress thee with their own flesh;
and they shall be drunken with their own blood, as with
sweet wine: and all flesh shall know that I the LORD am thy
Saviour and thy Redeemer, the mighty One of Jacob.

*　*　*

[Let Zion Rejoice]

52. Awake, awake; put on thy strength, O Zion; put on thy beautiful garments, O Jerusalem, the holy city: for henceforth there
shall no more come into thee the uncircumcised and the
unclean.
Shake thyself from the dust; arise, and sit down, O Jerusalem:
loose thyself from the bands of thy neck, O captive
daughter of Zion.

For thus saith the LORD, Ye have sold yourselves for nought; and ye shall be
redeemed without money. For thus saith the Lord GOD, My people went down
aforetime into Egypt to sojourn there; and the Assyrian oppressed them without cause. Now therefore, what have I here, saith the LORD, that my people is
taken away for nought? they that rule over them make them to howl, saith the
LORD; and my name continually every day is blasphemed. Therefore my people
shall know my name: therefore they shall know in that day that I am he that
doth speak: behold, it is I.

How beautiful upon the mountains are the feet of him that
bringeth good tidings, that publisheth peace; that bringeth
good tidings of good, that publisheth salvation; that saith
unto Zion, Thy God reigneth!
Thy watchmen shall lift up the voice; with the voice together
shall they sing: for they shall see eye to eye, when the LORD
shall bring again Zion.
Break forth into joy, sing together, ye waste places of Jerusalem: for the LORD hath comforted his people, he hath
redeemed Jerusalem.
The LORD hath made bare his holy arm in the eyes of all the
nations; and all the ends of the earth shall see the salvation
of our God.

Depart ye, depart ye, go ye out from thence, touch no unclean
thing; go ye out of the midst of her; be ye clean, that bear the
vessels of the LORD.
For ye shall not go out with haste, nor go by flight: for the
LORD will go before you; and the God of Israel will be your
rereward.

Behold, my servant shall deal prudently, he shall be exalted
and extolled, and be very high.
As many were astonied at thee; his visage was so marred more
than any man, and his form more than the sons of men:
So shall he sprinkle many nations; the kings shall shut their
mouths at him: for that which had not been told them shall
they see; and that which they had not heard shall they
consider.

THE NEW TESTAMENT†

ca. first century C.E.

From Luke

[*Jesus' Early Life*]

1. Forasmuch as many have taken in hand to set forth in order a declaration
of those things which are most surely believed among us, even as they delivered them unto us, which from the beginning were eyewitnesses, and ministers
of the word; it seemed good to me also, having had perfect understanding of all
things from the very first, to write unto thee in order, most excellent Theophilus, that thou mightest know the certainty of those things, wherein thou hast
been instructed.

There was in the days of Herod, the king of Judæa, a certain priest named
Zacharias, of the course of Abia: and his wife was of the daughters of Aaron,
and her name was Elisabeth. And they were both righteous before God, walking in all the commandments and ordinances of the Lord blameless. And they
had no child, because that Elisabeth was barren, and they both were now well
stricken in years.

And it came to pass, that while he executed the priest's office before God in
the order of his course, according to the custom of the priest's office, his lot
was to burn incense when he went into the temple of the Lord. And the whole
multitude of the people were praying without at the time of incense. And there

† The King James Version.

appeared unto him an angel of the Lord standing on the right side of the altar of incense. And when Zacharias saw him, he was troubled, and fear fell upon him. But the angel said unto him, Fear not, Zacharias: for thy prayer is heard; and thy wife Elisabeth shall bear thee a son, and thou shalt call his name John. And thou shalt have joy and gladness; and many shall rejoice at his birth. For he shall be great in the sight of the Lord, and shall drink neither wine nor strong drink; and he shall be filled with the Holy Ghost, even from his mother's womb. And many of the children of Israel shall he turn to the Lord their God. And he shall go before him in the spirit and power of Elias, to turn the hearts of the fathers to the children, and the disobedient to the wisdom of the just; to make ready a people prepared for the Lord. And Zacharias said unto the angel, Whereby shall I know this? for I am an old man, and my wife well stricken in years. And the angel answering said unto him, I am Gabriel, that stand in the presence of God; and am sent to speak unto thee, and to shew thee these glad tidings. And, behold, thou shalt be dumb, and not able to speak, until the day that these things shall be performed, because thou believest not my words, which shall be fulfilled in their season.

And the people waited for Zacharias, and marvelled that he tarried so long in the temple. And when he came out, he could not speak unto them: and they perceived that he had seen a vision in the temple: for he beckoned unto them, and remained speechless. And it came to pass, that, as soon as the days of his ministration were accomplished, he departed to his own house.

And after those days his wife Elisabeth conceived, and hid herself five months, saying, Thus hath the Lord dealt with me in the days wherein he looked on me, to take away my reproach among men.

And in the sixth month the angel Gabriel was sent from God unto a city of Galilee, named Nazareth, to a virgin espoused to a man whose name was Joseph, of the house of David; and the virgin's name was Mary. And the angel came in unto her, and said, Hail, thou that art highly favoured, the Lord is with thee: blessed art thou among women. And when she saw him, she was troubled at his saying, and cast in her mind what manner of salutation this should be. And the angel said unto her, Fear not, Mary: for thou hast found favour with God. And, behold, thou shalt conceive in thy womb, and bring forth a son, and shalt call his name Jesus. He shall be great, and shall be called the Son of the Highest: and the Lord God shall give unto him the throne of his father David: and he shall reign over the house of Jacob for ever; and of his kingdom there shall be no end.

Then said Mary unto the angel, How shall this be, seeing I know not a man? And the angel answered and said unto her, The Holy Ghost shall come upon thee, and the power of the Highest shall overshadow thee: therefore also that holy thing which shall be born of thee shall be called the Son of God. And, behold, thy cousin Elisabeth, she hath also conceived a son in her old age: and this is the sixth month with her, who was called barren. For with God nothing shall be impossible. And Mary said, Behold the handmaid of the Lord; be it unto me according to thy word. And the angel departed from her.

And Mary arose in those days, and went into the hill country with haste, into a city of Juda; and entered into the house of Zacharias, and saluted Elisabeth. And it came to pass, that, when Elisabeth heard the salutation of Mary, the babe leaped in her womb; and Elisabeth was filled with the Holy Ghost:

and she spake out with a loud voice, and said, Blessed art thou among women, and blessed is the fruit of thy womb. And whence is this to me, that the mother of my Lord should come to me? For, lo, as soon as the voice of thy salutation sounded in mine ears, the babe leaped in my womb for joy. And blessed is she that believed: for there shall be a performance of those things which were told her from the Lord.

And Mary said,

> My soul doth magnify the Lord,
> And my spirit hath rejoiced in God my Saviour.
> For he hath regarded the low estate of his handmaiden; for, behold, from henceforth all generations shall call me blessed.
> For he that is mighty hath done to me great things; and holy is his name.
> And his mercy is on them that fear him from generation to generation.
> He hath shewed strength with his arm; he hath scattered the proud in the imagination of their hearts.
> He hath put down the mighty from their seats and exalted them of low degree.
> He hath filled the hungry with good things; and the rich he hath sent empty away.
> He hath holpen his servant Israel, in remembrance of his mercy;
> As he spake to our fathers, to Abraham, and to his seed for ever.

And Mary abode with her about three months, and returned to her own house.

Now Elisabeth's full time came that she should be delivered; and she brought forth a son. And her neighbours and her cousins heard how the Lord had shewed great mercy upon her; and they rejoiced with her. And it came to pass, that on the eighth day they came to circumcise the child; and they called him Zacharias, after the name of his father. And his mother answered and said, Not so; but he shall be called John. And they said unto her, There is none of thy kindred that is called by this name. And they made signs to his father, how he would have him called. And he asked for a writing table, and wrote, saying, His name is John. And they marvelled all. And his mouth was opened immediately, and his tongue loosed, and he spake, and praised God. And fear came on all that dwelt round about them: and all these sayings were noised abroad throughout all the hill country of Judæa. And all they that heard them laid them up in their hearts, saying, What manner of child shall this be! And the hand of the Lord was with him.

And his father Zacharias was filled with the Holy Ghost, and prophesied, saying,

> Blessed be the Lord God of Israel; for he hath visited and redeemed his people,
> And hath raised up an horn of salvation for us in the house of his servant David;
> As he spake by the mouth of his holy prophets, which have been since the world began:

> That we should be saved from our enemies, and from the hand
> of all that hate us;
> To perform the mercy promised to our fathers, and to remem-
> ber his holy covenant;
> The oath which he sware to our father Abraham,
> That he would grant unto us, that we being delivered out of the
> hand of our enemies might serve him without fear,
> In holiness and righteousness before him, all the days of our
> life.
> And thou, child, shalt be called the prophet of the Highest: for
> thou shalt go before the face of the Lord to prepare his
> ways;
> To give knowledge of salvation unto his people by the remission
> of their sins,
> Through the tender mercy of our God; whereby the dayspring
> from on high hath visited us,
> To give light to them that sit in darkness and in the shadow of
> death, to guide our feet into the way of peace.

And the child grew, and waxed strong in spirit, and was in the deserts till the day of his shewing unto Israel.

2. And it came to pass in those days, that there went out a decree from Cæsar Augustus, that all the world should be taxed. (And this taxing was first made when Cyrenius was governor of Syria.) And all went to be taxed, every one into his own city. And Joseph also went up from Galilee, out of the city of Naza-reth, into Judæa, unto the city of David, which is called Bethlehem; (because he was of the house and lineage of David:) to be taxed with Mary his espoused wife, being great with child. And so it was, that, while they were there, the days were accomplished that she should be delivered. And she brought forth her first-born son, and wrapped him in swaddling clothes, and laid him in a manger; because there was no room for them in the inn.

And there were in the same country shepherds abiding in the field, keeping watch over their flock by night. And, lo, the angel of the Lord came upon them, and the glory of the Lord shone round about them: and they were sore afraid. And the angel said unto them, Fear not: for, behold, I bring you good tidings of great joy, which shall be to all people. For unto you is born this day in the city of David a Saviour, which is Christ the Lord. And this shall be a sign unto you; Ye shall find the babe wrapped in swaddling clothes, lying in a manger. And suddenly there was with the angel a multitude of the heavenly host praising God, and saying, Glory to God in the highest, and on earth peace, good will toward men.

And it came to pass, as the angels were gone away from them into heaven, the shepherds said one to another, Let us now go even unto Bethlehem, and see this thing which is come to pass, which the Lord hath made known unto us. And they came with haste, and found Mary, and Joseph, and the babe lying in a manger. And when they had seen it, they made known abroad the saying which was told them concerning this child. And all they that heard it won-dered at those things which were told them by the shepherds. But Mary kept all these things, and pondered them in her heart. And the shepherds returned, glorifying and praising God for all the things that they had heard and seen, as it was told unto them.

And when eight days were accomplished for the circumcising of the child, his name was called Jesus, which was so named of the angel before he was conceived in the womb. And when the days of her purification according to the law of Moses were accomplished, they brought him to Jerusalem, to present him to the Lord; (as it is written in the law of the Lord, Every male that openeth the womb shall be called holy to the Lord;) and to offer a sacrifice according to that which is said in the law of the Lord, A pair of turtledoves, or two young pigeons.

And, behold, there was a man in Jerusalem, whose name was Simeon; and the same man was just and devout, waiting for the consolation of Israel: and the Holy Ghost was upon him. And it was revealed unto him by the Holy Ghost, that he should not see death, before he had seen the Lord's Christ. And he came by the Spirit into the temple: and when the parents brought in the child Jesus, to do for him after the custom of the law, then took he him up in his arms, and blessed God, and said,

> Lord, now lettest thou thy servant depart in peace, according
> to thy word:
> For mine eyes have seen thy salvation,
> Which thou hast prepared before the face of all people;
> A light to lighten the Gentiles, and the glory of thy people
> Israel.

And Joseph and his mother marvelled at those things which were spoken of him. And Simeon blessed them, and said unto Mary his mother, Behold, this child is set for the fall and rising again of many in Israel; and for a sign which shall be spoken against; (yea, a sword shall pierce through thy own soul also,) that the thoughts of many hearts may be revealed.

And there was one Anna, a prophetess, the daughter of Phanuel, of the tribe of Aser: she was of a great age, and had lived with an husband seven years from her virginity; and she was a widow of about fourscore and four years, which departed not from the temple, but served God with fastings and prayers night and day. And she coming in that instant gave thanks likewise unto the Lord, and spake of him to all them that looked for redemption in Jerusalem. And when they had performed all things according to the law of the Lord, they returned into Galilee, to their own city Nazareth. And the child grew, and waxed strong in spirit, filled with wisdom: and the grace of God was upon him.

Now his parents went to Jerusalem every year at the feast of the passover. And when he was twelve years old, they went up to Jerusalem after the custom of the feast. And when they had fulfilled the days, as they returned, the child Jesus tarried behind in Jerusalem; and Joseph and his mother knew not of it. But they, supposing him to have been in the company, went a day's journey; and they sought him among their kinsfolk and acquaintance. And when they found him not, they turned back again to Jerusalem, seeking him.

And it came to pass, that after three days they found him in the temple, sitting in the midst of the doctors, both hearing them, and asking them questions. And all that heard him were astonished at his understanding and answers. And when they saw him, they were amazed: and his mother said unto him, Son, why hast thou thus dealt with us? behold, thy father and I have sought thee sorrowing. And he said unto them, How is it that ye sought me? wist ye not that I must be about my Father's business? And they understood not the saying which he spake unto them. And he went down with them, and came to Nazareth, and was subject unto them: but his mother kept all these sayings in her heart. And Jesus increased in wisdom and stature, and in favour with God and man.

3. Now in the fifteenth year of the reign of Tiberius Cæsar, Pontius Pilate being governor of Judæa, and Herod being tetrarch of Galilee, and his brother Philip tetrarch of Ituræa and of the region of Trachonitis, and Lysanias the tetrarch of Abilene, Annas and Caiaphas being the high priests, the word of God came unto John the son of Zacharias in the wilderness. And he came into all the country about Jordan, preaching the baptism of repentance for the remission of sins; as it is written in the book of the words of Esaias the prophet, saying, The voice of one crying in the wilderness, Prepare ye the way of the Lord, make his paths straight. Every valley shall be filled, and every mountain and hill shall be brought low; and the crooked shall be made straight, and the rough ways shall be made smooth; and all flesh shall see the salvation of God.

Then said he to the multitude that came forth to be baptized of him, O generation of vipers, who hath warned you to flee from the wrath to come? Bring forth therefore fruits worthy of repentance, and begin not to say within yourselves, We have Abraham to our father: for I say unto you, That God is able of these stones to raise up children unto Abraham. And now also the axe is laid unto the root of the trees: every tree therefore which bringeth not forth good fruit is hewn down, and cast into the fire.

And the people asked him, saying, What shall we do then? He answereth and saith unto them, He that hath two coats, let him impart to him that hath none; and he that hath meat, let him do likewise. Then came also publicans to be baptized, and said unto him, Master, what shall we do? And he said unto them, Exact no more than that which is appointed you. And the soldiers likewise demanded of him, saying, And what shall we do? And he said unto them, Do violence to no man, neither accuse any falsely; and be content with your wages.

And as the people were in expectation, and all men mused in their hearts of John, whether he were the Christ, or not; John answered, saying unto them all, I indeed baptize you with water; but one mightier than I cometh, the latchet of whose shoes I am not worthy to unloose: he shall baptize you with the Holy Ghost and with fire: whose fan is in his hand, and he will throughly purge his floor, and will gather the wheat into his garner; but the chaff he will burn with fire unquenchable. And many other things in his exhortation preached he unto the people. But Herod the tetrarch, being reproved by him for Herodias his brother Philip's wife, and for all the evils which Herod had done, added yet this above all, that he shut up John in prison.

Now when all the people were baptized, it came to pass, that Jesus also being baptized, and praying, the heaven was opened, and the Holy Ghost descended in a bodily shape like a dove upon him, and a voice came from heaven, which said, Thou art my beloved Son, in thee I am well pleased.

And Jesus himself began to be about thirty years of age, being (as was supposed) the son of Joseph, which was the son of Heli, which was the son of Matthat, which was the son of Levi, which was the son of Melchi, which was the son of Janna, which was the son of Joseph, which was the son of Mattathias, which was the son of Amos, which was the son of Naum, which was the son of Esli, which was the son of Nagge, which was the son of Maath, which was the son of Mattathias, which was the son of Semei, which was the son of Joseph, which was the son of Juda, which was the son of Joanna, which was the son of Rhesa, which was the son of Zorobabel, which was the son of Salathiel, which was the son of Neri, which was the son of Melchi, which was the son of Addi, which was the son of Cosam, which was the son of Elmodam, which was the son of Er, which was the son of Jose, which was the son of Eliezer, which was the son of Jorim, which was the son of Matthat, which was the son of Levi, which was the son of Simeon, which was the son of Juda, which was the son of Joseph, which was the son of Jonan, which was the son of Eliakim, which was the son of Melea, which was the son of Menan, which was the son of Mattatha, which was the son of Nathan, which was the son of David, which was the son of Jesse, which was the son of Obed, which was the son of Booz, which was the son of Salmon, which was the son of Naasson, which was the son of Aminadab, which was the son of Aram, which was the son of Esrom, which was the son of Phares, which was the son of Juda, which was the son of Jacob, which was the son of Isaac, which was the son of Abraham, which was the son of Thara, which was the son of Nachor, which was the son of Saruch, which was the son of Ragau, which was the son of Phalec, which was the son of Heber, which was the son of Sala, which was the son of Cainan, which was the son of Arphaxad, which was the son of Sem, which was the son of Noe, which was the son of Lamech, which was the son of Mathusala, which was the son of Enoch, which was the son of Jared, which was the son of Maleleel, which was the son of Cainan, which was the son of Enos, which was the son of Seth, which was the son of Adam, which was the son of God.

4. And Jesus being full of the Holy Ghost returned from Jordan, and was led by the Spirit into the wilderness, being forty days tempted of the devil. And in those days he did eat nothing: and when they were ended, he afterward hungered. And the devil said unto him, If thou be the Son of God, command this stone that it be made bread. And Jesus answered him, saying, It is written, That man shall not live by bread alone, but by every word of God. And the devil, taking him up into an high mountain, shewed unto him all the kingdoms of the world in a moment of time. And the devil said unto him, All this power will I give thee, and the glory of them: for that is delivered unto me; and to whomsoever I will I give it. If thou therefore wilt worship me, all shall be thine. And Jesus answered and said unto him, Get thee behind me, Satan: for it is written, Thou shalt worship the Lord thy God, and him only shalt thou serve. And he brought him to Jerusalem, and set him on a pinnacle of the temple, and said unto him, If thou be the Son of God, cast thyself down from hence: for it is written, He shall give his angels charge over thee, to keep thee: and in their hands they shall bear thee up, lest at any time thou dash thy foot against a stone. And Jesus answering said unto him, It is said, Thou shalt not tempt the Lord thy God. And when the devil had ended all the temptation, he departed from him for a season.

And Jesus returned in the power of the Spirit into Galilee: and there went out a fame of him through all the region round about. And he taught in their synagogues, being glorified of all.

And he came to Nazareth, where he had been brought up: and, as his custom was, he went into the synagogue on the sabbath day, and stood up for to read. And there was delivered unto him the book of the prophet Esaias. And when he had opened the book, he found the place where it was written, The Spirit of the Lord is upon me, because he hath anointed me to preach the gospel to the poor; he hath sent me to heal the brokenhearted, to preach deliverance to the captives, and recovering of sight to the blind, to set at liberty them that are bruised, to preach the acceptable year of the Lord. And he closed the book, and he gave it again to the minister, and sat down. And the eyes of all them that were in the synagogue were fastened on him.

And he began to say unto them, This day is this scripture fulfilled in your ears. And all bare him witness, and wondered at the gracious words which proceeded out of his mouth. And they said, Is not this Joseph's son? And he said unto them, Ye will surely say unto me this proverb, Physician, heal thyself: whatsoever we have heard done in Capernaum, do also here in thy country. And he said, Verily I say unto you, No prophet is accepted in his own country. But I tell you of a truth, many widows were in Israel in the days of Elias, when the heaven was shut up three years and six months, when great famine was throughout all the land; but unto none of them was Elias sent, save unto Sarepta, a city of Sidon, unto a woman that was a widow. And many lepers were in Israel in the time of Eliseus the prophet; and none of them was cleansed, saving Naaman the Syrian. And all they in the synagogue, when they heard these things, were filled with wrath, and rose up, and thrust him out of the city, and led him unto the brow of the hill whereon their city was built, that they might cast him down headlong. But he passing through the midst of them went his way, and came down to Capernaum, a city of Galilee, and taught them on the sabbath days. And they were astonished at his doctrine: for his word was with power.

And in the synagogue there was a man, which had a spirit of an unclean devil, and cried out with a loud voice, saying, Let us alone; what have we to do with thee, thou Jesus of Nazareth? art thou come to destroy us? I know thee who thou art; the Holy One of God. And Jesus rebuked him, saying, Hold thy peace, and come out of him. And when the devil had thrown him in the midst, he came out of him, and hurt him not. And they were all amazed, and spake among themselves, saying, What a word is this! for with authority and power he commandeth the unclean spirits, and they come out. And the fame of him went out into every place of the country round about.

And he arose out of the synagogue, and entered into Simon's house. And Simon's wife's mother was taken with a great fever; and they besought him for her. And he stood over her, and rebuked the fever; and it left her: and immediately she arose and ministered unto them.

Now when the sun was setting, all they that had any sick with divers diseases brought them unto him; and he laid his hands on every one of them, and healed them. And devils also came out of many, crying out, and saying, Thou art Christ the Son of God. And he rebuking them suffered them not to speak:

for they knew that he was Christ. And when it was day, he departed and went
into a desert place: and the people sought him, and came unto him, and stayed
him, that he should not depart from them. And he said unto them, I must
preach the kingdom of God to other cities also: for therefore am I sent. And he
preached in the synagogues of Galilee.

5. And it came to pass, that, as the people pressed upon him to hear the word
of God, he stood by the lake of Gennesaret, and saw two ships standing by the
lake: but the fishermen were gone out of them, and were washing their nets.
And he entered into one of the ships, which was Simon's, and prayed him that
he would thrust out a little from the land. And he sat down, and taught the
people out of the ship. Now when he had left speaking, he said unto Simon,
Launch out into the deep, and let down your nets for a draught. And Simon
answering said unto him, Master, we have toiled all the night, and have taken
nothing: nevertheless at thy word I will let down the net. And when they had
this done, they inclosed a great multitude of fishes: and their net brake. And
they beckoned unto their partners, which were in the other ship, that they
should come and help them. And they came, and filled both the ships, so that
they began to sink. When Simon Peter saw it, he fell down at Jesus' knees, saying, Depart from me; for I am a sinful man, O Lord. For he was astonished, and
all that were with him, at the draught of the fishes which they had taken: and
so was also James, and John, the sons of Zebedee, which were partners with
Simon. And Jesus said unto Simon, Fear not; from henceforth thou shalt catch
men. And when they had brought their ships to land, they forsook all, and followed him.

   And it came to pass, when he was in a certain city, behold a man full of leprosy: who seeing Jesus fell on his face, and besought him, saying, Lord, if thou
wilt, thou canst make me clean. And he put forth his hand, and touched him,
saying, I will: be thou clean. And immediately the leprosy departed from him.
And he charged him to tell no man: but go, and shew thyself to the priest, and
offer for thy cleansing, according as Moses commanded, for a testimony unto
them. But so much the more went there a fame abroad of him: and great multitudes came together to hear, and to be healed by him of their infirmities. And
he withdrew himself into the wilderness, and prayed.

   And it came to pass on a certain day, as he was teaching, that there were
Pharisees and doctors of the law sitting by, which were come out of every town
of Galilee, and Judæa, and Jerusalem: and the power of the Lord was present
to heal them. And, behold, men brought in a bed a man which was taken with
a palsy: and they sought means to bring him in, and to lay him before him. And
when they could not find by what way they might bring him in because of the
multitude, they went upon the housetop, and let him down through the tiling
with his couch into the midst before Jesus. And when he saw their faith, he
said unto him, Man, thy sins are forgiven thee. And the scribes and the Pharisees began to reason, saying, Who is this which speaketh blasphemies? Who
can forgive sins, but God alone? But when Jesus perceived their thoughts, he
answering said unto them, What reason ye in your hearts? Whether is easier,
to say, Thy sins be forgiven thee; or to say, Rise up and walk? But that ye may
know that the Son of man hath power upon earth to forgive sins, (he said unto
the sick of the palsy,) I say unto thee, Arise, and take up thy couch, and go into

thine house. And immediately he rose up before them, and took up that whereon he lay, and departed to his own house, glorifying God. And they were all amazed, and they glorified God, and were filled with fear, saying, We have seen strange things to day.

And after these things he went forth, and saw a publican, named Levi, sitting at the receipt of custom: and he said unto him, Follow me. And he left all, rose up, and followed him. And Levi made him a great feast in his own house: and there was a great company of publicans and of others that sat down with them. But their scribes and Pharisees murmured against his disciples, saying, Why do ye eat and drink with publicans and sinners? And Jesus answering said unto them, They that are whole need not a physician; but they that are sick. I came not to call the righteous, but sinners to repentance.

And they said unto him, Why do the disciples of John fast often, and make prayers, and likewise the disciples of the Pharisees; but thine eat and drink? And he said unto them, Can ye make the children of the bridechamber fast, while the bridegroom is with them? But the days will come, when the bridegroom shall be taken away from them, and then shall they fast in those days. And he spake also a parable unto them; No man putteth a piece of a new garment upon an old; if otherwise, then both the new maketh a rent, and the piece that was taken out of the new agreeth not with the old. And no man putteth new wine into old bottles; else the new wine will burst the bottles, and be spilled, and the bottles shall perish. But new wine must be put into new bottles; and both are preserved. No man also having drunk old wine straightway desireth new: for he saith, The old is better.

6. And it came to pass on the second sabbath after the first, that he went through the corn fields; and his disciples plucked the ears of corn, and did eat, rubbing them in their hands. And certain of the Pharisees said unto them, Why do ye that which is not lawful to do on the sabbath days? And Jesus answering them said, Have ye not read so much as this, what David did, when himself was an hungred, and they which were with him; how he went into the house of God, and did take and eat the shewbread, and gave also to them that were with him; which it is not lawful to eat but for the priests alone? And he said unto them, That the Son of man is Lord also of the sabbath.

And it came to pass also on another sabbath, that he entered into the synagogue and taught: and there was a man whose right hand was withered. And the scribes and Pharisees watched him, whether he would heal on the sabbath day; that they might find an accusation against him. But he knew their thoughts, and said to the man which had the withered hand, Rise up, and stand forth in the midst. And he arose and stood forth. Then said Jesus unto them, I will ask you one thing; Is it lawful on the sabbath days to do good, or to do evil? to save life, or to destroy it? And looking round about upon them all, he said unto the man, Stretch forth thy hand. And he did so: and his hand was restored whole as the other. And they were filled with madness; and communed one with another what they might do to Jesus.

And it came to pass in those days, that he went out into a mountain to pray, and continued all night in prayer to God. And when it was day, he called unto him his disciples: and of them he chose twelve, whom also he named apostles; Simon, (whom he also named Peter,) and Andrew his brother, James and John,

Philip and Bartholomew, Matthew and Thomas, James the son of Alphæus, and Simon called Zelotes, and Judas the brother of James, and Judas Iscariot, which also was the traitor.

And he came down with them, and stood in the plain, and the company of his disciples, and a great multitude of people out of all Judæa and Jerusalem, and from the sea coast of Tyre and Sidon, which came to hear him, and to be healed of their diseases; and they that were vexed with unclean spirits: and they were healed. And the whole multitude sought to touch him: for there went virtue out of him, and healed them all.

And he lifted up his eyes on his disciples, and said, Blessed be ye poor: for yours is the kingdom of God. Blessed are ye that hunger now: for ye shall be filled. Blessed are ye that weep now: for ye shall laugh. Blessed are ye, when men shall hate you, and when they shall separate you from their company, and shall reproach you, and cast out your name as evil, for the Son of man's sake. Rejoice ye in that day, and leap for joy: for, behold, your reward is great in heaven: for in the like manner did their fathers unto the prophets. But woe unto you that are rich! for ye have received your consolation. Woe unto you that are full! for ye shall hunger. Woe unto you that laugh now! for ye shall mourn and weep. Woe unto you, when all men shall speak well of you! for so did their fathers to the false prophets.

But I say unto you which hear, Love your enemies, do good to them which hate you, bless them that curse you, and pray for them which despitefully use you. And unto him that smiteth thee on the one cheek offer also the other; and him that taketh away thy cloke forbid not to take thy coat also. Give to every man that asketh of thee; and of him that taketh away thy goods ask them not again. And as ye would that men should do to you, do ye also to them likewise. For if ye love them which love you, what thank have ye? for sinners also love those that love them. And if ye do good to them which do good to you, what thank have ye? for sinners also do even the same. And if ye lend to them of whom ye hope to receive, what thank have ye? for sinners also lend to sinners, to receive as much again. But love ye your enemies, and do good, and lend, hoping for nothing again; and your reward shall be great, and ye shall be the children of the Highest: for he is kind unto the unthankful and to the evil. Be ye therefore merciful, as your Father also is merciful.

Judge not, and ye shall not be judged: condemn not, and ye shall not be condemned: forgive, and ye shall be forgiven: give, and it shall be given unto you; good measure, pressed down, and shaken together, and running over, shall men give into your bosom. For with the same measure that ye mete withal it shall be measured to you again. And he spake a parable unto them, Can the blind lead the blind? shall they not both fall into the ditch? The disciple is not above his master: but every one that is perfect shall be as his master. And why beholdest thou the mote that is in thy brother's eye, but perceivest not the beam that is in thine own eye? Either how canst thou say to thy brother, Brother, let me pull out the mote that is in thine eye, when thou thyself beholdest not the beam that is in thine own eye? Thou hypocrite, cast out first the beam out of thine own eye, and then shalt thou see clearly to pull out the mote that is in thy brother's eye.

For a good tree bringeth not forth corrupt fruit; neither doth a corrupt tree bring forth good fruit. For every tree is known by his own fruit. For of thorns men do not gather figs, nor of a bramble bush gather they grapes. A good man out of the good treasure of his heart bringeth forth that which is good; and an evil man out of the evil treasure of his heart bringeth forth that which is evil: for of the abundance of the heart his mouth speaketh.

And why call ye me, Lord, Lord, and do not the things which I say? Whosoever cometh to me, and heareth my sayings, and doeth them, I will shew you to whom he is like: he is like a man which built an house, and digged deep, and laid the foundation on a rock: and when the flood arose, the stream beat vehemently upon that house, and could not shake it: for it was founded upon a rock. But he that heareth, and doeth not, is like a man that without a foundation built an house upon the earth; against which the stream did beat vehemently, and immediately it fell; and the ruin of that house was great.

*   *   *

[The Good Samaritan]

10. After these things the Lord appointed other seventy also, and sent them two and two before his face into every city and place, whither he himself would come. Therefore said he unto them, The harvest truly is great, but the labourers are few: pray ye therefore the Lord of the harvest, that he would send forth labourers into his harvest. Go your ways: behold, I send you forth as lambs among wolves. Carry neither purse, nor scrip, nor shoes: and salute no man by the way. And into whatsoever house ye enter, first say, Peace be to this house. And if the son of peace be there, your peace shall rest upon it: if not, it shall turn to you again. And in the same house remain, eating and drinking such things as they give: for the labourer is worthy of his hire. Go not from house to house. And into whatsoever city ye enter, and they receive you, eat such things as are set before you: and heal the sick that are therein, and say unto them, The kingdom of God is come nigh unto you. But into whatsoever city ye enter, and they receive you not, go your ways out into the streets of the same, and say, Even the very dust of your city, which cleaveth on us, we do wipe off against you: notwithstanding be ye sure of this, that the kingdom of God is come nigh unto you. But I say unto you, that it shall be more tolerable in that day for Sodom, than for that city.

Woe unto thee, Chorazin! woe unto thee, Bethsaida! for if the mighty works had been done in Tyre and Sidon, which have been done in you, they had a great while ago repented, sitting in sackcloth and ashes. But it shall be more tolerable for Tyre and Sidon at the judgment, than for you. And thou, Capernaum, which art exalted to heaven, shalt be thrust down to hell. He that heareth you heareth me; and he that despiseth you despiseth me; and he that despiseth me despiseth him that sent me.

And the seventy returned again with joy, saying, Lord, even the devils are subject unto us through thy name. And he said unto them, I beheld Satan as lightning fall from heaven. Behold, I give unto you power to tread on serpents and scorpions, and over all the power of the enemy: and nothing shall by any means hurt you. Notwithstanding in this rejoice not, that the spirits are subject unto you; but rather rejoice, because your names are written in heaven.

In that hour Jesus rejoiced in spirit, and said, I thank thee, O Father, Lord of heaven and earth, that thou hast hid these things from the wise and prudent, and hast revealed them unto babes: even so, Father; for so it seemed good in thy sight. All things are delivered to me of my Father: and no man knoweth who the Son is, but the Father; and who the Father is, but the Son, and he to whom the Son will reveal him. And he turned him unto his disciples, and said privately, Blessed are the eyes which see the things that ye see: for I tell you, that many prophets and kings have desired to see those things which ye see, and have not seen them; and to hear those things which ye hear, and have not heard them.

And, behold, a certain lawyer stood up, and tempted him, saying, Master, what shall I do to inherit eternal life? He said unto him, What is written in the law? how readest thou? And he answering said, Thou shalt love the Lord thy God with all thy heart, and with all thy soul, and with all thy strength, and with all thy mind; and thy neighbour as thyself. And he said unto him, Thou hast answered right: this do, and thou shalt live. But he, willing to justify himself, said unto Jesus, And who is my neighbour? And Jesus answering said, A certain man went down from Jerusalem to Jericho, and fell among thieves, which stripped him of his raiment, and wounded him, and departed, leaving him half dead. And by chance there came down a certain priest that way: and when he saw him, he passed by on the other side. And likewise a Levite, when he was at the place, came and looked on him, and passed by on the other side. But a certain Samaritan, as he journeyed, came where he was: and when he saw him, he had compassion on him, and went to him, and bound up his wounds, pouring in oil and wine, and set him on his own beast, and brought him to an inn, and took care of him. And on the morrow when he departed, he took out two pence, and gave them to the host, and said unto him, Take care of him; and whatsoever thou spendest more, when I come again, I will repay thee. Which now of these three, thinkest thou, was neighbour unto him that fell among the thieves? And he said, He that shewed mercy on him. Then said Jesus unto him, Go, and do thou likewise.

Now it came to pass, as they went, that he entered into a certain village: and a certain woman named Martha received him into her house. And she had a sister called Mary, which also sat at Jesus' feet, and heard his word. But Martha was cumbered about much serving, and came to him, and said, Lord, dost thou not care that my sister hath left me to serve alone? bid her therefore that she help me. And Jesus answered and said unto her, Martha, Martha, thou art careful and troubled about many things: but one thing is needful: and Mary hath chosen that good part, which shall not be taken away from her.

*   *   *

[The Prodigal Son and Other Parables]

15. Then drew near unto him all the publicans and sinners for to hear him. And the Pharisees and scribes murmured, saying, This man receiveth sinners, and eateth with them.

And he spake this parable unto them, saying, What man of you, having an hundred sheep, if he lose one of them, doth not leave the ninety and nine in the wilderness, and go after that which is lost, until he find it? And when he hath found it, he layeth it on his shoulders, rejoicing. And when he cometh home, he calleth together his friends and neighbours, saying unto them, Rejoice with me; for I have found my sheep which was lost. I say unto you, that likewise joy shall be in heaven over one sinner that repenteth, more than over ninety and nine just persons, which need no repentance.

Either what woman having ten pieces of silver, if she lose one piece, doth not light a candle, and sweep the house, and seek diligently till she find it? And when she hath found it, she calleth her friends and her neighbours together, saying, Rejoice with me; for I have found the piece which I had lost. Likewise, I say unto you, there is joy in the presence of the angels of God over one sinner that repenteth.

And he said, A certain man had two sons: and the younger of them said to his father, Father, give me the portion of goods that falleth to me. And he divided unto them his living. And not many days after the younger son gathered all together, and took his journey into a far country, and there wasted his substance with riotous living. And when he had spent all, there arose a mighty famine in that land; and he began to be in want. And he went and joined himself to a citizen of that country; and he sent him into his fields to feed swine. And he would fain have filled his belly with the husks that the swine did eat: and no man gave unto him. And when he came to himself, he said, How many hired servants of my father's have bread enough and to spare, and I perish with hunger! I will arise and go to my father, and will say unto him, Father, I have sinned against heaven, and before thee, and am no more worthy to be called thy son: make me as one of thy hired servants. And he arose, and came to his father. But when he was yet a great way off, his father saw him, and had compassion, and ran, and fell on his neck, and kissed him. And the son said unto him, Father, I have sinned against heaven, and in thy sight, and am no more worthy to be called thy son. But the father said to his servants, Bring forth the best robe, and put it on him; and put a ring on his hand, and shoes on his feet: and bring hither the fatted calf, and kill it; and let us eat, and be merry: for this my son was dead, and is alive again; he was lost, and is found. And they began to be merry.

Now his elder son was in the field: and as he came and drew nigh to the house, he heard musick and dancing. And he called one of the servants, and asked what these things meant. And he said unto him, Thy brother is come; and thy father hath killed the fatted calf, because he hath received him safe and sound. And he was angry, and would not go in: therefore came his father out, and intreated him. And he answering said to his father, Lo, these many years do I serve thee, neither transgressed I at any time thy commandment: and yet thou never gavest me a kid, that I might make merry with my friends: but as soon as this thy son was come, which hath devoured thy living with harlots, thou hast killed for him the fatted calf. And he said unto him, Son, thou art ever with me, and all that I have is thine. It was meet that we should make merry, and be glad: for this thy brother was dead, and is alive again; and was lost, and is found.

16. And he said also unto his disciples, There was a certain rich man, which had a steward; and the same was accused unto him that he had wasted his goods. And he called him, and said unto him, How is it that I hear this of thee? give an account of thy stewardship; for thou mayest be no longer steward. Then the steward said within himself, What shall I do? for my lord taketh away from me the stewardship: I cannot dig; to beg I am ashamed. I am resolved what to

do, that, when I am put out of the stewardship, they may receive me into their houses. So he called every one of his lord's debtors unto him, and said unto the first, How much owest thou unto my lord? And he said, An hundred measures of oil. And he said unto him, Take thy bill, and sit down quickly, and write fifty. Then said he to another, And how much owest thou? And he said, An hundred measures of wheat. And he said unto him, Take thy bill, and write fourscore. And the lord commended the unjust steward, because he had done wisely: for the children of this world are in their generation wiser than the children of light.

And I say unto you, Make to yourselves friends of the mammon of unrighteousness; that, when ye fail, they may receive you into everlasting habitations. He that is faithful in that which is least is faithful also in much: and he that is unjust in the least is unjust also in much. If therefore ye have not been faithful in the unrighteous mammon, who will commit to your trust the true riches? And if ye have not been faithful in that which is another man's, who shall give you that which is your own? No servant can serve two masters: for either he will hate the one, and love the other; or else he will hold to the one, and despise the other. Ye cannot serve God and mammon.

And the Pharisees also, who were covetous, heard all these things: and they derided him. And he said unto them, Ye are they which justify yourselves before men; but God knoweth your hearts: for that which is highly esteemed among men is abomination in the sight of God. The law and the prophets were until John: since that time the kingdom of God is preached, and every man presseth into it. And it is easier for heaven and earth to pass, than one tittle of the law to fail. Whosoever putteth away his wife, and marrieth another, committeth adultery: and whosoever marrieth her that is put away from her husband committeth adultery.

There was a certain rich man, which was clothed in purple and fine linen, and fared sumptuously every day: and there was a certain beggar named Lazarus, which was laid at his gate, full of sores, and desiring to be fed with the crumbs which fell from the rich man's table: moreover the dogs came and licked his sores. And it came to pass, that the beggar died, and was carried by the angels into Abraham's bosom: the rich man also died, and was buried; and in hell he lift up his eyes, being in torments, and seeth Abraham afar off, and Lazarus in his bosom. And he cried and said, Father Abraham, have mercy on me, and send Lazarus, that he may dip the tip of his finger in water, and cool my tongue; for I am tormented in this flame. But Abraham said, Son, remember that thou in thy lifetime receivedst thy good things, and likewise Lazarus evil things: but now he is comforted, and thou art tormented. And beside all this, between us and you there is a great gulf fixed: so that they which would pass from hence to you cannot; neither can they pass to us, that would come from thence. Then he said, I pray thee therefore, father, that thou wouldest send him to my father's house: for I have five brethren; that he may testify unto them, lest they also come into this place of torment. Abraham saith unto him, They have Moses and the prophets; let them hear them. And he said, Nay, father Abraham: but if one went unto them from the dead, they will repent. And he said unto him, If they hear not Moses and the prophets, neither will they be persuaded, though one rose from the dead.

17. Then said he unto the disciples, It is impossible but that offences will come: but woe unto him, through whom they come! It were better for him that a millstone were hanged about his neck, and he cast into the sea, than that he should offend one of these little ones.

Take heed to yourselves: If thy brother trespass against thee, rebuke him; and if he repent, forgive him. And if he trespass against thee seven times in a day, and seven times in a day turn again to thee, saying, I repent; thou shalt forgive him.

And the apostles said unto the Lord, Increase our faith. And the Lord said, If ye had faith as a grain of mustard seed, ye might say unto this sycamine tree, Be thou plucked up by the root, and be thou planted in the sea; and it should obey you.

But which of you, having a servant plowing or feeding cattle, will say unto him by and by, when he is come from the field, Go and sit down to meat? And will not rather say unto him, Make ready wherewith I may sup, and gird thyself, and serve me, till I have eaten and drunken; and afterward thou shalt eat and drink? Doth he thank that servant because he did the things that were commanded him? I trow not. So likewise ye, when ye shall have done all those things which are commanded you, say, We are unprofitable servants: we have done that which was our duty to do.

And it came to pass, as he went to Jerusalem, that he passed through the midst of Samaria and Galilee. And as he entered into a certain village, there met him ten men that were lepers, which stood afar off: and they lifted up their voices, and said, Jesus, Master, have mercy on us. And when he saw them, he said unto them, Go shew yourselves unto the priests. And it came to pass, that, as they went, they were cleansed. And one of them, when he saw that he was healed, turned back, and with a loud voice glorified God, and fell down on his face at his feet, giving him thanks: and he was a Samaritan. And Jesus answering said, Were there not ten cleansed? but where are the nine? There are not found that returned to give glory to God, save this stranger. And he said unto him, Arise, go thy way: thy faith hath made thee whole.

And when he was demanded of the Pharisees, when the kingdom of God should come, he answered them and said, The kingdom of God cometh not with observation: neither shall they say, Lo here! or, lo there! for, behold, the kingdom of God is within you.

And he said unto the disciples, The days will come, when ye shall desire to see one of the days of the Son of man, and ye shall not see it. And they shall say to you, See here; or, see there: go not after them, nor follow them. For as the lightning, that lighteneth out of the one part under heaven, shineth unto the other part under heaven; so shall also the Son of man be in his day. But first must he suffer many things, and be rejected of this generation. And as it was in the days of Noe, so shall it be also in the days of the Son of man. They did eat, they drank, they married wives, they were given in marriage, until the day that Noe entered into the ark, and the flood came, and destroyed them all. Likewise also as it was in the days of Lot; they did eat, they drank, they bought, they sold, they planted, they builded; but the same day that Lot went out of Sodom it rained fire and brimstone from heaven, and destroyed them all. Even thus shall it be in the day when the Son of man is revealed. In that day, he which shall be upon the housetop, and his stuff in the house, let him not come down to take it away: and he that is in the field, let him likewise not return back. Remember Lot's wife. Whosoever shall seek to save his life shall lose it; and whosoever shall lose his life shall preserve it. I tell you, in that night there shall be two men in one bed; the one shall be taken, and the other shall be left. Two women shall be grinding together; the one shall be taken, and the other left. Two men shall be in the field; the one shall be taken, and the other left. And they answered and said unto him, Where, Lord? And he said unto them, Wheresoever the body is, thither will the eagles be gathered together.

18. And he spake a parable unto them to this end, that men ought always to pray, and not to faint; saying, There was in a city a judge, which feared not God, neither regarded man: and there was a widow in that city; and she came unto him, saying, Avenge me of mine adversary. And he would not for a while: but afterward he said within himself, Though I fear not God, nor regard man; yet because this widow troubleth me, I will avenge her, lest by her continual coming she weary me. And the Lord said, Hear what the unjust judge saith. And shall not God avenge his own elect, which cry day and night unto him, though he bear long with them? I tell you that he will avenge them speedily. Nevertheless when the Son of man cometh, shall he find faith on the earth?

And he spake this parable unto certain which trusted in themselves that they were righteous, and despised others: Two men went up into the temple to pray; the one a Pharisee, and the other a publican. The Pharisee stood and prayed thus with himself, God, I thank thee, that I am not as other men are, extortioners, unjust, adulterers, or even as this publican. I fast twice in the week, I give tithes of all that I possess. And the publican, standing afar off, would not lift up so much as his eyes unto heaven, but smote upon his breast, saying, God be merciful to me a sinner. I tell you, this man went down to his house justified rather than the other: for every one that exalteth himself shall be abased; and he that humbleth himself shall be exalted.

And they brought unto him also infants, that he would touch them: but when his disciples saw it, they rebuked them. But Jesus called them unto him, and said, Suffer little children to come unto me, and forbid them not: for of such is the kingdom of God. Verily I say unto you, Whosoever shall not receive the kingdom of God as a little child shall in no wise enter therein.

And a certain ruler asked him, saying, Good Master, what shall I do to inherit eternal life? And Jesus said unto him, Why callest thou me good? none is good, save one, that is, God. Thou knowest the commandments, Do not commit adultery, Do not kill, Do not steal, Do not bear false witness, Honour thy father and thy mother. And he said, All these have I kept from my youth up. Now when Jesus heard these things, he said unto him, Yet lackest thou one thing: sell all that thou hast, and distribute unto the poor, and thou shalt have treasure in heaven: and come, follow me. And when he heard this, he was very sorrowful: for he was very rich. And when Jesus saw that he was very sorrowful, he said, How hardly shall they that have riches enter into the kingdom of God! For it is easier for a camel to go through a needle's eye, than for a rich man to enter into the kingdom of God. And they that heard it said, Who then can be saved? And he said, The things which are impossible with men are possible with God. Then Peter said, Lo, we have left all, and followed thee. And he said unto them, Verily I say unto you, There is no man that hath left house, or parents, or brethren, or wife, or children, for the kingdom of God's sake, who shall not receive manifold more in this present time, and in the world to come life everlasting.

Then he took unto him the twelve, and said unto them, Behold, we go up to Jerusalem, and all things that are written by the prophets concerning the Son of man shall be accomplished. For he shall be delivered unto the Gentiles, and shall be mocked, and spitefully entreated, and spitted on: and they shall scourge him, and put him to death: and the third day he shall rise again. And they understood none of these things: and this saying was hid from them, neither knew they the things which were spoken.

And it came to pass, that as he was come nigh unto Jericho, a certain blind man sat by the way side begging: and hearing the multitude pass by, he asked what it meant. And they told him, that Jesus of Nazareth passeth by. And he cried, saying, Jesus, thou Son of David, have mercy on me. And they which went before rebuked him, that he should hold his peace: but he cried so much the more, Thou Son of David, have mercy on me. And Jesus stood, and commanded him to be brought unto him: and when he was come near, he asked him, saying, What wilt thou that I shall do unto thee? And he said, Lord, that I may receive my sight. And Jesus said unto him, Receive thy sight: thy faith hath saved thee. And immediately he received his sight, and followed him, glorifying God: and all the people, when they saw it, gave praise unto God.

19. And Jesus entered and passed through Jericho. And, behold, there was a man named Zacchæus, which was the chief among the publicans, and he was rich. And he sought to see Jesus who he was; and could not for the press, because he was little of stature. And he ran before, and climbed up into a sycomore tree to see him: for he was to pass that way. And when Jesus came to the place, he looked up, and saw him, and said unto him, Zacchæus, make haste, and come down; for to day I must abide at thy house. And he made haste, and came down, and received him joyfully. And when they saw it, they all murmured, saying, That he was gone to be guest with a man that is a sinner. And Zacchæus stood, and said unto the Lord; Behold, Lord, the half of my goods I give to the poor; and if I have taken any thing from any man by false accusation, I restore him fourfold. And Jesus said unto him, This day is salvation come to this house, forsomuch as he also is a son of Abraham. For the Son of man is come to seek and to save that which was lost.

And as they heard these things, he added and spake a parable, because he was nigh to Jerusalem, and because they thought that the kingdom of God should immediately appear. He said therefore, A certain nobleman went into a far country to receive for himself a kingdom, and to return. And he called his ten servants, and delivered them ten pounds, and said unto them, Occupy till I come. But his citizens hated him, and sent a message after him, saying, We will not have this man to reign over us. And it came to pass, that when he was returned, having received the kingdom, then he commanded these servants to be called unto him, to whom he had given the money, that he might know how much every man had gained by trading. Then came the first, saying, Lord, thy pound hath gained ten pounds. And he said unto him, Well, thou good servant: because thou hast been faithful in a very little, have thou authority over ten cities. And the second came, saying, Lord, thy pound hath gained five pounds. And he said likewise to him, Be thou also over five cities. And another came, saying, Lord, behold, here is thy pound, which I have kept laid up in a napkin: for I feared thee, because thou art an austere man: thou takest up that thou layedst not down, and reapest that thou didst not sow. And he saith unto him, Out of thine own mouth will I judge thee, thou wicked servant. Thou knewest that I was an austere man, taking up that I laid not down, and reaping that I did not sow: wherefore then gavest not thou my money into the bank, that at my coming I might have required mine own with usury? And he said unto them that stood by, Take from him the pound, and give it to him that hath ten pounds. (And they said unto him, Lord, he hath ten pounds.) For I say unto you, That unto every one which hath shall be given; and from him that hath not, even that he hath shall be taken away from him. But those mine enemies, which would not that I should reign over them, bring hither, and slay them before me.

And when he had thus spoken, he went before, ascending up to Jerusalem. And it came to pass, when he was come nigh to Bethphage and Bethany, at the mount called the mount of Olives, he sent two of his disciples, saying, Go ye into the village over against you; in the which at your entering ye shall find a colt tied, whereon yet never man sat: loose him, and bring him hither. And if any man ask you, Why do ye loose him? thus shall ye say unto him, Because the Lord hath need of him. And they that were sent went their way, and found even as he had said unto them. And as they were loosing the colt, the owners thereof said unto them, Why loose ye the colt? And they said, The Lord hath need of him. And they brought him to Jesus: and they cast their garments upon the colt, and they set Jesus thereon. And as he went, they spread their clothes in the way.

And when he was come nigh, even now at the descent of the mount of Olives, the whole multitude of the disciples began to rejoice and praise God with a loud voice for all the mighty works that they had seen; saying, Blessed be the King that cometh in the name of the Lord: peace in heaven, and glory in the highest. And some of the Pharisees from among the multitude said unto him, Master, rebuke thy disciples. And he answered and said unto them, I tell you that, if these should hold their peace, the stones would immediately cry out.

And when he was come near, he beheld the city, and wept over it, saying, If thou hadst known, even thou, at least in this thy day, the things which belong unto thy peace! but now they are hid from thine eyes. For the days shall come upon thee, that thine enemies shall cast a trench about thee, and compass thee round, and keep thee in on every side, and shall lay thee even with the ground, and thy children within thee; and they shall not leave in thee one stone upon another; because thou knewest not the time of thy visitation.

And he went into the temple, and began to cast out them that sold therein, and them that bought; saying unto them, It is written, My house is the house of prayer: but ye have made it a den of thieves. And he taught daily in the temple. But the chief priests and the scribes and the chief of the people sought to destroy him, and could not find what they might do: for all the people were very attentive to hear him.

20. And it came to pass, that on one of those days, as he taught the people in the temple, and preached the gospel, the chief priests and the scribes came upon him with the elders, and spake unto him, saying, Tell us, by what authority doest thou these things? or who is he that gave thee this authority? And he answered and said unto them, I will also ask you one thing; and answer me: The baptism of John, was it from heaven, or of men? And they reasoned with themselves, saying, If we shall say, From heaven; he will say, Why then believed ye him not? But and if we say, Of men; all the people will stone us: for they be persuaded that John was a prophet. And they answered, that they could not tell whence it was. And Jesus said unto them, Neither tell I you by what authority I do these things.

Then began he to speak to the people this parable; A certain man planted a vineyard, and let it forth to husbandmen, and went into a far country for a long time. And at the season he sent a servant to the husbandmen, that they should give him of the fruit of the vineyard: but the husbandmen beat him, and sent him away empty. And again he sent another servant: and they beat him also, and entreated him shamefully, and sent him away empty. And again he sent a third: and they wounded him also, and cast him out. Then said the lord of the vineyard, What shall I do? I will send my beloved son: it may be they will reverence him when they see him. But when the husbandmen saw him, they reasoned among themselves, saying, This is the heir: come, let us kill him, that the inheritance may be ours. So they cast him out of the vineyard, and killed him. What therefore shall the lord of the vineyard do unto them? He shall come and destroy these husbandmen, and shall give the vineyard to others. And when they heard it, they said, God forbid. And he beheld them, and said, What is this then that is written, The stone which the builders rejected, the same is become the head of the corner? Whosoever shall fall upon that stone shall be broken; but on whomsoever it shall fall, it will grind him to powder. And the chief priests and the scribes the same hour sought to lay hands on him; and they feared the people: for they perceived that he had spoken this parable against them.

And they watched him, and sent forth spies, which should feign themselves just men, that they might take hold of his words, that so they might deliver him unto the power and authority of the governor. And they asked him, saying, Master, we know that thou sayest and teachest rightly, neither acceptest thou the person of any, but teachest the way of God truly: is it lawful for us to give tribute unto Cæsar, or no? But he perceived their craftiness, and said unto them, Why tempt ye me? Shew me a penny. Whose image and superscription hath it? They answered and said, Cæsar's. And he said unto them, Render therefore unto Cæsar the things which be Cæsar's, and unto God the things which be God's. And they could not take hold of his words before the people: and they marvelled at his answer, and held their peace.

Then came to him certain of the Sadducees, which deny that there is any resurrection; and they asked him, saying, Master, Moses wrote unto us, If any man's brother die, having a wife, and he die without children, that his brother should take his wife, and raise up seed unto his brother. There were therefore seven brethren: and the first took a wife, and died without children. And the second took her to wife, and he died childless. And the third took her; and in like manner the seven also: and they left no children, and died. Last of all the woman died also. Therefore in the resurrection whose wife of them is she? for seven had her to wife. And Jesus answering said unto them, The children of this world marry, and are given in marriage: but they which shall be accounted worthy to obtain that world, and the resurrection from the dead, neither marry, nor are given in marriage: neither can they die any more: for they are equal unto the angels; and are the children of God, being the children of the resurrection. Now that the dead are raised, even Moses shewed at the bush, when he calleth the Lord the God of Abraham, and the God of Isaac, and the God of Jacob. For he is not a God of the dead, but of the living: for all live unto him. Then certain of the scribes answering said, Master, thou hast well said. And after that they durst not ask him any question at all.

And he said unto them, How say they that Christ is David's son? And David himself saith in the book of Psalms, The Lord said unto my Lord, Sit thou on my right hand, till I make thine enemies thy footstool. David therefore calleth him Lord, how is he then his son?

Then in the audience of all the people he said unto his disciples, Beware of the scribes, which desire to walk in long robes, and love greetings in the markets, and the highest seats in the synagogues, and the chief rooms at feasts; which devour widows' houses, and for a shew make long prayers: the same shall receive greater damnation.

21. And he looked up, and saw the rich men casting their gifts into the treasury. And he saw also a certain poor widow casting in thither two mites. And he said, Of a truth I say unto you, that this poor widow hath cast in more than they all: for all these have of their abundance cast in unto the offerings of God: but she of her penury hath cast in all the living that she had.

And as some spake of the temple, how it was adorned with goodly stones and gifts, he said, As for these things which ye behold, the days will come, in the which there shall not be left one stone upon another, that shall not be thrown down. And they asked him, saying, Master, but when shall these things be? and what sign will there be when these things shall come to pass?

And he said, Take heed that ye be not deceived: for many shall come in my name, saying, I am Christ; and the time draweth near: go ye not therefore after them. But when ye shall hear of wars and commotions, be not terrified: for these things must first come to pass; but the end is not by and by. Then said he unto them, Nation shall rise against nation, and kingdom against kingdom: and great earthquakes shall be in divers places, and famines, and pestilences; and fearful sights and great signs shall there be from heaven.

But before all these, they shall lay their hands on you, and persecute you, delivering you up to the synagogues, and into prisons, being brought before kings and rulers for my name's sake. And it shall turn to you for a testimony. Settle it therefore in your hearts, not to meditate before what ye shall answer: for I will give you a mouth and wisdom, which all your adversaries shall not be able to gainsay nor resist. And ye shall be betrayed both by parents, and brethren, and kinsfolks, and friends; and some of you shall they cause to be put to death. And ye shall be hated of all men for my name's sake. But there shall not an hair of your head perish. In your patience possess ye your souls.

And when ye shall see Jerusalem compassed with armies, then know that the desolation thereof is nigh. Then let them which are in Judæa flee to the mountains; and let them which are in the midst of it depart out; and let not them that are in the countries enter thereinto. For these be the days of vengeance, that all things which are written may be fulfilled. But woe unto them that are with child, and to them that give suck, in those days! for there shall be great distress in the land, and wrath upon this people. And they shall fall by the edge of the sword, and shall be led away captive into all nations: and Jerusalem shall be trodden down of the Gentiles, until the times of the Gentiles be fulfilled.

And there shall be signs in the sun, and in the moon, and in the stars; and upon the earth distress of nations, with perplexity; the sea and the waves roaring; men's hearts failing them for fear, and for looking after those things which are coming on the earth: for the powers of heaven shall be shaken. And then shall they see the Son of man coming in a cloud with power and great glory. And when these things begin to come to pass, then look up, and lift up your heads; for your redemption draweth nigh.

And he spake to them a parable; Behold the fig tree, and all the trees; when they now shoot forth, ye see and know of your own selves that summer is now nigh at hand. So likewise ye, when ye see these things come to pass, know ye that the kingdom of God is nigh at hand. Verily I say unto you, This generation shall not pass away, till all be fulfilled. Heaven and earth shall pass away: but my words shall not pass away.

And take heed to yourselves, lest at any time your hearts be overcharged with surfeiting, and drunkenness, and cares of this life, and so that day come upon you unawares. For as a snare shall it come on all them that dwell on the face of the whole earth. Watch ye therefore, and pray always, that ye may be accounted worthy to escape all these things that shall come to pass, and to stand before the Son of man.

And in the day time he was teaching in the temple; and at night he went out, and abode in the mount that is called the mount of Olives. And all the people came early in the morning to him in the temple, for to hear him.

Acts of the Apostles

[Pentecost and the Early Church]

1. The former treatise have I made, O Theophilus, of all that Jesus began both to do and teach, until the day in which he was taken up, after that he through the Holy Ghost had given commandments unto the apostles whom he had chosen: to whom also he shewed himself alive after his passion by many infallible proofs, being seen of them forty days, and speaking of the things pertaining to the kingdom of God: and, being assembled together with them, commanded them that they should not depart from Jerusalem, but wait for the promise of the Father, which, saith he, ye have heard of me. For John truly baptized with water; but ye shall be baptized with the Holy Ghost not many days hence.

When they therefore were come together, they asked of him, saying, Lord, wilt thou at this time restore again the kingdom to Israel? And he said unto them, It is not for you to know the times or the seasons, which the Father hath put in his own power. But ye shall receive power, after that the Holy Ghost is come upon you: and ye shall be witnesses unto me both in Jerusalem, and in all Judæa, and in Samaria, and unto the uttermost part of the earth. And when he had spoken these things, while they beheld, he was taken up; and a cloud received him out of their sight. And while they looked stedfastly toward heaven as he went up, behold, two men stood by them in white apparel; which also said, Ye men of Galilee, why stand ye gazing up into heaven? this same Jesus, which is taken up from you into heaven, shall so come in like manner as ye have seen him go into heaven.

Then returned they unto Jerusalem from the mount called Olivet, which is from Jerusalem a sabbath day's journey. And when they were come in, they went up into an upper room, where abode both Peter, and James, and John, and Andrew, Philip, and Thomas, Bartholomew, and Matthew, James the son of Alphæus, and Simon Zelotes, and Judas the brother of James. These all continued with one accord in prayer and supplication, with the women, and Mary the mother of Jesus, and with his brethren.

And in those days Peter stood up in the midst of the disciples, and said, (the number of names together were about an hundred and twenty,) Men and brethren, this scripture must needs have been fulfilled, which the Holy Ghost by the mouth of David spake before concerning Judas, which was guide to them that took Jesus. For he was numbered with us, and had obtained part of this ministry. Now this man purchased a field with the reward of iniquity; and falling headlong, he burst asunder in the midst, and all his bowels gushed out. And it was known unto all the dwellers at Jerusalem; insomuch as that field is called in their proper tongue, Aceldama, that is to say, The field of blood. For it is written in the book of Psalms, Let his habitation be desolate, and let no man dwell therein: and his bishoprick let another take. Wherefore of these men which have companied with us all the time that the Lord Jesus went in and out among us, beginning from the baptism of John, unto that same day that he was taken up from us, must one be ordained to be a witness with us of his resurrection. And they appointed two, Joseph called Barsabas, who was surnamed Justus, and Matthias. And they prayed, and said, Thou, Lord, which knowest the hearts of all men, shew whether of these two thou hast chosen, that he may take part of this ministry and apostleship, from which Judas by transgression fell, that he might go to his own place. And they gave forth their lots; and the lot fell upon Matthias; and he was numbered with the eleven apostles.

2. And when the day of Pentecost was fully come, they were all with one accord in one place. And suddenly there came a sound from heaven as of a rushing mighty wind, and it filled all the house where they were sitting. And there appeared unto them cloven tongues like as of fire, and it sat upon each of them. And they were all filled with the Holy Ghost, and began to speak with other tongues, as the Spirit gave them utterance.

And there were dwelling at Jerusalem Jews, devout men, out of every nation under heaven. Now when this was noised abroad, the multitude came together, and were confounded, because that every man heard them speak in his own language. And they were all amazed and marvelled, saying one to another, Behold, are not all these which speak Galilæans? And how hear we every man in our own tongue, wherein we were born? Parthians, and Medes, and Elamites, and the dwellers in Mesopotamia, and in Judæa, and Cappadocia, in Pontus, and Asia, Phrygia, and Pamphylia, in Egypt, and in the parts of Libya about Cyrene, and strangers of Rome, Jews and proselytes, Cretes and Arabians, we do hear them speak in our tongues the wonderful works of God. And they were all amazed, and were in doubt, saying one to another, What meaneth this? Others mocking said, These men are full of new wine.

But Peter, standing up with the eleven, lifted up his voice, and said unto them, Ye men of Judæa, and all ye that dwell at Jerusalem, be this known unto you, and hearken to my words: for these are not drunken, as ye suppose, seeing it is but the third hour of the day. But this is that which was spoken by the prophet Joel; and it shall come to pass in the last days, saith God, I will pour out of my Spirit upon all flesh: and your sons and your daughters shall prophesy, and your young men shall see visions, and your old men shall dream dreams: and on my servants and on my handmaidens I will pour out in those days of my Spirit; and they shall prophesy: and I will shew wonders in heaven above, and signs in the earth beneath; blood, and fire, and vapour of smoke: the sun shall be turned into darkness, and the moon into blood, before that great and notable day of the Lord come: and it shall come to pass, that whosoever shall call on the name of the Lord shall be saved.

Ye men of Israel, hear these words; Jesus of Nazareth, a man approved of God among you by miracles and wonders and signs, which God did by him in the midst of you, as ye yourselves also know: him, being delivered by the determinate counsel and foreknowledge of God, ye have taken, and by wicked hands have crucified and slain: whom God hath raised up, having loosed the pains of death: because it was not possible that he should be holden of it. For David speaketh concerning him, I foresaw the Lord always before my face, for he is on my right hand, that I should not be moved: therefore did my heart rejoice, and my tongue was glad; moreover also my flesh shall rest in hope: because thou wilt not leave my soul in hell, neither wilt thou suffer thine Holy One to see corruption. Thou hast made known to me the ways of life; thou shalt make me full of joy with thy countenance.

Men and brethren, let me freely speak unto you of the patriarch David, that he is both dead and buried, and his sepulchre is with us unto this day. Therefore being a prophet, and knowing that God had sworn with an oath to him, that of the fruit of his loins, according to the flesh, he would raise up Christ to sit on his throne; he seeing this before spake of the resurrection of Christ, that his soul was not left in hell, neither his flesh did see corruption. This Jesus hath God raised up, whereof we all are witnesses. Therefore being by the right hand of God exalted, and having received of the Father the promise of the Holy Ghost, he hath shed forth this, which ye now see and hear. For David is not ascended into the heavens: but he saith himself, The LORD said unto my Lord, Sit thou on my right hand, until I make thy foes thy footstool. Therefore let all the house of Israel know assuredly, that God hath made that same Jesus, whom ye have crucified, both Lord and Christ.

Now when they heard this, they were pricked in their heart, and said unto Peter and to the rest of the apostles, Men and brethren, what shall we do? Then Peter said unto them, Repent, and be baptized every one of you in the name of Jesus Christ for the remission of sins, and ye shall receive the gift of the Holy

Ghost. For the promise is unto you, and to your children, and to all that are afar off, even as many as the Lord our God shall call. And with many other words did he testify and exhort, saying, Save yourselves from this untoward generation. Then they that gladly received his word were baptized: and the same day there were added unto them about three thousand souls.

And they continued stedfastly in the apostles' doctrine and fellowship, and in breaking of bread, and in prayers. And fear came upon every soul: and many wonders and signs were done by the apostles. And all that believed were together, and had all things common; and sold their possessions and goods, and parted them to all men, as every man had need. And they, continuing daily with one accord in the temple, and breaking bread from house to house, did eat their meat with gladness and singleness of heart, praising God, and having favour with all the people. And the Lord added to the church daily such as should be saved.

3. Now Peter and John went up together into the temple at the hour of prayer, being the ninth hour. And a certain man lame from his mother's womb was carried, whom they laid daily at the gate of the temple which is called Beautiful, to ask alms of them that entered into the temple; who seeing Peter and John about to go into the temple asked an alms. And Peter, fastening his eyes upon him with John, said, Look on us. And he gave heed unto them, expecting to receive something of them. Then Peter said, Silver and gold have I none; but such as I have give I thee: In the name of Jesus Christ of Nazareth rise up and walk. And he took him by the right hand, and lifted him up: and immediately his feet and ancle bones received strength. And he leaping up stood, and walked, and entered with them into the temple, walking, and leaping, and praising God. And all the people saw him walking and praising God: and they knew that it was he which sat for alms at the Beautiful gate of the temple: and they were filled with wonder and amazement at that which had happened unto him. And as the lame man which was healed held Peter and John, all the people ran together unto them in the porch that is called Solomon's, greatly wondering.

And when Peter saw it, he answered unto the people, Ye men of Israel, why marvel ye at this? or why look ye so earnestly on us, as though by our own power or holiness we had made this man to walk? The God of Abraham, and of Isaac, and of Jacob, the God of our fathers, hath glorified his Son Jesus; whom ye delivered up, and denied him in the presence of Pilate, when he was determined to let him go. But ye denied the Holy One and the Just, and desired a murderer to be granted unto you; and killed the Prince of life, whom God hath raised from the dead; whereof we are witnesses. And his name through faith in his name hath made this man strong, whom ye see and know: yea, the faith which is by him hath given him this perfect soundness in the presence of you all. And now, brethren, I wot that through ignorance ye did it, as did also your rulers. But those things, which God before had shewed by the mouth of all his prophets, that Christ should suffer, he hath so fulfilled.

Repent ye therefore, and be converted, that your sins may be blotted out, when the times of refreshing shall come from the presence of the Lord; and he shall send Jesus Christ, which before was preached unto you: whom the heaven must receive until the times of restitution of all things, which God hath spoken by the mouth of all his holy prophets since the world began. For Moses truly said unto the fathers, A prophet shall the Lord your God raise up unto you of your brethren, like unto me; him shall ye hear in all things whatsoever he shall say unto you. And it shall come to pass, that every soul, which will not hear that prophet, shall be destroyed from among the people. Yea, and all the prophets from Samuel and those that follow after, as many as have spoken, have likewise foretold of these days. Ye are the children of the prophets, and of the covenant which God made with our fathers, saying unto Abraham, And in thy seed shall all the kindreds of the earth be blessed. Unto you first God, having raised up his Son Jesus, sent him to bless you, in turning away every one of you from his iniquities.

4. And as they spake unto the people, the priests, and the captain of the temple, and the Sadducees, came upon them, being grieved that they taught the people, and preached through Jesus the resurrection from the dead. And they laid hands on them, and put them in hold unto the next day: for it was now eventide. Howbeit many of them which heard the word believed; and the number of the men was about five thousand.

And it came to pass on the morrow, that their rulers, and elders, and scribes, and Annas the high priest, and Caiaphas, and John, and Alexander, and as many as were of the kindred of the high priest, were gathered together at Jerusalem. And when they had set them in the midst, they asked, By what power, or by what name, have ye done this? Then Peter, filled with the Holy Ghost, said unto them, Ye rulers of the people, and elders of Israel, if we this day be examined of the good deed done to the impotent man, by what means he is made whole; be it known unto you all, and to all the people of Israel, that by the name of Jesus Christ of Nazareth, whom ye crucified, whom God raised from the dead, even by him doth this man stand here before you whole. This is the stone which was set at nought of you builders, which is become the head of the corner. Neither is there salvation in any other: for there is none other name under heaven given among men, whereby we must be saved.

Now when they saw the boldness of Peter and John, and perceived that they were unlearned and ignorant men, they marvelled; and they took knowledge of them, that they had been with Jesus. And beholding the man which was healed standing with them, they could say nothing against it. But when they had commanded them to go aside out of the council, they conferred among themselves, saying, What shall we do to these men? for that indeed a notable miracle hath been done by them is manifest to all them that dwell in Jerusalem; and we cannot deny it. But that it spread no further among the people, let us straitly threaten them, that they speak henceforth to no man in this name.

And they called them, and commanded them not to speak at all nor teach in the name of Jesus. But Peter and John answered and said unto them, Whether it be right in the sight of God to hearken unto you more than unto God, judge ye. For we cannot but speak the things which we have seen and heard. So when they had further threatened them, they let them go, finding nothing how they might punish them, because of the people: for all men glorified God for that which was done. For the man was above forty years old, on whom this miracle of healing was shewed.

And being let go, they went to their own company, and reported all that the chief priests and elders had said unto them. And when they heard that, they lifted up their voice to God with one accord, and said, Lord, thou art God, which hast made heaven, and earth, and the sea, and all that in them is: who by the mouth of thy servant David hast said, Why did the heathen rage, and the people imagine vain things? The kings of the earth stood up, and the rulers were gathered together against the Lord, and against his Christ. For of a truth against thy holy child Jesus, whom thou hast anointed, both Herod, and Pontius Pilate, with the Gentiles, and the people of Israel, were gathered together, for to do whatsoever thy hand and thy counsel determined before to be done. And now, Lord, behold their threatenings: and grant unto thy servants, that with all boldness they may speak thy word, by stretching forth thine hand to heal; and that signs and wonders may be done by the name of thy holy child Jesus. And when they had prayed, the place was shaken where they were assembled together; and they were all filled with the Holy Ghost, and they spake the word of God with boldness.

And the multitude of them that believed were of one heart and of one soul: neither said any of them that ought of the things which he possessed was his own; but they had all things common. And with great power gave the apostles witness of the resurrection of the Lord Jesus: and great grace was upon them all. Neither was there any among them that lacked: for as many as were possessors of lands or houses sold them, and brought the prices of the things that were sold, and laid them down at the apostles' feet: and distribution was made unto every man according as he had need.

And Joses, who by the apostles was surnamed Barnabas, (which is, being interpreted, The son of consolation,) a Levite, and of the country of Cyprus, having land, sold it, and brought the money, and laid it at the apostles' feet.

5. But a certain man named Ananias, with Sapphira his wife, sold a possession, and kept back part of the price, his wife also being privy to it, and brought a certain part, and laid it at the apostles' feet. But Peter said, Ananias, why hath Satan filled thine heart to lie to the Holy Ghost, and to keep back part of the price of the land? Whiles it remained, was it not thine own? and after it was sold, was it not in thine own power? why hast thou conceived this thing in thine heart? thou hast not lied unto men, but unto God. And Ananias hearing these words fell down, and gave up the ghost: and great fear came on all them that heard these things. And the young men arose, wound him up, and carried him out, and buried him.

And it was about the space of three hours after, when his wife, not knowing what was done, came in. And Peter answered unto her, Tell me whether ye sold the land for so much? And she said, Yea, for so much. Then Peter said unto her, How is it that ye have agreed together to tempt the Spirit of the Lord? behold, the feet of them which have buried thy husband are at the door, and shall carry thee out. Then fell she down straightway at his feet, and yielded up the ghost: and the young men came in, and found her dead, and, carrying her forth, buried her by her husband. And great fear came upon all the church, and upon as many as heard these things.

And by the hands of the apostles were many signs and wonders wrought among the people; (and they were all with one accord in Solomon's porch. And of the rest durst no man join himself to them: but the people magnified them. And believers were the more added to the Lord, multitudes both of men and women.) Insomuch that they brought forth the sick into the streets, and laid them on beds and couches, that at the least the shadow of Peter passing by might overshadow some of them. There came also a multitude out of the cities round about unto Jerusalem, bringing sick folks, and them which were vexed with unclean spirits: and they were healed every one.

Then the high priest rose up, and all they that were with him, (which is the sect of the Sadducees,) and were filled with indignation, and laid their hands on the apostles, and put them in the common prison. But the angel of the Lord by night opened the prison doors, and brought them forth, and said, Go, stand and speak in the temple to the people all the words of this life. And when they heard that, they entered into the temple early in the morning, and taught. But the high priest came, and they that were with him, and called the council together, and all the senate of the children of Israel, and sent to the prison to have them brought. But when the officers came, and found them not in the prison, they returned, and told, saying, The prison truly found we shut with all safety, and the keepers standing without before the doors: but when we had opened, we found no man within.

Now when the high priest and the captain of the temple and the chief priests heard these things, they doubted of them whereunto this would grow. Then came one and told them, saying, Behold, the men whom ye put in prison are standing in the temple, and teaching the people. Then went the captain with the officers, and brought them without violence: for they feared the people, lest they should have been stoned. And when they had brought them, they set them before the council: and the high priest asked them, saying, Did not we straitly command you that ye should not teach in this name? and, behold, ye have filled Jerusalem with your doctrine, and intend to bring this man's blood upon us.

Then Peter and the other apostles answered and said, We ought to obey God rather than men. The God of our fathers raised up Jesus, whom ye slew and hanged on a tree. Him hath God exalted with his right hand to be a Prince and a Saviour, for to give repentance to Israel, and forgiveness of sins. And we are his witnesses of these things; and so is also the Holy Ghost, whom God hath given to them that obey him.

When they heard that, they were cut to the heart, and took counsel to slay them. Then stood there up one in the council, a Pharisee, named Gamaliel, a doctor of the law, had in reputation among all the people, and commanded to put the apostles forth a little space; and said unto them, Ye men of Israel, take heed to yourselves what ye intend to do as touching these men. For before these days rose up Theudas, boasting himself to be somebody; to whom a number of men, about four hundred, joined themselves: who was slain; and all, as many as obeyed him, were scattered, and brought to nought. After this man rose up Judas of Galilee in the days of the taxing, and drew away much people after him: he also perished; and all, even as many as obeyed him, were dispersed. And now I say unto you, Refrain from these men, and let them alone: for if this counsel or this work be of men, it will come to nought: but if it be of God, ye cannot overthrow it; lest haply ye be found even to fight against God. And to him they agreed: and when they had called the apostles, and beaten them, they commanded that they should not speak in the name of Jesus, and let them go.

And they departed from the presence of the council, rejoicing that they were counted worthy to suffer shame for his name. And daily in the temple, and in every house, they ceased not to teach and preach Jesus Christ.

6. And in those days, when the number of the disciples was multiplied, there arose a murmuring of the Grecians against the Hebrews, because their widows were neglected in the daily ministration. Then the twelve called the multitude of the disciples unto them, and said, It is not reason that we should leave the word of God, and serve tables. Wherefore, brethren, look ye out among you seven men of honest report, full of the Holy Ghost and wisdom, whom we may appoint over this business. But we will give ourselves continually to prayer, and to the ministry of the word. And the saying pleased the whole multitude: and they chose Stephen, a man full of faith and of the Holy Ghost, and Philip, and Prochorus, and Nicanor, and Timon, and Parmenas, and Nicolas a proselyte of Antioch: whom they set before the apostles: and when they had prayed, they laid their hands on them. And the word of God increased; and the number of the disciples multiplied in Jerusalem greatly; and a great company of the priests were obedient to the faith. And Stephen, full of faith and power, did great wonders and miracles among the people.

Then there arose certain of the synagogue, which is called the synagogue of the Libertines, and Cyrenians, and Alexandrians, and of them of Cilicia and of Asia, disputing with Stephen. And they were not able to resist the wisdom and the spirit by which he spake. Then they suborned men, which said, We have heard him speak blasphemous words against Moses, and against God. And they stirred up the people, and the elders, and the scribes, and came upon him, and caught him, and brought him to the council, and set up false witnesses, which said, This man ceaseth not to speak blasphemous words against this holy place, and the law: for we have heard him say, that this Jesus of Nazareth shall destroy this place, and shall change the customs which Moses delivered us. And all that sat in the council, looking stedfastly on him, saw his face as it had been the face of an angel.

7. Then said the high priest, Are these things so? And he said, Men, brethren, and fathers, hearken; The God of glory appeared unto our father Abraham, when he was in Mesopotamia, before he dwelt in Charran, and said unto him, Get thee out of thy country, and from thy kindred, and come into the land which I shall shew thee. Then came he out of the land of the Chaldæans, and dwelt in Charran: and from thence, when his father was dead, he removed him into this land, wherein ye now dwell. And he gave him none inheritance in it, no, not so much as to set his foot on: yet he promised that he would give it to him for a possession, and to his seed after him, when as yet he had no child. And God spake on this wise, That his seed should sojourn in a strange land; and that they should bring them into bondage, and entreat them evil four hundred years. And the nation to whom they shall be in bondage will I judge, said God: and after that shall they come forth, and serve me in this place. And he gave him the covenant of circumcision: and so Abraham begat Isaac, and circumcised him the eighth day; and Isaac begat Jacob; and Jacob begat the twelve patriarchs.

And the patriarchs, moved with envy, sold Joseph into Egypt: but God was with him, and delivered him out of all his afflictions, and gave him favour and wisdom in the sight of Pharaoh king of Egypt; and he made him governor over Egypt and all his house. Now there came a dearth over all the land of Egypt and Chanaan, and great affliction: and our fathers found no sustenance. But when Jacob heard that there was corn in Egypt, he sent out our fathers first. And at the second time Joseph was made known to his brethren; and Joseph's kindred was made known unto Pharaoh. Then sent Joseph, and called his father Jacob to him, and all his kindred, threescore and fifteen souls. So Jacob went down into Egypt, and died, he, and our fathers, and were carried over into Sychem, and laid in the sepulchre that Abraham bought for a sum of money of the sons of Emmor the father of Sychem.

But when the time of the promise drew nigh, which God had sworn to Abraham, the people grew and multiplied in Egypt. till another king arose, which knew not Joseph. The same dealt subtilly with our kindred, and evil entreated our fathers, so that they cast out their young children, to the end they might not live. In which time Moses was born, and was exceeding fair, and nourished up in his father's house three months: and when he was cast out, Pharaoh's daughter took him up, and nourished him for her own son. And Moses was learned in all the wisdom of the Egyptians, and was mighty in words and in deeds.

And when he was full forty years old, it came into his heart to visit his brethren the children of Israel. And seeing one of them suffer wrong, he defended him, and avenged him that was oppressed, and smote the Egyptian: for he supposed his brethren would have understood how that God by his hand would deliver them: but they understood not. And the next day he shewed himself unto them as they strove, and would have set them at one again, saying, Sirs, ye are brethren; why do ye wrong one to another? But he that did his neighbour wrong thrust him away, saying, Who made thee a ruler and a judge over us? Wilt thou kill me, as thou diddest the Egyptian yesterday? Then fled Moses at this saying, and was a stranger in the land of Madian, where he begat two sons.

And when forty years were expired, there appeared to him in the wilderness of mount Sina an angel of the Lord in a flame of fire in a bush. When Moses saw it, he wondered at the sight: and as he drew near to behold it, the voice of the Lord came unto him, saying, I am the God of thy fathers, the God of Abraham, and the God of Isaac, and the God of Jacob. Then Moses trembled, and durst not behold. Then said the Lord to him, Put off thy shoes from thy feet: for the place where thou standest is holy ground. I have seen, I have seen the affliction of my people which is in Egypt, and I have heard their groaning, and am come down to deliver them. And now come, I will send thee into Egypt.

This Moses whom they refused, saying, Who made thee a ruler and a judge? the same did God send to be a ruler and a deliverer by the hand of the angel which appeared to him in the bush. He brought them out, after that he had shewed wonders and signs in the land of Egypt, and in the Red sea, and in the wilderness forty years. This is that Moses, which said unto the children of Israel, A prophet shall the Lord your God raise up unto you of your brethren, like unto me; him shall ye hear. This is he, that was in the church in the wilderness with the angel which spake to him in the mount Sina, and with our fathers: who received the lively oracles to give unto us: to whom our fathers would not obey, but thrust him from them, and in their hearts turned back again into Egypt, saying unto Aaron, Make us gods to go before us: for as for this Moses, which brought us out of the land of Egypt, we wot not what is become of him. And they made a calf in those days, and offered sacrifice unto the idol, and rejoiced in the works of their own hands.

Then God turned, and gave them up to worship the host of heaven; as it is written in the book of the prophets, O ye house of Israel, have ye offered to me slain beasts and sacrifices by the space of forty years in the wilderness? Yea, ye took up the tabernacle of Moloch, and the star of your god Remphan, figures which ye made to worship them: and I will carry you away beyond Babylon. Our fathers had the tabernacle of witness in the wilderness, as he had appointed, speaking unto Moses, that he should make it according to the fashion that he had seen. Which also our fathers that came after brought in with Jesus into the possession of the Gentiles, whom God drave out before the face of our fathers, unto the days of David; who found favour before God, and desired to find a tabernacle for the God of Jacob. But Solomon built him an house. Howbeit the most High dwelleth not in temples made with hands; as saith the prophet, Heaven is my throne, and earth is my footstool: what house will ye build me? saith the Lord: or what is the place of my rest? Hath not my hand made all these things?

Ye stiffnecked and uncircumcised in heart and ears, ye do always resist the Holy Ghost: as your fathers did, so do ye. Which of the prophets have not your fathers persecuted? and they have slain them which shewed before of the coming of the Just One; of whom ye have been now the betrayers and murderers: who have received the law by the disposition of angels, and have not kept it.

When they heard these things, they were cut to the heart, and they gnashed on him with their teeth. But he, being full of the Holy Ghost, looked up stedfastly into heaven, and saw the glory of God, and Jesus standing on the right hand of God, and said, Behold, I see the heavens opened, and the Son of man standing on the right hand of God. Then they cried out with a loud voice, and stopped their ears, and ran upon him with one accord, and cast him out of the city, and stoned him: and the witnesses laid down their clothes at a young man's feet, whose name was Saul. And they stoned Stephen, calling upon God, and saying, Lord Jesus, receive my spirit. And he kneeled down, and cried with a loud voice, Lord, lay not this sin to their charge. And when he had said this, he fell asleep. And Saul was consenting unto his death.

8. And at that time there was a great persecution against the church which was at Jerusalem; and they were all scattered abroad throughout the regions of Judæa and Samaria, except the apostles. And devout men carried Stephen to his burial, and made great lamentation over him. As for Saul, he made havock of the church, entering into every house, and haling men and women committed them to prison. Therefore they that were scattered abroad went every where preaching the word.

Then Philip went down to the city of Samaria, and preached Christ unto them. And the people with one accord gave heed unto those things which Philip spake, hearing and seeing the miracles which he did. For unclean spirits, crying with loud voice, came out of many that were possessed with them: and many taken with palsies, and that were lame, were healed. And there was great joy in that city.

But there was a certain man, called Simon, which beforetime in the same city used sorcery, and bewitched the people of Samaria, giving out that himself was some great one: to whom they all gave heed, from the least to the greatest, saying, This man is the great power of God. And to him they had regard, because that of long time he had bewitched them with sorceries. But when they believed Philip preaching the things concerning the kingdom of God, and the name of Jesus Christ, they were baptized, both men and women. Then Simon himself believed also: and when he was baptized, he continued with Philip, and wondered, beholding the miracles and signs which were done.

Now when the apostles which were at Jerusalem heard that Samaria had received the word of God, they sent unto them Peter and John: who, when they were come down, prayed for them, that they might receive the Holy Ghost: (for as yet he was fallen upon none of them: only they were baptized in the name of the Lord Jesus.) Then laid they their hands on them, and they received the Holy Ghost.

And when Simon saw that through laying on of the apostles' hands the Holy Ghost was given, he offered them money, saying, Give me also this power, that on whomsoever I lay hands, he may receive the Holy Ghost. But Peter said unto him, Thy money perish with thee, because thou hast thought that the gift of God may be purchased with money. Thou hast neither part nor lot in this matter: for thy heart is not right in the sight of God. Repent therefore of this thy wickedness, and pray God, if perhaps the thought of thine heart may be forgiven thee. For I perceive that thou art in the gall of bitterness, and in the bond of iniquity. Then answered Simon, and said, Pray ye to the Lord for me, that none of these things which ye have spoken come upon me. And they, when they had testified and preached the word of the Lord, returned to Jerusalem, and preached the gospel in many villages of the Samaritans.

And the angel of the Lord spake unto Philip, saying, Arise, and go toward the south unto the way that goeth down from Jerusalem unto Gaza, which is desert. And he arose and went: and, behold, a man of Ethiopia, an eunuch of great authority under Candace queen of the Ethiopians, who had the charge of all her treasure, and had come to Jerusalem for to worship, was returning, and sitting in his chariot read Esaias the prophet. Then the Spirit said unto Philip, Go near, and join thyself to this chariot. And Philip ran thither to him, and heard him read the prophet Esaias, and said, Understandest thou what thou readest? And he said, How can I, except some man should guide me? And he desired Philip that he would come up and sit with him. The place of the scripture which he read was this, He was led as a sheep to the slaughter; and like a lamb dumb before his shearer, so opened he not his mouth: in his humiliation his judgment was taken away: and who shall declare his generation? for his life is taken from the earth. And the eunuch answered Philip, and said, I pray thee, of whom speaketh the prophet this? of himself, or of some other man? Then Philip opened his mouth, and began at the same scripture, and preached unto him Jesus.

And as they went on their way, they came unto a certain water: and the eunuch said, See, here is water; what doth hinder me to be baptized? And Philip said, If thou believest with all thine heart, thou mayest. And he answered and said, I believe that Jesus Christ is the Son of God. And he commanded the chariot to stand still: and they went down both into the water, both Philip and the eunuch; and he baptized him. And when they were come up out of the water, the Spirit of the Lord caught away Philip, that the eunuch saw him no more: and he went on his way rejoicing. But Philip was found at Azotus: and passing through he preached in all the cities, till he came to Cæsarea.

9. And Saul, yet breathing out threatenings and slaughter against the disciples of the Lord, went unto the high priest, and desired of him letters to Damascus to the synagogues, that if he found any of this way, whether they were men or women, he might bring them bound unto Jerusalem. And as he journeyed, he came near Damascus: and suddenly there shined round about him a light from heaven: and he fell to the earth, and heard a voice saying unto him, Saul, Saul, why persecutest thou me? And he said, Who art thou, Lord? And the Lord said, I am Jesus whom thou persecutest: it is hard for thee to kick against the pricks. And he trembling and astonished said, Lord, what wilt thou have me to do? And the Lord said unto him, Arise, and go into the city, and it shall be told thee what thou must do. And the men which journeyed with him stood speechless, hearing a voice, but seeing no man. And Saul arose from the earth; and when his eyes were opened, he saw no man: but they led him by the hand, and brought him into Damascus. And he was three days without sight, and neither did eat nor drink.

And there was a certain disciple at Damascus, named Ananias; and to him said the Lord in a vision, Ananias. And he said, Behold, I am here, Lord. And the Lord said unto him, Arise, and go into the street which is called Straight, and inquire in the house of Judas for one called Saul, of Tarsus: for, behold, he prayeth, and hath seen in a vision a man named Ananias coming in, and putting his hand on him, that he might receive his sight. Then Ananias answered, Lord, I have heard by many of this man, how much evil he hath done to thy saints at Jerusalem: and here he hath authority from the chief priests to bind all that call on thy name. But the Lord said unto him, Go thy way: for he is a chosen vessel unto me, to bear my name before the Gentiles, and kings, and the children of Israel: for I will shew him how great things he must suffer for my name's sake. And Ananias went his way, and entered into the house; and putting his hands on him said, Brother Saul, the Lord, even Jesus, that appeared unto thee in the way as thou camest, hath sent me, that thou mightest receive thy sight, and be filled with the Holy Ghost. And immediately there fell from his eyes as it had been scales: and he received sight forthwith, and arose, and was baptized. And when he had received meat, he was strengthened.

Then was Saul certain days with the disciples which were at Damascus. And straightway he preached Christ in the synagogues, that he is the Son of God. But all that heard him were amazed, and said; Is not this he that destroyed them which called on this name in Jerusalem, and came hither for that intent, that he might bring them bound unto the chief priests? But Saul increased the more in strength, and confounded the Jews which dwelt at Damascus, proving that this is very Christ.

And after that many days were fulfilled, the Jews took counsel to kill him: but their laying await was known of Saul. And they watched the gates day and night to kill him. Then the disciples took him by night, and let him down by the wall in a basket. And when Saul was come to Jerusalem, he assayed to join himself to the disciples: but they were all afraid of him, and believed not that he was a disciple. But Barnabas took him, and brought him to the apostles, and declared unto them how he had seen the Lord in the way, and that he had spoken to him, and how he had preached boldly at Damascus in the name of Jesus. And he was with them coming in and going out at Jerusalem. And he spake boldly in the name of the Lord Jesus, and disputed against the Grecians: but they went about to slay him. Which when the brethren knew, they brought him down to Cæsarea, and sent him forth to Tarsus. Then had the churches rest throughout all Judæa and Galilee and Samaria, and were edified; and walking in the fear of the Lord, and in the comfort of the Holy Ghost, were multiplied.

And it came to pass, as Peter passed throughout all quarters, he came down also to the saints which dwelt at Lydda. And there he found a certain man named Æneas, which had kept his bed eight years, and was sick of the palsy. And Peter said unto him, Æneas, Jesus Christ maketh thee whole: arise, and make thy bed. And he arose immediately. And all that dwelt at Lydda and Saron saw him, and turned to the Lord.

Now there was at Joppa a certain disciple named Tabitha, which by interpretation is called Dorcas: this woman was full of good works and almsdeeds which she did. And it came to pass in those days, that she was sick, and died: whom when they had washed, they laid her in an upper chamber. And forasmuch as Lydda was nigh to Joppa, and the disciples had heard that Peter was there, they sent unto him two men, desiring him that he would not delay to come to them. Then Peter arose and went with them. When he was come, they brought him into the upper chamber: and all the widows stood by him weeping, and shewing the coats and garments which Dorcas made, while she was with them. But Peter put them all forth, and kneeled down, and prayed; and turning him to the body said, Tabitha, arise. And she opened her eyes: and when she saw Peter, she sat up. And he gave her his hand, and lifted her up, and when he had called the saints and widows, presented her alive. And it was known throughout all Joppa; and many believed in the Lord. And it came to pass, that he tarried many days in Joppa with one Simon a tanner.

10. There was a certain man in Cæsarea called Cornelius, a centurion of the band called the Italian band, a devout man, and one that feared God with all his house, which gave much alms to the people, and prayed to God alway. He saw in a vision evidently about the ninth hour of the day an angel of God coming in to him, and saying unto him, Cornelius. And when he looked on him, he was afraid, and said, What is it, Lord? And he said unto him, Thy prayers and thine alms are come up for a memorial before God. And now send men to Joppa, and call for one Simon, whose surname is Peter: he lodgeth with one Simon a tanner, whose house is by the sea side: he shall tell thee what thou oughtest to do. And when the angel which spake unto Cornelius was departed, he called two of his household servants, and a devout soldier of them that waited on him continually; and when he had declared all these things unto them, he sent them to Joppa.

On the morrow, as they went on their journey, and drew nigh unto the city, Peter went up upon the housetop to pray about the sixth hour: and he became very hungry, and would have eaten: but while they made ready, he fell into a trance, and saw heaven opened, and a certain vessel descending unto him, as it had been a great sheet knit at the four corners, and let down to the earth: wherein were all manner of fourfooted beasts of the earth, and wild beasts, and creeping things, and fowls of the air. And there came a voice to him, Rise, Peter; kill, and eat. But Peter said, Not so, Lord; for I have never eaten any thing that is common or unclean. And the voice spake unto him again the second time, What God hath cleansed, that call not thou common. This was done thrice: and the vessel was received up again into heaven.

Now while Peter doubted in himself what this vision which he had seen should mean, behold, the men which were sent from Cornelius had made inquiry for Simon's house, and stood before the gate, and called, and asked whether Simon, which was surnamed Peter, were lodged there. While Peter thought on the vision, the Spirit said unto him, Behold, three men seek thee. Arise therefore, and get thee down, and go with them, doubting nothing: for I have sent them. Then Peter went down to the men which were sent unto him from Cornelius; and said, Behold, I am he whom ye seek: what is the cause wherefore ye are come? And they said, Cornelius the centurion, a just man, and one that feareth God, and of good report among all the nation of the Jews, was warned from God by an holy angel to send for thee into his house, and to hear words of thee. Then called he them in, and lodged them.

And on the morrow Peter went away with them, and certain brethren from Joppa accompanied him. And the morrow after they entered into Cæsarea. And Cornelius waited for them, and had called together his kinsmen and near friends. And as Peter was coming in, Cornelius met him, and fell down at his feet, and worshipped him. But Peter took him up, saying, Stand up; I myself also am a man. And as he talked with him, he went in, and found many that were come together. And he said unto them, Ye know how that it is an unlawful thing for a man that is a Jew to keep company, or come unto one of another nation; but God hath shewed me that I should not call any man common or unclean. Therefore came I unto you without gainsaying, as soon as I was sent for: I ask therefore for what intent ye have sent for me? And Cornelius said, Four days ago I was fasting until this hour; and at the ninth hour I prayed in my house, and, behold, a man stood before me in bright clothing, and said, Cornelius, thy prayer is heard, and thine alms are had in remembrance in the sight of God. Send therefore to Joppa, and call hither Simon, whose surname is Peter; he is lodged in the house of one Simon a tanner by the sea side: who, when he cometh, shall speak unto thee. Immediately therefore I sent to thee; and thou hast well done that thou art come. Now therefore are we all here present before God, to hear all things that are commanded thee of God.

Then Peter opened his mouth, and said, Of a truth I perceive that God is no respecter of persons: but in every nation he that feareth him, and worketh righteousness, is accepted with him. The word which God sent unto the children of Israel, preaching peace by Jesus Christ: (he is Lord of all:) that word, I say, ye know, which was published throughout all Judæa, and began from Galilee, after the baptism which John preached; how God anointed Jesus of Nazareth with the Holy Ghost and with power: who went about doing good, and healing all that were oppressed of the devil; for God was with him. And we are witnesses of all things which he did both in the land of the Jews, and in Jerusalem; whom they slew and hanged on a tree: him God raised up the third day, and shewed him openly; not to all the people, but unto witnesses chosen before of God, even to us, who did eat and drink with him after he rose from the dead. And he commanded us to preach unto the people, and to testify that it is he which was ordained of God to be the Judge of quick and dead. To him give all the prophets witness, that through his name whosoever believeth in him shall receive remission of sins.

While Peter yet spake these words, the Holy Ghost fell on all them which heard the word. And they of the circumcision which believed were astonished, as many as came with Peter, because that on the Gentiles also was poured out the gift of the Holy Ghost. For they heard them speak with tongues, and magnify God. Then answered Peter, Can any man forbid water, that these should not be baptized, which have received the Holy Ghost as well as we? And he commanded them to be baptized in the name of the Lord. Then prayed they him to tarry certain days.

11. And the apostles and brethren that were in Judæa heard that the Gentiles had also received the word of God. And when Peter was come up to Jerusalem, they that were of the circumcision contended with him, saying, Thou wentest in to men uncircumcised, and didst eat with them. But Peter rehearsed the matter from the beginning, and expounded it by order unto them, saying, I was in the city of Joppa praying: and in a trance I saw a vision, A certain vessel descend, as it had been a great sheet, let down from heaven by four corners; and it came even to me: upon the which when I had fastened mine eyes, I considered, and saw fourfooted beasts of the earth, and wild beasts, and creeping things, and fowls of the air. And I heard a voice saying unto me, Arise, Peter; slay and eat. But I said, Not so, Lord: for nothing common or unclean hath at any time entered into my mouth. But the voice answered me again from heaven, What God hath cleansed, that call not thou common. And this was done three times: and all were drawn up again into heaven.

And, behold, immediately there were three men already come unto the house where I was, sent from Cæsarea unto me. And the spirit bade me go with them, nothing doubting. Moreover these six brethren accompanied me, and we entered into the man's house: and he shewed us how he had seen an angel in his house, which stood and said unto him, Send men to Joppa, and call for Simon, whose surname is Peter; who shall tell thee words, whereby thou and all thy house shall be saved. And as I began to speak, the Holy Ghost fell on them, as on us at the beginning. Then remembered I the word of the Lord, how that he said, John indeed baptized with water; but ye shall be baptized with the Holy Ghost. Forasmuch then as God gave them the like gift as he did unto us, who believed on the Lord Jesus Christ; what was I, that I could withstand God? When they heard these things, they held their peace, and glorified God, saying, Then hath God also to the Gentiles granted repentance unto life.

Now they which were scattered abroad upon the persecution that arose about Stephen travelled as far as Phenice, and Cyprus, and Antioch, preaching the word to none but unto the Jews only. And some of them were men of Cyprus and Cyrene, which, when they were come to Antioch, spake unto the Grecians, preaching the Lord Jesus. And the hand of the Lord was with them: and a great number believed, and turned unto the Lord.

Then tidings of these things came unto the ears of the church which was in Jerusalem: and they sent forth Barnabas, that he should go as far as Antioch. Who, when he came, and had seen the grace of God, was glad, and exhorted them all, that with purpose of heart they would cleave unto the Lord.

For he was a good man, and full of the Holy Ghost and of faith: and much people was added unto the Lord. Then departed Barnabas to Tarsus, for to seek Saul: and when he had found him, he brought him unto Antioch. And it came to pass, that a whole year they assembled themselves with the church, and taught much people. And the disciples were called Christians first in Antioch.

And in these days came prophets from Jerusalem unto Antioch. And there stood up one of them named Agabus, and signified by the spirit that there should be great dearth throughout all the world: which came to pass in the days of Claudius Cæsar. Then the disciples, every man according to his ability, determined to send relief unto the brethren which dwelt in Judæa: which also they did, and sent it to the elders by the hands of Barnabas and Saul.

First Epistle of Paul to the Corinthians

[*The Gift of Love*]

13. Though I speak with the tongues of men and of angels, and have not charity, I am become as sounding brass, or a tinkling cymbal. And though I have the gift of prophecy, and understand all mysteries, and all knowledge; and though I have all faith, so that I could remove mountains, and have not charity, I am nothing. And though I bestow all my goods to feed the poor, and though I give my body to be burned, and have not charity, it profiteth me nothing.

Charity suffereth long, and is kind; charity envieth not; charity vaunteth not itself, is not puffed up, doth not behave itself unseemly, seeketh not her own, is not easily provoked, thinketh no evil; rejoiceth not in iniquity, but rejoiceth in the truth; beareth all things, believeth all things, hopeth all things, endureth all things.

Charity never faileth: but whether there be prophecies, they shall fail; whether there be tongues, they shall cease; whether there be knowledge, it shall vanish away. For we know in part, and we prophesy in part. But when that which is perfect is come, then that which is in part shall be done away. When I was a child, I spake as a child, I understood as a child, I thought as a child: but when I became a man, I put away childish things. For now we see through a glass, darkly; but then face to face: now I know in part; but then shall I know even as also I am known. And now abideth faith, hope, charity, these three; but the greatest of these is charity.

SUPPLEMENTAL TEXTS FOR ENGLISH 232

HENRIK IBSEN

1828–1906

A Doll House†

CHARACTERS

TORVALD HELMER, a lawyer	THE HELMERS' THREE SMALL
NORA, his wife	CHILDREN
DR. RANK	ANNE-MARIE, their nurse
MRS. LINDE	HELENE, a maid
NILS KROGSTAD, a bank clerk	A DELIVERY BOY

Act One

A comfortable, tasteful, but not expensively furnished room. A door to the right in the back wall leads out to the hall; another door to the left leads in to Helmer's study. Between these doors is a piano. In the middle of the left wall, a door, and farther back, a window. Near the window a round table with armchairs and a small sofa. In the right wall, upstage, a door and, on this same side nearer the foreground, a porcelain stove with a pair of armchairs and a rocking chair. Between the stove and the door, a little table. Engravings on the walls. An étagère with porcelain figures and other small art objects; a small bookcase with books in rich bindings. Carpet on the floor; the fire burns in the stove. A winter's day.

(A bell rings in the hallway; soon after, we hear the door being opened. Nora, cheerfully humming, enters the room; she is dressed in outdoor clothes and carries a great number of packages, which she sets down on the table, right. She lets the door to the hall stand open and we see a Porter carrying a Christmas tree and a basket, which he hands to the Maid, who had opened the door for them.)

† Translated by Rick Davis and Brian Johnston.

NORA   Be sure you hide the tree, Helene. We can't let the children see it before it's decorated tonight. (*To the Porter as she takes out her purse.*) How much—? Oh yes, I know, half a krone—here's one—no, keep the change. (*The Porter thanks her and leaves, Nora closes the door. She continues laughing softly to herself while she takes off her outdoor clothes. She takes a bag of macaroons from her pocket and eats a couple; then she walks cautiously and listens outside her husband's door.*) He's home, all right.
(*Humming again, she goes over to the table, right.*)

HELMER   (*From within the study.*)   Do I hear a skylark singing out there?

NORA   (*Busy opening some packages.*)   Yes, you do.

HELMER   Is there by any chance a squirrel rummaging around?

NORA   Yes!

HELMER   When did the squirrel get home?

NORA   Just this second. (*She puts the bag of macaroons in her pocket and wipes her mouth.*) Come out here, Torvald, and look at what I've bought.

HELMER   Can't be disturbed! (*After a moment, he opens the door and looks in, his pen in his hand.*) Did you say bought? All that? Has the little spendthrift been out wasting money again?

NORA   Oh, Torvald—this year we really ought to let ourselves go a little bit. It's the first Christmas we haven't had to watch our money.

HELMER   But we still can't go around wasting it, you know.

NORA   Yes, Torvald, now we can afford to waste a little bit here and there. Isn't that right? Just a teeny little bit. Now that you've got such a big salary and we've got heaps and heaps of money coming in?

HELMER   Yes, after New Year's. And then it's three whole months before the first paycheck.

NORA   Fuff! We can borrow till then.

HELMER   Nora! (*Goes over to her and takes her playfully by the ear.*) Is that dizzy little head of yours spinning around again? Suppose I borrowed a thousand today, and you wasted it all on Christmas, and then on New Year's Eve I got hit in the head by a falling brick and lay there—

NORA   (*Covering his mouth.*)   Ugh! Don't say awful things like that!

HELMER   Well, suppose it happened—what then?

NORA   If anything that awful happened, some silly loan would be the least of my worries.

HELMER   What about the people I'd borrowed from?

NORA   Them? Who cares about them! They're only strangers.

HELMER   Nora, Nora, you are such a woman! Seriously, Nora, you know what I think about these things. No debts! Never borrow! Some freedom's lost, and because of that some beauty too, from a home that's built on borrowing and debt. The two of us have managed to hold out bravely until now; and we'll stay the course for the little time remaining.

NORA   (*Goes over to the stove.*)   All right, Torvald, whatever you want.

HELMER   (*Following.*)   Now, now; the little songbird mustn't droop its wings. Right? Is the squirrel standing there sulking? (*Taking out his wallet.*) Nora, guess what I have?

NORA   (*Turning quickly.*)   Money!

HELMER There, see? (*Handing her some bills.*) For Heaven's sake, I know how much a house goes through at Christmastime.

NORA (*Counting.*) Ten—twenty—thirty—forty—Oh, thank you, thank you, Torvald. This will help me no end.

HELMER It had certainly better.

NORA Yes, yes, I'll make sure it does. But come here so I can show you what I've bought. And so cheap! Look—new clothes for Ivar, also a sword. Here's a horse and trumpet for Bob. And for Emmy, a doll and a doll bed. They're pretty plain, but she'll just tear them to pieces anyway before you know it. And here's some dress material and some handkerchiefs for the maids— even though old Anne-Marie really deserves a little more.

HELMER And what's in that package there?

NORA (*With a cry.*) No, Torvald! Not till tonight!

HELMER Aha! But tell me, you little spendthrift, what did you think of for yourself?

NORA For me? Oh, I don't need anything.

HELMER You most certainly do. Tell me what you'd like most of all—within reason.

NORA Oh, I really don't know. Yes—listen, Torvald—

HELMER Well?

NORA (*Fumbling with his button; not looking at him.*) If you want to give me something, you could—you could—

HELMER Well, say it.

NORA (*Quickly.*) You could give me money, Torvald. Only what you can spare; then one of these days I could buy something with it.

HELMER No, but Nora—

NORA Yes, do it, Torvald, darling. I'm begging you. And I'll hang the money in pretty gilt paper on the tree. Wouldn't that be lovely?

HELMER What do we call those little birds that are always spending their money?

NORA Spendthrifts—yes, I know, I know. But let's do what I say, Torvald; then I'll have time to think about what I really need. That's pretty practical, isn't it?

HELMER (*Smiling.*) Absolutely—if you could only hold on to the money I give you, and if you actually bought something for yourself with it. But it will go for the house, for a lot of things we don't need, and I'll just have to shell out again.

NORA Oh, Torvald—

HELMER Can't be denied, my dear little Nora. (*Puts his arm around her waist.*) Spendthrifts are sweet; but they go through an awful lot of money. It's unbelievable how expensive it is to keep a spendthrift.

NORA Oh, fuff—how can you say that? I save absolutely everything I can.

HELMER (*Laughing.*) Yes, that's true—everything you *can*. But the trouble is, you *can't*.

NORA (*Humming and smiling with quiet complacency.*) Hmm. You just can't imagine what kinds of expenses larks and squirrels have, Torvald.

HELMER You are a strange little one. Just like your father was. You'll try anything you can think of to get hold of some money; but the moment you get some, it slips through your fingers. You never know what you've done with it. But you are what you are. It's in your blood—these things are hereditary, Nora.

NORA I wish I'd inherited a lot of Papa's qualities.

HELMER Well I don't want you to be anything but what you are: my sweet little songbird. But listen—I'm getting the distinct impression—you've got a sort of a—what can I call it—a kind of a guilty look today.

NORA I do?

HELMER You certainly do. Look me straight in the eye.

NORA (*Looking at him.*) Well?

HELMER (*Wagging his finger.*) Our sweet tooth wouldn't have been running wild in town today, would it?

NORA No, what makes you think that?

HELMER You're sure that sweet tooth didn't make a little stop at the bakery?

NORA No, Torvald, I swear—

HELMER Didn't nibble a little candy?

NORA No, absolutely not.

HELMER Not even munched on a macaroon or two?

NORA No, Torvald, honestly, I promise—

HELMER Now, now—of course I'm only joking.

NORA (*Going to the table, right.*) I'd never dream of going against you.

HELMER No, I know that. And after all, you've given me your word. (*Goes to her.*) Well, you keep your little Christmas secrets to yourself, then, my dearest Nora. I guess everything will be revealed this evening when we light the tree.

NORA Did you remember to invite Doctor Rank?

HELMER No—there's no need; it's taken for granted. But I'll ask him again when he stops in this morning. I've ordered the very best wine. Nora, you can't imagine how excited I am about tonight.

NORA Me too! And the children are just going to love it!

HELMER Ah, it's so marvelous to have a secure position and a comfortable income. Isn't it fun just to think about that?

NORA Oh, it's wonderful!

HELMER Do you remember last Christmas? Three whole weeks beforehand, you locked yourself up every evening, till way past midnight, making flowers for the Christmas tree, and all the other little surprises you had for us. Uch—I've never been so bored in my whole life.

NORA I wasn't bored at all.

HELMER (*Smiling.*) But it didn't amount to much after all, Nora.

NORA Oh, are you going to tease me with that again? I couldn't help it that the cat came in and tore everything to bits.

HELMER No, that's right, you couldn't, my poor little Nora. You worked so hard to make us happy, that's the main thing. But it's good that those hard times are behind us.

NORA Yes, it's really wonderful.

HELMER Now I don't have to sit here all alone boring myself, and you don't have to torture your precious eyes and your delicate little fingers—

NORA (*Clapping her hands.*) No, is that true, Torvald, I really don't have to? How wonderful to hear that! (*Takes his arm.*) Now I'll tell you what I thought we should do—as soon as Christmas is over—(*The doorbell rings.*) Oh, that doorbell. (*Tidying up the room.*) That means a visitor—what a bore!

HELMER   I'm not at home to visitors, remember that.

MAID (*In the doorway.*)   Madam, there's a strange lady here to see you.

NORA   Show her in.

MAID (*To Helmer.*)   And the Doctor arrived at the same time.

HELMER   He went straight to my study?

MAID   Yes, sir, he did.

(*Helmer goes into his room. The Maid shows Mrs. Linde, dressed in traveling clothes, into the room and closes the door after her.*)

MRS. LINDE (*Timidly and somewhat hesitantly.*)   Good day, Nora.

NORA (*Uncertainly.*)   Good day—

MRS. LINDE   You don't recognize me.

NORA   No; I don't know—I think—(*Bursting out.*) Kristine! Is it really you?

MRS. LINDE   Yes, it is.

NORA   Kristine! How could I not recognize you? But then how could I—? (*Quieter.*) You've changed, Kristine.

MRS. LINDE   Yes, I expect I have. In nine—ten—long years—

NORA   Is it that long? Yes, that's right. Oh, the last eight years have been happy ones, believe me. And now you've come to town as well. Made the long trip in winter. That was brave.

MRS. LINDE   I just got here this morning on the steamer.

NORA   To enjoy yourself at Christmas, of course. That's a lovely idea! Yes, enjoy ourselves—we will certainly do that. But take off your coat. You're not too cold? (*Helps her.*) That's it; now let's settle down and be cozy here by the stove. No, take the armchair there. I'll sit here in the rocking chair. (*Gripping her hands.*) Yes, now you look more like yourself again; it was just those first few moments—you have gotten a bit paler, Kristine—and maybe a little thinner.

MRS. LINDE   And much, much older, Nora.

NORA   Well, maybe a little older, a tiny little bit; but not too much. (*Drawing back, suddenly serious.*) Oh, I can't believe how thoughtless I am, sitting here chattering—Kristine, can you forgive me?

MRS. LINDE   What do you mean, Nora?

NORA (*Quietly.*)   Poor Kristine, you're a widow.

MRS. LINDE   Yes, for three years now.

NORA   I knew it of course, I read it in the paper. Oh, Kristine, you have to believe me, I was always going to write you at the time, but I kept putting it off, and things kept getting in the way.

MRS. LINDE   Nora, dear, I understood completely.

NORA   No, it was horrible of me. You poor thing, it must have been so hard for you—and he didn't leave you anything to live on?

MRS. LINDE   No.

NORA   And no children?

MRS. LINDE   No.

NORA   So, nothing at all.

MRS. LINDE   No—not even a sense of grief to hold on to.

NORA (*Looking at her in disbelief.*) Kristine, how is that possible?

MRS. LINDE (*Smiles sadly, stroking Nora's hair.*) Ah, sometimes it happens that way, Nora.

NORA So completely alone. That must be terribly sad for you. I have three lovely children—you can't see them right now, they're out with Anne-Marie. But now you have to tell me everything.

MRS. LINDE No, no, I'd rather hear about you.

NORA No, you have to go first. Today I'm not going to be selfish. Today I'm only going to think about you. But I have to tell you *one* thing. Did you hear about the great luck we just had?

MRS. LINDE No, what is it?

NORA My husband has been made manager of the Bank.

MRS. LINDE Your husband? That is lucky!

NORA Isn't it? The law is such a chancy business, especially when you won't take the ugly cases. Torvald would never do that, of course, and I agree with him completely. So you can imagine how happy we are! He starts at the Bank right after New Year's, and then he'll be getting a huge salary and lots of commissions. From now on we'll be able to live quite differently—we can actually do what we want. Oh, Kristine, I feel so light and happy! Isn't it lovely to have lots of money, and not have to worry about anything?

MRS. LINDE It's lovely just to have enough.

NORA No, not just enough, but lots and lots of money!

MRS. LINDE (*Smiling.*) Nora, Nora, haven't you gotten over that yet? You were such a spendthrift in school.

NORA (*Laughing softly.*) Yes, Torvald still says the same thing. (*Wagging her finger.*) But "Nora, Nora" hasn't been as wild as you all think. We haven't exactly been in a position where I could waste any money. We've both had to work.

MRS. LINDE You too?

NORA Yes, odd jobs—sewing, embroidery, work like that—(*Casually.*) and also other things. You know Torvald left the government when we got married; he saw he'd never be promoted, and he needed to earn more money than before. In that first year he worked himself to the bone, always looking for extra income, day and night. But he couldn't keep it up, and he got deathly sick. The doctor said he absolutely had to move south.

MRS. LINDE Didn't you stay a whole year in Italy?

NORA That's right. It wasn't that easy to get away, as you can imagine. Ivar had just been born. But we had to go, there was no question about it. Ah, it was a wonderful trip, and it saved Torvald's life. But it was incredibly expensive.

MRS. LINDE I believe you.

NORA Four thousand, eight hundred kroner. That's a lot of money.

MRS. LINDE It's just lucky you had it when the emergency came up.

NORA Well, I can tell you, we had to get it from Papa.

MRS. LINDE So that's how. That was about the time your father died, I think.

NORA Yes, Kristine, it was right then. Just think, I couldn't go and be with him. I stayed right here and waited every day for little Ivar to come into the world. And I had my poor, sick Torvald to take care of. Dear, sweet Papa! I never saw him again, Kristine. That was the saddest time in my whole marriage.

MRS. LINDE   I know how much he meant to you. But then you left for Italy?

NORA   Yes, we had the money then, and the doctors insisted. So we left in a month.

MRS. LINDE   And your husband came back completely cured?

NORA   Right as rain!

MRS. LINDE   But—the doctor—?

NORA   What do you mean?

MRS. LINDE   I thought the maid said the man who came in with me was a doctor.

NORA   Yes, Doctor Rank. He's not here on a house call, he's our best friend—he comes by at least once a day. No, Torvald hasn't been sick a day since then. And the children are strong and sound and so am I. (*Jumping up and clapping her hands.*) Oh God, oh God, Kristine, it's so wonderful to live and be happy! But I'm being hateful here, only talking about myself. (*Sits on a stool close by Kristine and lays her arms on her knees.*) Please don't be mad at me! Tell me something—is it really true that you didn't love your husband? So why did you marry him?

MRS. LINDE   My mother was still alive, but she was bedridden and couldn't take care of herself; and I also had to look after my two younger brothers. I couldn't justify refusing his offer.

NORA   No, no, you were right. He was rich at the time, wasn't he?

MRS. LINDE   He was pretty well-off, I think. But the business wasn't very solid, Nora: when he died it all went to pieces, nothing was left.

NORA   And then—?

MRS. LINDE   Well, I had to do what I could for myself—a little shop, a few students, whatever else I could find. These last three years have been like one long workday without a break. But now it's over, Nora. My poor mother doesn't need me anymore, she's gone. And the boys are working now, they're on their own.

NORA   You must feel such relief—

MRS. LINDE   No, not at all. Only inexpressibly empty. Nothing more to live for. (*Stands uneasily.*) So I couldn't stand it any longer out in that little backwater. It's got to be easier here to find something to do, something to keep my mind working. If only I could be lucky enough to find a steady job, some office work—

NORA   But Kristine, that's so exhausting, and you're tired enough to begin with. You'd be better off if you could get away to a spa for a while.

MRS. LINDE (*Going over to window.*)   I don't have a papa to send me on a trip, Nora.

NORA (*Getting up.*)   Oh, don't be mad at me!

MRS. LINDE   Nora, dear, don't you be mad at me. That's the worst thing about this situation of mine; it leaves you with so much bitterness. You've got nothing to work for, but you still have to watch out for every opportunity. You have to live, so you become selfish. When you told me your news, I was more excited for my own sake than yours.

NORA   Why? Oh, I see—you mean maybe Torvald can do something for you.

MRS. LINDE   That's exactly what I was thinking.

NORA   And so he will, Kristine! Leave it to me—I'll suggest it so beautifully, so beautifully—find something charming that he'll really appreciate. Oh, I can't wait to help you.

MRS. LINDE   You're so kind, Nora, to take such an interest in me—doubly kind, since you don't know much about life's hardships yourself.

NORA   I—? Don't know much—?

MRS. LINDE   (*Smiling.*)   Well, good Lord, a little sewing and things like that—you're such a child, Nora.

NORA   (*Tosses her head, walks across the room.*)   You shouldn't be so sure about that.

MRS. LINDE   Oh?

NORA   You're like everyone else. You all think I'm not capable of anything serious—

MRS. LINDE   Now, now—

NORA   That I've never been put to the test in the cold, hard world.

MRS. LINDE   Nora, you've just been telling me all about your troubles.

NORA   Fuff! Trifles! (*Quietly.*) I haven't told you the big thing.

MRS. LINDE   What big thing? What do you mean?

NORA   You look down on me an awful lot, Kristine, but you really shouldn't. You're proud that you've worked so hard for your mother all these years.

MRS. LINDE   I don't look down on anyone. But it's true that I'm proud—and happy—that I was given the chance to ease my mother's sorrow in her last days.

NORA   And when you think about what you've done for your brothers, you're proud of that as well.

MRS. LINDE   I think I'm entitled to that.

NORA   So do I. But now you'll hear, Kristine. I also have something to be proud and happy about.

MRS. LINDE   I don't doubt it. But how do you mean?

NORA   Let's talk quietly. What if Torvald heard? He mustn't, not for anything in the world. Nobody can find out about this, nobody but you.

MRS. LINDE   What is it?

NORA   Come over here. (*Pulls her down on the sofa beside her.*) Now then: here's what I have to be proud and happy about. I saved Torvald's life.

MRS. LINDE   Saved—? How did you save—?

NORA   I told you about the trip to Italy. Torvald would never have survived if he hadn't gone down there—

MRS. LINDE   Yes, well, your father gave you all the money you needed—

NORA   (*Smiling.*)   Yes, that's what Torvald and everyone else believe, but—

MRS. LINDE   But—?

NORA   Papa never gave anything. I got the money myself.

MRS. LINDE   You? That was a lot of money.

NORA   Four thousand, eight hundred kroner. What do you say to that?

MRS. LINDE   But Nora, how was that possible? Did you win the lottery?

NORA   (*Disdainfully.*)   The lottery. (*Snorting.*) What kind of art would *that* have taken?

MRS. LINDE   Then where did you get it from?

NORA   (*Humming and smiling secretively.*)   Hmm; tra la la la la!

MRS. LINDE Because you certainly couldn't have borrowed it.

NORA Oh? Why not?

MRS. LINDE No, a wife can't get a loan without her husband's permission.

NORA (*Tossing her head.*) Well, but a wife with a head for business, a wife who knows how to be a little clever—

MRS. LINDE Nora, I just don't understand—

NORA And you don't need to. Nobody said anything about *borrowing* the money. Maybe I got it some other way. (*Throwing herself back on the sofa.*) Maybe I got it from one of my admirers. When you're as alluring as I am—

MRS. LINDE You're crazy.

NORA I've got you really curious now, haven't I?

MRS. LINDE Listen to me, Nora: you haven't done anything foolish, have you?

NORA (*Sitting up again.*) Is it foolish to save your husband's life?

MRS. LINDE I think it's foolish that without his knowledge you—

NORA But that's just it—he mustn't know anything! Good Lord, can't you see that? He can never know how bad off he was. The doctors came to *me* to say his life was in jeopardy—that only a trip south could save him. At first I tried to coax him into it—I told him how lovely it would be to take a trip abroad like other young wives—then I begged and cried—I said he should be kind and indulge a woman in my condition—and I hinted that he could easily take out a loan. That really set him off, Kristine. He told me I was being frivolous, and that it was his duty as a husband not to indulge my every whim and caprice—I think that's what he called them. Well, well, I thought, saved you must be and saved you shall be—and that's when I came up with my plan.

MRS. LINDE Didn't your husband ever find out that the money wasn't your father's?

NORA Never. Papa died right after that. I thought about letting him in on it and asking him not to say anything. But with him lying there so sick—and finally it wasn't necessary.

MRS. LINDE And you've never confided in your husband?

NORA No, for heaven's sake, how can you even imagine that? He's so strict about those things. And besides, Torvald's a man—he'd be so humiliated if he knew he owed me anything. It could even spoil our relationship; it would be the end of our beautiful, happy home.

MRS. LINDE So you'll never tell him?

NORA (*Reflectively, half-smiling.*) Yes, maybe someday; years from now, when I can't count on my looks anymore. Don't laugh! I mean when Torvald's not as attracted to me as he is now—when my dancing and dressing-up and reciting for him don't interest him any more. Then it'll be good to have something to fall back on. (*Breaking off.*) Dumb, dumb, dumb! That'll never happen. So what do you think of my big secret, Kristine? I can do things after all, can't I? But as you can imagine, it's been a big worry for me. It hasn't been that easy to make the payments on time. So I had to save a little, here and there, whenever I could. I couldn't really take anything out of the housekeeping budget, because Torvald has to live in a certain style. And I couldn't scrimp on the children's clothes; I used up whatever I got for them—the angels!

MRS. LINDE Poor Nora! So it came out of your allowance?

NORA   Yes, of course. But then it was mostly my problem. Whenever Torvald gave me money for new clothes or whatever, I'd only use half; I always bought the simplest, cheapest things. I'm lucky that everything looks good on me, so Torvald never noticed. But it made me sad sometimes, Kristine—because it's so nice to dress up now and then, isn't it?

MRS. LINDE   Yes it is.

NORA   But I found other ways to make some money too. Last winter I was lucky enough to get a big copying job to do. So I shut myself in and wrote every evening till late at night. Ah, I'd get so tired, so tired—but it was also great fun, sitting and working and earning money like that. Almost like being a man.

MRS. LINDE   How much have you managed to pay off like that?

NORA   Well, I can't really say exactly. This kind of account is very hard to keep track of. I only know that I've paid back everything I can scrape together. A lot of times I didn't know which way to turn. (*Smiling.*) I'd sit here and imagine that a rich old man had fallen in love with me.

MRS. LINDE   What? Which man?

NORA   Oh, come on! And that he'd just died and when they read his will, there it was in big letters: "My entire fortune is to be paid in cash, immediately, to the delightful Mrs. Nora Helmer."

MRS. LINDE   But Nora, who is he?

NORA   Good Lord, don't you get it? There never was any such person; it was just something I'd sit here and dream about when I couldn't think of any other way to get the money. But now it doesn't matter, the old bore can go back where he came from; I don't need him or his will, because my troubles are over. Oh, God, it's so lovely to think of, Kristine! Carefree! To be carefree, completely carefree! To run around and play with the children; to make everything in the house warm and beautiful, just the way Torvald likes it! Then maybe we can travel a little. Maybe I'll get down to the ocean again. Oh yes, it is so wonderful to live and be happy!

(*The bell rings in the hallway.*)

MRS. LINDE   (*Rising.*)   The bell—maybe I should go.

NORA   No, stay here. It won't be for me. It's probably for Torvald.

MAID   (*From the hall doorway.*)   Excuse me, ma'am. There's a gentleman here to speak with the lawyer.

NORA   With the Bank Manager, you mean.

MAID   Yes, with the Bank Manager. But I didn't know if—since the Doctor's in there—

NORA   Who is the gentleman?

KROGSTAD   (*From the doorway.*)   It's me, Mrs. Helmer.

(*Mrs. Linde starts, checks herself, and turns toward the window.*)

NORA   (*A step towards him, tense, in a low voice.*)   You? What is it? What do you want to talk to my husband about?

KROGSTAD   Bank matters—more or less. I have a minor position on the bank staff, and I hear your husband is our new chief.

NORA   And so it's—

KROGSTAD   Just dry business, Mrs. Helmer. Absolutely nothing else.

NORA Then would you please be good enough to step into his study? (*She nods indifferently and shuts the hallway door; then she goes and tends the stove.*)

MRS. LINDE Nora—who was that man?

NORA That was a lawyer named Krogstad.

MRS. LINDE So it really was him.

NORA Do you know that man?

MRS. LINDE I used to know him—a long time ago. He was a law clerk for a while up in our area.

NORA Yes, that's right, he was.

MRS. LINDE He certainly has changed.

NORA He had a very unhappy marriage.

MRS. LINDE And now he's a widower?

NORA With several children. There we go, now it's burning. (*She closes the stove door and moves the rocking chair a little to the side.*)

MRS. LINDE He's got himself involved in all kinds of businesses, they say.

NORA Oh yes? Probably; I really wouldn't know. But let's not think about business—it's so boring!

(*Doctor Rank comes out from Helmer's study.*)

RANK (*Still in the doorway.*) No, no, Torvald: I don't want to be in the way; I'd just as soon go talk to your wife for a while. (*Closing the door and noticing Mrs. Linde.*) I'm sorry—I'm in the way here too.

NORA You certainly are not. (*Introducing him.*) Doctor Rank, Mrs. Linde.

RANK Aha! That's an oft-mentioned name in this house. I think I passed you on the stairs when I arrived.

MRS. LINDE Yes, I don't handle stairs very well.

RANK Aha—are you having some kind of trouble?

MRS. LINDE Probably just overwork.

RANK Nothing more? So you've probably come to town to catch your breath in the holiday parties.

MRS. LINDE I'm looking for a job.

RANK Is that the prescription for overwork?

MRS. LINDE One has to live, Doctor.

RANK Yes, there's general agreement on that point.

NORA Oh, come on now, Doctor Rank, you want to live as much as anyone.

RANK Yes, I really do. Wretched as I am, I really want to stretch my torment to the limit. All my patients feel the same way. And it's the same with the morally diseased—right now there's a terminal moral case in there with Helmer—

MRS. LINDE (*Quietly.*) Ah—!

NORA Who's that?

RANK Oh, just a certain lawyer Krogstad, no one you'd know anything about. His character, my ladies, is rotten right down to the roots—but even he began making speeches—as if it were self-evident—that he had to *live.*

NORA Oh? What did he want to talk to Torvald about?

RANK I don't know for sure. All I heard was something about the bank.

NORA I didn't know Krog—that this lawyer Krogstad had anything to do with the bank.

RANK   Yes, he's got some kind of position down there. (*To Mrs. Linde.*) I don't know if you have, in your part of the country, any of these moral detectives, these investigators who go around sniffing out moral corruption and then get their victims into a safe place where they can keep them under constant surveillance—it's a lucrative business these days. The healthy ones get left out in the cold—no room for them!

MRS. LINDE   And yet it's the sick ones who need to be brought inside.

RANK   (*Shrugs his shoulders.*)   There you have it. That's the philosophy that's turning our whole world into a hospital.

(*Nora, lost in thought, breaks into quiet laughter, clapping her hands.*)

RANK   Why do you laugh? Do you really know what the world is?

NORA   What do I care about the boring old world? I was laughing at something else—something terribly funny. Tell me, Doctor Rank, all those people who work at the bank—are they all under Torvald now?

RANK   Is *that* what's so terribly funny to you?

NORA   (*Smiling and humming.*)   Never mild! Never mind! (*Walking around the room.*) Yes, it is extremely amusing that we—that Torvald has so much influence over so many people. (*Takes a bag from her pocket.*) Doctor Rank, how about a little macaroon?

RANK   Aha! Macaroons! I thought they were illegal here.

NORA   Yes, but Kristine gave me these—

MRS. LINDE   What? I—?

NORA   Now, now, now, don't worry. How could you know that Torvald made a law against them? You see, he's afraid they'll rot my teeth. But, fuff—just this once—don't you agree, Doctor Rank? There you are! (*She pops a macaroon into his mouth.*) You too, Kristine. And I'll have one too, just a little one—or two at the most. (*Walking around again.*) Yes, now I am really tremendously happy. There's just one last thing in the world I have a tremendous desire to do.

RANK   Oh? What's that?

NORA   I have this tremendous desire to say something so that Torvald can hear it.

RANK   So why can't you say it?

NORA   No, I don't dare. It's too horrible.

MRS. LINDE   Horrible?

RANK   Well, then, maybe you'd better not. But with us—can't you? What do you want to say so Torvald can hear?

NORA   I have a tremendous desire to say: To hell with everything!

RANK   Are you crazy?

MRS. LINDE   For heaven' sake, Nora.

RANK   Say it—here he is.

NORA   (*Hiding the macaroons.*)   Shh, shh, shh!

(*Helmer enters from his study, hat in hand and overcoat on his arm.*)

NORA   Well, my dear, are you through with him?

HELMER   Yes, he just left.

NORA   Let me introduce you—this is Kristine, who's just come to town.

HELMER   Kristine? I'm sorry, but I don't know—

NORA   Mrs. Linde, Torvald dear, Mrs. Kristine Linde.

HELMER   Oh, I see. A childhood friend?

MRS. LINDE   Yes, we knew each other back then.

NORA   And just think, she made the long trip here just to talk to you.

MRS. LINDE   Well, actually, I didn't—

NORA   Kristine, you see, is extremely good at office work, and so she's tre-mendously eager to place herself under the direction of a capable man so that she can learn even more than she—

HELMER   Very sensible, Mrs. Linde.

NORA   So that when she heard you'd been made bank manager—there was a bulletin about it in all the papers—she started out as fast as she could, and—it's true, isn't it, Torvald? You could do something for Kristine for my sake, yes?

HELMER   It's not completely out of the question. You are, I suppose, a widow?

MRS. LINDE   Yes.

HELMER   And you have experience in office work?

MRS. LINDE   Yes, quite a bit.

HELMER   Well then, it's entirely possible that I can offer you a position—

NORA (*Clapping her hands.*)   You see, you see!

HELMER   You appeared at a lucky moment, Mrs. Linde.

MRS. LINDE   How can I thank you—

HELMER   Not at all necessary. (*Puts on overcoat.*) But today I'll have to ask you to excuse me—

RANK   Wait—I'll go with you.

(*Rank gets his fur coat from the hall and warms it at the stove.*)

NORA   Don't be out long, Torvald my dear.

HELMER   Just an hour, no more.

NORA   Are you leaving too, Kristine?

MRS. LINDE (*Putting on her outdoor things.*)   Yes, now I've got to find myself a room.

HELMER   Then maybe we can all walk together for a while.

NORA (*Helping her.*)   It's so boring that we don't have space here, but it's just impossible for us to—

MRS. LINDE   Don't even think of it! Goodbye, Nora, and thank you for everything.

NORA   Goodbye for now. But I'll see you again this evening. You too, Doctor Rank. What? If you feel well? Of course you will! Wrap yourself up nice and warm.

(*They all go out together into the hall. Children's voices are heard on the stairs*)

NORA   There they are! There they are!

(*She runs to open the front door. Anne-Marie, their nanny, enters with the children.*)

NORA   Come in, come in! (*Bends down and kisses them.*)
Oh, you sweet little darlings! Look at them, Kristine, aren't they lovely!

RANK   No loitering out here in the draft!

HELMER   Let's go, Mrs. Linde; this place is unbearable now for anyone but mothers.

(*Doctor Rank, Helmer, Mrs. Linde go down the stairs. The nursemaid goes into the living room with the children. Nora goes in also, after shutting the door to the hallway.*)

NORA   You look so clean and healthy! Your cheeks are all red! Like apples and roses. (*The children chatter away to her throughout the following.*) Was it fun? That's great. Really? You pulled both Emmy and Bob on the sled? My goodness, both of them together! You're a clever boy, Ivar. Here, let me hold her for a little while, Anne-Marie. My sweet little doll-baby! (*Takes the smallest child from Anne-Marie and dances with her.*) Yes, yes, Mommy will dance with Bob too. What? A snowball fight? Oh, I wish I was there with you! No, don't bother, I'll undress them myself, Anne-Marie. Yes, let me do it, it's so much fun. Go in for a while—you look frozen. There's warm coffee for you on the stove. (*Anne-Marie goes into the room on the left. Nora takes off the children's outdoor clothes and throws them around while the children all talk at the same time.*) Is that so? A great big dog came running after you? But it didn't bite? No, dogs never bite lovely little doll-babies. Stop peeking into the packages, Ivar! What is it? Oh, wouldn't you like to know? No, it's something awful! Well? Do you want to play? What'll we play? Hide-and-seek. Yes, let's play hide-and-seek. Bob, you hide first. Me? All right, I'll hide first.

(*She and the children play, laughing and shouting, in the living room and the adjoining room to the right. At last Nora hides under the table; the children come storming in, searching, not finding her; then, hearing her muffled laughter, rush to the table, lift the tablecloth, and discover her. A storm of delight. Meanwhile, there has been a knocking at the front door; no one has noticed it. Now the door half opens, and Krogstad appears. He waits a little while the game continues.*)

KROGSTAD   I beg your pardon, Mrs. Helmer.
NORA   (*Turns, with a stifled cry, half jumps up.*)   Ah! What do you want?
KROGSTAD   Excuse me. The front door was open—somebody must have forgotten to shut it.
NORA   (*Rising.*)   My husband's not here, Mr. Krogstad.
KROGSTAD   I know that.
NORA   Well—what do you want?
KROGSTAD   A word with you.
NORA   With—? (*To the children, quietly.*) Go in with Anne-Marie. No, the strange man won't hurt Mama. When he's gone we can play some more. (*She leads the children in to the room on the left and closes the door after them. Now, tense and nervous.*) You want to speak with me?
KROGSTAD   Yes, I do.
NORA   Today—? But it's not the first of the month yet—
KROGSTAD   No, it's Christmas Eve. It's up to you how much Christmas cheer you'll have.
NORA   What do you want? Today I can't possibly—
KROGSTAD   We won't talk about that right now. It's something else. I suppose you have a moment?
NORA   Well, yes; all right—though—
KROGSTAD   Good. I was sitting over at Olsen's Restaurant and I saw your husband going down the street—
NORA   Oh yes.
KROGSTAD   With a lady.

NORA So?

KROGSTAD I wonder if you'll allow me to ask if that lady was Mrs. Linde?

NORA Yes.

KROGSTAD Just arrived in town?

NORA Yes, today.

KROGSTAD She's a good friend of yours?

NORA Yes, she is. But I can't see—

KROGSTAD I also knew her at one time.

NORA I'm aware of that.

KROGSTAD Really? That's what I thought. Well, then, let me get right to the point: Is Mrs. Linde getting a job at the bank?

NORA Why do you think you can cross-examine me, Mr. Krogstad? You, who's just one of my husband's employees? But since you ask, you might as well know: yes, Mrs. Linde got a job. And I arranged it all for her, Mr. Krogstad. Now you know.

KROGSTAD As I thought.

NORA (*Pacing the floor.*) Oh, I should hope that one always has a little bit of influence. Just because one is a woman, it doesn't follow that—when one is in an inferior position, Mr. Krogstad, one ought to be very careful with somebody who—

KROGSTAD Who has influence?

NORA Exactly.

KROGSTAD (*Changing tone.*) Mrs. Helmer, would you be good enough to use your influence on my behalf?

NORA What? What do you mean?

KROGSTAD Would you be kind enough to make sure that I keep my inferior position at the bank?

NORA What do you mean? Who's trying to take it away from you?

KROGSTAD Oh, you don't have to play the innocent with me. I understand perfectly well that your friend doesn't want to run the risk of seeing me again; and now I also understand who to thank for being let go.

NORA But I promise you—

KROGSTAD Yes, yes, yes. But here's the point: there's still time, and I'd advise you to use your influence to prevent it.

NORA But, Mr. Krogstad, I have no influence at all.

KROGSTAD No? I thought a minute ago you said—

NORA I didn't mean it that way. What makes you think I've got any sort of influence over my husband in things like that?

KROGSTAD Oh, I've known your husband since we were students together— and I don't believe our Bank Manager has any more willpower than any other married man.

NORA You talk like that about my husband and I'll show you the door.

KROGSTAD The lady has courage.

NORA I'm not afraid of you any more. Soon after New Year's I'll be done with the whole business.

KROGSTAD Now listen to me, Mrs. Helmer. If it becomes necessary, I'll fight to the death for my little job at the bank.

NORA Yes, it looks that way.

KROGSTAD   And not just for the money—that's the least of my concerns. It's something else—well, all right—you know, of course, like everyone else, that some years ago I was guilty of an indiscretion.

NORA   I think I heard something about it.

KROGSTAD   The case never came to trial, but even so every door was closed to me. So I had to go into the sort of business you're familiar with. I had to find something—and I think I can say that I've been far from the worst in that line of work. But now I want to put all of it behind me. My sons are growing up. For their sake I want to win back as much respect as I can in the community. That position in the bank was the first rung in the ladder for me. Now your husband wants to kick me right back off the ladder and into the mud again.

NORA   But for God's sake, Mr. Krogstad, it's just not in my power to help you.

KROGSTAD   That's because you don't have the will to do it—but I can force you to.

NORA   You wouldn't tell my husband that I owe you money?

KROGSTAD   Hmm—what if I did?

NORA   That would be shameful. (*Choking with tears.*) That secret—my pride and my joy—if he learned about it in such a horrible way—learned it from you—. You'd put me through such an incredibly unpleasant scene—

KROGSTAD   Only unpleasant?

NORA   (*Vehemently.*)   Just try it! It'll only be worse for you. Because then my husband will really get to see what kind of man you are, and you'll have no chance of keeping your job.

KROGSTAD   I asked you if all you were afraid of was this unpleasant scene here at home?

NORA   If my husband finds out about it, of course he'll pay you off immediately, and we'd have nothing more to do with you.

KROGSTAD   (*A step nearer.*)   Listen, Mrs. Helmer: either you've got a terrible memory or a very shaky grasp of business. Let me get a few facts straight for you.

NORA   How do you mean?

KROGSTAD   When your husband was sick, you came to me for four thousand, eight hundred kroner.

NORA   I didn't know where else to go.

KROGSTAD   I promised to get it for you—

NORA   And you did.

KROGSTAD   I promised to get it for you on certain conditions. At the time you were so wrapped up in your husband's illness that I suppose you didn't think through all the details. Maybe I'd better remind you of them. Now: I promised to get you the money based on a note that I drafted.

NORA   Yes, which I signed.

KROGSTAD   Very good. But below your signature I added some lines to the effect that your father would guarantee the loan. Your father was to sign there.

NORA   Was to—? He signed it.

KROGSTAD   I left out the date. Your father was supposed to date his own signature. Do you remember that?

NORA   Yes, I think so—

KROGSTAD   Then I handed the note over to you so you could mail it to your father. Isn't that the case?

NORA   Yes.

KROGSTAD   And of course you did that right away—because only about five, six days later, you brought me the note, with your father's signature. And then you got your money.

NORA   Well? Haven't I been meeting my payments?

KROGSTAD   Yes, more or less. But to return to the question: that was a difficult time for you, wasn't it, Mrs. Helmer?

NORA   Yes, it was.

KROGSTAD   Your father was very ill, I believe.

NORA   He was very near the end.

KROGSTAD   He died soon after that?

NORA   Yes.

KROGSTAD   Tell me, Mrs. Helmer, do you by any chance recall the date of your father's death? Which day of the month, I mean.

NORA   Papa died on the twenty-ninth of September.

KROGSTAD   Quite correct; I've already confirmed that. That brings us to an oddity that I simply cannot account for.

NORA   What kind of oddity? I don't understand—

KROGSTAD   Here's the oddity, Mrs. Helmer: your father countersigned the note three days after his death.

NORA   How? I don't understand—

KROGSTAD   Your father died on the twenty-ninth of September. But look at this. Here your father has dated his signature "October 2nd." Isn't that odd, Mrs. Helmer? (*Nora is silent.*) Can you explain it to me? (*Nora remains silent.*) Here's another remarkable thing: the date "October 2nd" and the year are not written in your father's hand, but in a hand that I ought to know. Now, that could be explained; your father forgot to date his signature, and someone else did it for him, somewhat carelessly, before anyone knew of his death. Nothing wrong with that. Everything hinges on the signature. And that *is* genuine, isn't it, Mrs. Helmer? It really was your father himself who signed his name there?

NORA   (*After a short silence, throws back her head and looks firmly at him.*) No, it wasn't. *I* signed Papa's name.

KROGSTAD   Listen, Mrs. Helmer—do you understand that this is a dangerous confession?

NORA   Why? You'll get your money soon enough.

KROGSTAD   Can I ask you—why didn't you send the note to your father?

NORA   Impossible. Papa was so sick. If I had asked him for his signature, I'd have had to tell him what the money was for. I just couldn't tell him, in his condition, that my husband was dying. It was just impossible.

KROGSTAD   Then it would have been better for you to give up the trip.

NORA   No, impossible again. That trip was to save my husband's life. I couldn't give that up.

KROGSTAD   But didn't it occur to you that you were committing a fraud against me?

NORA   I couldn't worry about that. I certainly wasn't concerned about you. I could hardly stand you, making up all those cold conditions when you knew perfectly well how much danger my husband was in.

KROGSTAD   Mrs. Helmer, you obviously don't have any idea what you've implicated yourself in. But let me tell you this: what I once did was nothing more, and nothing worse, and it destroyed me.

NORA   You? Are you trying to get me to believe that you risked everything to save your wife?

KROGSTAD   Laws don't much care about motives.

NORA   Then they must be very bad laws.

KROGSTAD   Bad or not, if I produce this paper in court, you'll be judged by those laws.

NORA   I don't believe it. Doesn't a daughter have the right to spare her dying father from worry and anxiety? Shouldn't a wife have the right to save her husband's life? I don't know the law very well, but I'm sure it must say somewhere in there that these things are legal. You must be a very bad lawyer, Mr. Krogstad.

KROGSTAD   Maybe so. But business—this kind of business we're in—don't you think I know something about that? Good. Do what you want. But hear this: if I get thrown down a second time, you're coming with me. (*He bows and goes out through the hall door.*)

NORA   (*Stands for a moment, reflecting, then tosses her head.*)   Nonsense! He's trying to frighten me! I'm not all that naïve. (*Starts gathering up the children's clothes, but soon stops.*) But—? No, impossible. I did it out of love.

CHILDREN   (*In the doorway, left.*)   Mama, the strange man's going down the street.

NORA   Yes, I know. But don't mention the strange man to anyone. You hear? Not even Papa.

CHILDREN   No, Mama. Now can we play again?

NORA   No, no. Not now.

CHILDREN   But Mama, you promised.

NORA   Yes, but right now I can't. Go inside; I've got too much to do. Go in, go in, my dear, sweet little ones. (*She herds them carefully into the room and closes the door after them. She sits on the sofa, takes up her embroidery, makes some stitches, but soon stops.*) Helene! Let me have the tree in here. (*Goes to the table at left and opens a drawer, pauses again.*) No, that's completely impossible!

MAID   (*With the spruce tree.*)   Where should I put it, Ma'am?

NORA   There—in the middle of the floor.

MAID   Anything else?

NORA   No, thank you. I have what I need.

(*The Maid, having set the tree down, goes out.*)

NORA   (*Busy decorating the tree.*)   Candles here, flowers here—that horrible man! Talk, talk, talk. Nothing's going to happen. The Christmas tree will be just lovely. I'll do anything you want me to, Torvald—I'll sing for you, dance for you—

(*Helmer, with a packet of papers under his arm, comes in through the hall.*)

NORA   Ah! Back already?

HELMER   Yes. Has someone been here?

NORA   Here? No.

HELMER   That's strange. I just saw Krogstad going out the door.

NORA   Really? Oh, of course. Krogstad was here for a moment.

HELMER   Nora, I can see it in your eyes, he's been here asking you to put in a good word for him.

NORA   Yes.

HELMER   And you were going to pretend it was your own idea. You'd pretend he'd never been here. Did he ask you to do that as well?

NORA   Yes, Torvald, but—

HELMER   Nora, Nora, you could go along with that? Do business with that sort of person, and make promises to him? And then, on top of it all, tell me a lie!

NORA   A lie?

HELMER   Didn't you tell me no one had been here? (*Wagging his finger.*) My little songbird mustn't ever do a thing like that again. A songbird needs a clean beak to chirp with. No false notes. (*Takes her by the waist.*) Isn't that the way it should be? Yes, of course it is. So lets not talk about it any more. (*Sits by the stove.*) Ah, it's so snug and cozy here.

NORA   (*Working on the tree; after a short pause.*)   Torvald!

HELMER   Yes?

NORA   I'm terribly excited about the Stenborg's party the day after tomorrow.

HELMER   And I'm terribly curious to see what you'll surprise me with.

NORA   Oh, that stupid nonsense!

HELMER   What?

NORA   I can't find anything I like; everything seems so pointless, so idiotic.

HELMER   Is that what little Nora thinks?

NORA   (*Behind his chair, her arms on its back.*)   Are you very busy, Torvald?

HELMER   Well—

NORA   What are those papers?

HELMER   Bank business.

NORA   Already?

HELMER   I've convinced the retiring manager to give me full authority to make changes in personnel and procedure. I'll have to use Christmas week for that. I want everything in order for the New Year.

NORA   So that's why this poor Krogstad—

HELMER   Hm.

NORA   (*Still leaning on the back of his chair, stroking the hair on his neck.*)   If you weren't so busy, I would ask you for a terribly big favor.

HELMER   Let's hear it. What can it be?

NORA   No one has your good taste. I really want to look my best at the costume party. Torvald, couldn't you take over from me and advise me what to wear and how to design my costume?

HELMER   So our little rebel's ready for a cease-fire?

NORA   Yes, Torvald. I can't get anywhere without your help.

HELMER   All right. I'll think about it. We'll come up with something.

NORA   How sweet of you! (*Goes over to the Christmas tree; pause.*) These red flowers are so pretty—But tell me, was what that Krogstad did really such a crime?

HELMER   He forged people's names. Do you know what that means?

NORA   Maybe he did it out of need.

HELMER   Yes, or thoughtlessness, like so many others. And I wouldn't condemn a man categorically because of one isolated incident.

NORA   No, you wouldn't, would you, Torvald?

HELMER   Men can often redeem themselves by openly confessing their guilt and accepting their punishment.

NORA   Punishment?

HELMER   But Krogstad didn't do that. He got himself off the hook with tricks and loopholes. That's what's corrupted him.

NORA   Do you think that would—?

HELMER   Imagine what life is like for a man like that: he has to lie and dissemble and cheat everyone he meets—has to wear a mask in front of his nearest and dearest—yes, even his wife and children. And the children—that's the most terrible part of it.

NORA   Why?

HELMER   Because an atmosphere so filled with lies brings pestilence and disease into every corner of a home. Every breath the children take carries the infection.

NORA   (*Closer behind him.*)   Are you sure about that?

HELMER   Ah, my dear, I'm a lawyer—I've seen it often enough. Almost everyone who turns bad as a youth has had a compulsive liar for a mother.

NORA   Why just—a mother?

HELMER   Usually you can trace it to the mother, but fathers have the same effect; it's something every lawyer knows. And yet this Krogstad has been living at home, poisoning his children with lies and deceit; that's why I call him morally corrupt. And that's why my sweet little Nora must promise me not to plead his case. Your hand on that. Now, now, what's this? Give me your hand. There. That's settled. And let me tell you, it would be impossible for me to work with him; I literally feel sick when I'm around someone like that.

NORA   (*Withdraws her hand and goes over to the other side of the Christmas tree.*) It's so hot in here! And I've got so much to pull together!

HELMER   (*Rising and gathering his papers.*)   Yes, I've got to try to get through some of these before dinner. I'll also give some thought to your costume. And I might also be thinking about something to hang on the tree in gilt paper—. (*Lays his hand on her head.*) Oh, my sweet little songbird. (*He goes into his room and closes the door.*)

NORA   (*Softly, after a silence.*)   No, no! It's not true. It's impossible. It just can't be possible.

ANNE-MARIE   (*In doorway, left.*)   The children are asking if they can come in to Mama.

NORA   No, no, no, don't let them in here with me! You stay with them, Anne-Marie.

ANNE-MARIE   Very well, Ma'am.

NORA   (*Pale with terror.*)   Harm my children—! Poison my home? (*Short pause; she tosses her head.*) It's not true. It could never be true!

Act Two

The same room in the corner by the piano stands the Christmas tree, stripped, bedraggled, with its candle-stumps all burned down. Nora's outdoor clothing lies on the sofa.

(Nora, alone, walks restlessly around the room. Finally she stands by the sofa and picks up her coat.)

NORA (*Dropping the coat again.*)   Somebody's coming! (*Goes to the door, listens.*) No, nobody there. Naturally—nobody's coming on Christmas Day—or tomorrow either. But maybe— (*She opens the door and looks out.*) No, nothing in the mailbox—perfectly empty. (*Comes forward.*) Oh, nonsense! Of course he wasn't serious about it. Nothing like that could happen. After all, I have three small children.

(Anne-Marie, carrying a large carton, comes in from the room on the left.)

ANNE-MARIE   Well, I finally found the box of masquerade costumes.

NORA   Thanks. Put it on the table.

ANNE-MARIE (*Does so.*)   But it's a terrible mess.

NORA   Ah, I wish I could rip them into a million pieces.

ANNE-MARIE   Lord bless us—they can be fixed up again. Just have a little patience.

NORA   Yes, I'll go and get Mrs. Linde to help.

ANNE-MARIE   You're not going out again now? In this horrible weather? Mrs. Nora will catch cold—get sick.

NORA   Worse things could happen. How are the children?

ANNE-MARIE   The poor little things are playing with their Christmas presents, but—

NORA   Are they always asking for me?

ANNE-MARIE   They're so used to having their Mama with them.

NORA   Yes, Anne-Marie, but I can't be with them as much as before.

ANNE-MARIE   Well, little children get used to anything.

NORA   Do you think so? Do you think they'd forget their mama if she were really gone?

ANNE-MARIE   Lord help us—gone?

NORA   Listen—tell me, Anne-Marie—I've wondered about this a lot—how could you ever, in your heart of hearts, stand to give your child away to strangers?

ANNE-MARIE   But I just had to when I became little Nora's wet nurse.

NORA   Yes, but how could you actually do it?

ANNE-MARIE   When I could get such a good place? A poor girl in trouble has to jump at a chance like that. Because that slick good-for-nothing wouldn't do anything for me.

NORA   But your daughter's completely forgotten you.

ANNE-MARIE   Oh no, not really. She wrote to me when she was confirmed, and when she got married.

NORA (*Clasps her around the neck.*)   Dear old Anne-Marie—you were a good mother for me when I was little.

ANNE-MARIE   Poor little Nora, with me as her only mother.

NORA   And if my little ones didn't have a mother, I know that you—stupid, stupid, stupid! (*Opening the carton.*) Go to them. Right now I have to— tomorrow you'll see how beautiful I look.

ANNE-MARIE   Yes, Mrs. Nora will be the most beautiful woman at the party. (*Anne-Marie goes into the room on the left.*)

NORA   (*Begins to unpack the box, but soon throws the whole thing aside.*)   Ah, if I had the nerve to go out. If only nobody would come. If only nothing happened here at home in the meantime. Stupid talk; nobody's coming. Just don't think. I have to brush out this muff. Beautiful gloves, beautiful gloves. Get it out, get it out! One, two, three, four, five, six, (*Screams.*) Oh, here they come. (*Goes toward the door, but stops, irresolute. Mrs. Linde comes in from the hall where she has removed her outdoor clothes.*) So it's you, Kristine. No one else out there? I'm glad you're here.

MRS. LINDE   I heard you were asking for me.

NORA   Yes, I happened to be passing by. I need your help with something. Come sit with me by the sofa. Look at this. There's going to be a costume party tomorrow over at Consul Stenborg's, and Torvald wants me to go as a Neapolitan fisher girl and dance the tarantella—I learned it in Capri.

MRS. LINDE   Well, well—you're giving a real performance?

NORA   Yes, Torvald says I should. Look—here's my costume. Torvald had it made for me down there. But it's all torn now and I just don't know—

MRS. LINDE   We'll get that fixed up in no time; the trimmings are just coming loose here and there, that's all. Needle and thread? There, now we have what we need.

NORA   This is so nice of you.

MRS. LINDE   (*Sewing.*)   So you're going in disguise tomorrow. Nora? You know what? I'll come by for a minute and look at you when you're all dressed up. You know I've completely forgotten to thank you for the lovely evening yesterday.

NORA   (*Gets up and crosses the floor.*)   Oh, I don't think it was as nice yesterday as it usually is. You should have gotten here a little earlier, Kristine. Torvald really knows how to make a home charming and elegant.

MRS. LINDE   So do you, just as much, I'd say. You're not your father's daughter for nothing. Tell me—is Doctor Rank always so depressed?

NORA   No, yesterday he was particularly low. But he's got a very serious illness—tuberculosis of the spine, poor man. You know his father was a disgusting creature who kept mistresses and things like that—that's how poor Doctor Rank got to be so sickly.

MRS. LINDE   (*Dropping her sewing to her lap.*)   Nora, my dear, how do you know about these things?

NORA   (*Walking around.*)   Fuff. When you've had three children you end up meeting some women who know a little about medicine, and they tell you a few things.

MRS. LINDE   (*Sewing again, short silence.*)   Does Doctor Rank come to the house every day?

NORA   Every single day. He's Torvald's best friend ever since they were children, and he's my good friend too. Doctor Rank sort of belongs to the house.

MRS. LINDE   But tell me this—is he honest? I mean, doesn't he like to tell people what they want to hear?

NORA   No, not at all. What makes you think that?

MRS. LINDE   When you introduced us yesterday he said he'd heard my name here so often—but then I noticed that your husband didn't have any idea who I was. So how could Doctor Rank—

NORA   That's right, Kristine. Torvald is so unbelievably devoted to me—he says he wants me all to himself. When we were first married he'd get jealous if I so much as mentioned any of my old friends from back home. So, of course, I stopped. But with Doctor Rank I can talk about all those things, because he enjoys hearing about them.

MRS. LINDE   Listen to me, Nora: in many ways you're still a child. I'm quite a bit older than you and I have a little more experience. Let me tell you something: you should put an end to all this with Doctor Rank.

NORA   What should I put an end to?

MRS. LINDE   All of it, I think. Yesterday you said something about a rich admirer who was going to give you money—

NORA   Yes, but unfortunately he doesn't exist. So what?

MRS. LINDE   Is Doctor Rank rich?

NORA   Yes.

MRS. LINDE   No one to care for?

NORA   No, no one—but—?

MRS. LINDE   And he comes by every day?

NORA   Yes, that's what I told you.

MRS. LINDE   How can such a cultivated man be so obvious?

NORA   I really don't understand you.

MRS. LINDE   Don't play games, Nora. Don't you think I know who lent you the money?

NORA   Are you out of your mind? How can you even think that? A good friend of ours, who comes over here every single day! That would have been horrible!

MRS. LINDE   So it really wasn't him?

NORA   No, I promise you. I would never have thought of that—anyway, he didn't have any money to lend back then—he inherited it all later.

MRS. LINDE   Well, that was just as well for you, I think.

NORA   No, I would never have thought of asking Doctor Rank. Even though I'm sure that if I did—

MRS. LINDE   But of course you wouldn't.

NORA   No, of course not. I can't imagine how it would be necessary. On the other hand, I'm sure that if I even mentioned it to him—

MRS. LINDE   Behind your husband's back?

NORA   I've got to get out of this other thing—that's also behind his back. I've really got to get out of that.

MRS. LINDE   Yes, that's what I said yesterday. But—

NORA   (*Walking up and down.*)   A man can deal with these things so much better than a woman—

MRS. LINDE   Your own husband can, yes.

NORA   Nonsense. (*Stopping.*) When you pay back everything you owe you get your note back.

MRS. LINDE   That's right.

NORA   And you can tear it up in a hundred thousand pieces and burn it—that disgusting piece of paper!

MRS. LINDE (*Looking straight at her, putting the sewing down, rising slowly.*) Nora—you're hiding something from me.

NORA   Can you see that?

MRS. LINDE   Something's happened since yesterday morning. Nora, what is it?

NORA (*Going to her.*)   Kristine! (*Listens.*) Ssh! Torvald's home. Look—go in there with the children for a while. Torvald can't stand to see people sewing. Let Anne-Marie help you.

MRS. LINDE (*Gathering some of her things.*)   Yes, all right, but I'm not leaving before we talk all this through. (*She goes into the room at left; at the same time, Helmer comes in from the hall.*)

NORA (*Goes to meet him.*)   Oh, I've been waiting for you, Torvald my dear.

HELMER   Was that the dressmaker?

NORA   No, it's Kristine; she's helping me with my costume. You know, I think I'm going to outdo myself this time.

HELMER   Yes, that was a pretty good idea I had, wasn't it?

NORA   Brilliant. But wasn't it also nice of me to agree to it?

HELMER (*Taking her under the chin.*)   Nice of you? Agreeing with your husband? All right, you crazy thing, I know you didn't mean it that way. But I don't want to disturb you; I suppose you'll want to try it on.

NORA   Will you be working?

HELMER   Yes. (*Shows her a bundle of papers.*) See. I've been down to the bank— (*He is about to go into his study.*)

NORA   Torvald.

HELMER   Yes.

NORA   If your little squirrel were to beg you ever so nicely for something—?

HELMER   Well?

NORA   Would you do it?

HELMER   First, of course, I'd need to know what it is.

NORA   The squirrel would romp around and do tricks if you'd be sweet and say yes.

HELMER   Come on, what is it?

NORA   The lark would sing high and low in every room—

HELMER   So what, she does that anyway.

NORA   I'd pretend I was a fairy child and dance for you in the moonlight, Torvald.

HELMER   Nora, I hope this isn't that same business from this morning.

NORA (*Coming closer.*)   Yes, Torvald, please, I beg you!

HELMER   You really have the nerve to drag that up again.

NORA   Yes, yes, you've got to do what I say; you've got to let Krogstad keep his job in the bank.

HELMER   But Nora, I'm giving his job to Mrs. Linde.

NORA   That's very sweet of you; but can't you get rid of another clerk, someone besides Krogstad?

HELMER   I can't believe how stubborn you're being! Just because you went ahead and made a foolish promise to speak up for him, now I'm supposed to—

NORA   That's not why, Torvald. It's for your own sake. That man writes articles for some horrible newspapers; you've said so yourself. He can do you an awful lot of harm. I'm scared to death of him—

HELMER Aha—I understand. You're frightened of the old memories.

NORA What do you mean by that?

HELMER You're thinking about your father.

NORA That's right. Remember how those horrible people wrote about Papa in the papers and slandered him so terribly. I believe they'd have gotten him fired if the government hadn't sent you up there to investigate and if you hadn't been so kind and fair to him.

HELMER My little Nora, there is a considerable difference between your father and me. Your father's public life was not exactly beyond reproach—but mine is. And that's how I plan to keep it for as long as I hold my position.

NORA Oh, you can never tell what spiteful people might do. It could be so nice and quiet and happy in our home—so peaceful and carefree—you and me and the children, Torvald—

HELMER And precisely by continuing to plead for him like this you're making it impossible for me to keep him on. It's already known around the bank that I'm letting Krogstad go. What if the rumor got around that the new bank manager was letting himself be overruled by his wife—

NORA Yes, so what?

HELMER Oh, of course—as long as our little rebel here gets her way—I should make myself look silly in front of my whole staff—make people think I can be influenced by all kinds of outside pressures—you can bet that would come back to haunt me soon enough. Besides—there's one thing that makes it impossible to have Krogstad in the bank as long as I'm the manager.

NORA What's that?

HELMER I might be able to overlook his moral failings if I had to—

NORA Yes, Torvald, isn't that right?

HELMER And I hear he's quite good at his job too. But he was a boyhood friend of mine—one of those stupid friendships you get into without thinking, and end up regretting later in life. I might just as well tell you—we're on a first-name basis. And that tactless idiot makes no secret of it in front of people. The opposite, in fact—he thinks it entitles him to take a familiar tone with me, so he's always coming out with "Hey, Torvald—Torvald, can I talk to you, Torvald—" and I can tell you I find it excruciating. He'll make my life at the bank completely intolerable.

NORA Torvald, you can't be serious.

HELMER Oh? Why not?

NORA No, because these are such petty things.

HELMER What are you saying? Petty? Do you think I'm petty?

NORA Not at all, Torvald, and that's just the reason—

HELMER All right; you call me petty, I might as well be just that. Petty! Very well! Now we'll put a stop to all of this. (*Goes to the door and calls.*) Helene!

NORA What are you doing?

HELMER (*Searching through his papers.*) A decision. (*The Maid enters.*) See this letter? Find a messenger right away and have him deliver it. Quickly. The address is on the envelope. There—here's some money.

MAID Yes sir. (*She leaves with the letter.*)

HELMER (*Tidying up his papers.*) So that's that, my little Miss Stubborn.

NORA (*Breathless.*)   Torvald, what was that letter?

HELMER   Krogstad's notice.

NORA   Get it back, Torvald! There's still time. Oh, Torvald, get it back! Do it for my sake—for your own sake—for the children's sake! Listen, Torvald, do it! You don't realize what can happen to all of us.

HELMER   Too late.

NORA   Yes, too late.

HELMER   Nora, I forgive you for being nervous about this, even though you're really insulting me. Yes, you are. Isn't it insulting to think that *I* would be afraid of what some hack journalist might do for revenge? But I forgive you, all the same, because it shows so beautifully how much you love me. That's how it should be, my own darling Nora. Come what may! When things get tough, I've got the courage—and the strength, you can believe it. I'm the kind of man who can take it all on himself.

NORA (*Terrified.*)   What do you mean by that?

HELMER   The whole thing, like I said.

NORA (*Resolutely.*)   You'll never have to do that, never.

HELMER   Good—so we'll share it, Nora, as man and wife. That's the way it should be. (*Fondling her.*)   Happy now? Well, well, well—enough of those frightened dove's eyes. It's nothing but empty fantasy. Now you should run through your tarantella and try the tambourine. I won't hear a thing in the office, so you can make all the noise you want. (*Turning in the doorway.*) And when Rank comes, tell him where he can find me. (*He nods to her, goes to his study with his papers, and closes the door behind him.*)

NORA (*Distracted with fear, standing as though glued to the spot, whispering.*) He's really going to do it. He will do it. He'll do it in spite of everything—No, never, never in this world! Anything but that—escape! A way out—(*The bell rings in the hall.*) Doctor Rank! Anything but that! Whatever else happens! (*She brushes her hands over her face, pulls herself together and goes to open the door in the hall. Doctor Rank is standing outside hanging up his fur coat. During the following, it begins to grow dark.*)

NORA   Doctor Rank, I recognized your ring. But you can't see Torvald quite yet; I think he's busy.

RANK   And you?

NORA (*While he comes into the room and she closes the door after him.*)   Oh, as you know perfectly well, I always have an hour to spare for you.

RANK   Thanks. I shall make use of it as long as I can.

NORA   What do you mean? As long as you can?

RANK   Yes, does that worry you?

NORA   Well, it's such a strange way to talk. Is anything going to happen?

RANK   Something that I've been expecting for a long time. But I didn't think it would come so soon.

NORA (*Gripping his arm.*)   What have you found out? Doctor Rank, you have to tell me!

RANK (*Sitting by the stove.*)   It's all over. There's no point in lying to myself.

NORA (*Breathing easier.*)   Is it you—?

RANK   Who else? I'm the worst of all my patients, Mrs. Helmer. Over the last few days I've done a general audit of my internal account. Bankrupt. Within a month I'll probably be rotting in the churchyard.

NORA   Oh, really. What a horrible thing to say.

RANK   It *is* a horrible thing. But the worst of it all is the horror beforehand. There's one more examination to go; when I've done that I'll know when the disintegration will begin. There is something I want to ask you. Helmer is so sensitive; he can't stand to be around anything ugly. I won't let him come to my sickroom.

NORA   Oh, but Doctor Rank—

RANK   I won't allow him in there. Under any circumstances. I'll lock the door to him. As soon as I'm absolutely certain of the worst, I'll send you my card with a black cross on it; then you'll know that it's begun.

NORA   No, you are completely unreasonable today. And I especially wanted you to be in a really good mood.

RANK   When I hold death in my hands? And to suffer like this for someone else's guilt? Is there any justice in that? In every family—every single one—somehow this inexorable retribution is taking its course.

NORA   (*Stopping her ears.*)   La la la la la! Cheer up! Cheer up!

RANK   Yes, finally even I can only laugh at the whole thing. My poor, innocent back has to pay for my father's career as a lascivious lieutenant.

NORA   (*By the table to the left.*)   Was he that addicted to asparagus and *pâté de foie gras*?

RANK   Yes, and truffles.

NORA   Truffles, yes. And also oysters, I believe.

RANK   Yes, oysters, oysters, of course.

NORA   And port and champagne too. It's so sad that all these delicious things have to go and attack our bones.

RANK   Especially when they attack the unfortunate bones that never got the slightest pleasure from them.

NORA   Ah, yes—that's the greatest sadness of all.

RANK   (*Looks searchingly at her.*)   Hmm—

NORA   (*Shortly after.*)   Why did you smile?

RANK   No, no—you laughed.

NORA   No, you smiled, Doctor Rank!

RANK   (*Getting up.*)   You're an even bigger flirt than I thought!

NORA   I'm full of crazy ideas today.

RANK   So it seems.

NORA   (*With both hands on his shoulders.*)   Dear, dear Doctor Rank: for Torvald and me, you simply will not die.

RANK   Oh, you'll soon get over that loss. Those who go away are soon forgotten.

NORA   (*Looking anxiously at him.*)   Do you think so?

RANK   You make new relationships, and then—

NORA   Who makes new relationships?

RANK   Both you and Helmer will, after I'm gone. You're well on your way already, I'd say. What was that Mrs. Linde doing here last night?

NORA   Come on now—you're not telling me you're jealous of poor Kristine?

RANK   Yes I am. She'll be my successor here in this house. When my time is up, I'll bet that woman will—

NORA   Ssh—don't talk so loud—she's in there.

RANK   Again today! There, you see?

NORA   She's just fixing my costume. Good Lord, you're unreasonable today. (*Sits on the sofa.*)   Now be nice, Doctor Rank. Tomorrow you'll see how beautifully I'll dance—and you can imagine I'm doing it just for you—yes, for Torvald too, of course. (*Takes various things out of a carton.*) Doctor Rank, sit here. I want to show you something.

RANK (*Sitting.*)   What is it?

NORA   Look here. Look!

RANK   Silk stockings.

NORA   Flesh-colored. Lovely, aren't they? It's so dark in here now, but in the morning—no, no, no, only the feet. Oh, well, you might as well go ahead and look higher up.

RANK   Hmm.

NORA   What's this critical stare? Don't you think they'll fit?

RANK   I couldn't possibly have an accurate opinion on that.

NORA (*Glancing at him for a moment.*)   Shame on you. (*Hits him lightly on the ear with the stockings.*) That's what you get. (*Puts them away again.*)

RANK   And what other splendors do I get to see?

NORA   Not a thing—you're being bad. (*She hums a little and rummages through her things.*)

RANK (*After a short pause.*)   When I'm sitting here like this, so close to you, I can't imagine—I can't begin to comprehend—what would have become of me if I had never found my way to this house.

NORA (*Smiling.*)   Yes, I believe you really enjoy being here with us.

RANK (*Quietly, looking ahead.*)   And to have to leave it all behind—

NORA   Nonsense, you're not leaving us behind.

RANK (*As before.*)   And to think that nothing remains after you're gone—no little gesture of gratitude—hardly even a passing regret—just a vacant place that the first person who comes along can fill.

NORA   And what if I were to ask you now for—? No—

RANK   For what?

NORA   For a great proof of your friendship.

RANK   Yes, yes?

NORA   I mean a tremendously big favor—

RANK   Would you really let me be so happy, just this once?

NORA   You have no idea what it is.

RANK   All right—so tell me.

NORA   No, Doctor Rank, I can't. It's too big, too unreasonable. It's advice, and help, and a great service too.

RANK   So much the better. I can't imagine what you mean. But keep talking. Don't you have confidence in me?

NORA   Yes, in you before anyone else. You're my best and truest friend, you know that. That's why I can tell you. All right, Doctor Rank: there's something you've got to help me prevent. You know how intensely, how indescribably deeply Torvald loves me—he'd give his life for my sake without a moment's thought.

RANK (*Bending toward her.*)   Nora—do you think he's the only one?

NORA (*With a slight start.*)   Who—?

RANK   Who would gladly give his life for you?

NORA (*Heavily.*)   I see.

RANK   I promised myself that you'd know before the end. I'll never find a better chance than this. Yes, Nora, now you know. And you also know that you can trust me like nobody else.

NORA (*Rises and speaks, evenly and calmly.*)   Let me through.

RANK (*Makes way for her, but remains seated.*)   Nora—

NORA (*In the hall doorway.*)   Helene, bring in the lamp. (*She goes over to the stove.*)   Ah, dear Doctor Rank, that was really awful of you.

RANK (*Rising.*)   That I've loved you just as much as anyone? Was *that* awful?

NORA   No, but that you felt you had to tell me. That was just not necessary.

RANK   What do you mean? You mean that you knew—?
(*The Maid enters with the lamp, sets it on the table, and goes out again.*)

RANK   Nora—Mrs. Helmer—I'm asking you. Did you know?

NORA   Oh, how do I know what I knew or didn't know? I can't say. How could you be so clumsy, Doctor Rank! When everything was so nice.

RANK   Well, in any case now you know that I'm at your service with body and soul. So please go on.

NORA (*Looking at him.*)   After this?

RANK   Please, please tell me what it is.

NORA   Now I can't tell you anything.

RANK   Yes, yes. Don't torment me like this. Let me do whatever is humanly possible for you.

NORA   You can't do anything for me now. In fact, I really don't need any help. You'll see—it was just my imagination. It really is. Of course! (*Sits in the rocking chair, looks at him, smiling.*)   Well, you are a piece of work, Doctor Rank. Don't you think you should be a little ashamed, now that the lamp is here?

RANK   No, not really. But maybe I'd better go—for good?

NORA   No, you certainly will not do that. Of course you'll keep coming here just like before. You know perfectly well that Torvald can't do without you.

RANK   Yes, but what about you?

NORA   Oh, I always enjoy your visits very much.

RANK   That's exactly what set me off on the wrong track. You're an enigma to me. I've often felt you'd almost rather be with me than with Helmer.

NORA   Well, you see, there are the people you love the most, and the people you'd almost rather be with.

RANK   Ah yes, you're on to something there.

NORA   When I was at home, of course I loved Papa the most. But I always had the most fun sneaking into the maids' rooms, because they never tried to teach me anything and they always had so much fun talking to each other.

RANK   Ah—so *they're* the ones that I've replaced.

NORA (*Jumping up and going to him.*)   Oh, dear Doctor Rank, I didn't mean that at all. But you can see that with Torvald it's a lot like it was with Papa—
(*The Maid enters from the hall.*)

MAID   Ma'am. (*Whispers and hands Nora a card.*)

NORA (*Glancing at the card.*) Ah! (*Puts it in her pocket.*)

RANK Something wrong?

NORA No, no, not at all. It's just—it's about my new costume.

RANK How could that be? Your costume's in there.

NORA Oh, yes—that one. But this is a different one, I ordered it—Torvald can't find out—

RANK Aha—there's our great secret.

NORA That's right. Go on in to him. He's working in the inner room. Keep him there as long as—

RANK Don't worry—he won't get by me. (*He goes into Helmer's study.*)

NORA (*To the Maid.*) And he's waiting in the kitchen?

MAID Yes, he came up the back stairs.

NORA Did you tell him somebody was here?

MAID I did, but that didn't help.

NORA He won't go away?

MAID No, he won't leave until he's talked to you.

NORA Let him come in then; but quietly. Helene, not a word of this to anyone; it's a surprise for my husband.

MAID Oh, yes, I understand. (*She goes out.*)

NORA This terrible thing is really happening. It's coming no matter what. No, no, no. It can't happen. It must not happen.

(*She goes and bolts Helmer's door. The Maid opens the hall door for Krogstad and closes it after him. He's dressed in traveling clothes, a fur coat, overshoes, and a fur cap.*)

NORA (*Goes toward him.*) Talk quietly—my husband's home.

KROGSTAD I don't care.

NORA What do you want from me?

KROGSTAD Some answers.

NORA Quick, then. What?

KROGSTAD You know, of course, I got my notice.

NORA I couldn't stop it, Mr. Krogstad. I fought for you as hard as I could, but it was no use.

KROGSTAD Does your husband really love you so little? He knows what I can do to you, and he still dares—

NORA How can you imagine he knows about it?

KROGSTAD No, I didn't think he did. It's not like my fine Torvald Helmer to show that kind of strength.

NORA Mr. Krogstad, I demand respect for my husband.

KROGSTAD Good Lord, of course, all due respect. But since the lady has kept all this so carefully hidden, might I ask if you've also come to understand a little better than yesterday what you've actually done?

NORA Better than you could ever teach me.

KROGSTAD Yes, I'm such a terrible lawyer—

NORA What do you want with me?

KROGSTAD Just to see how things are with you, Mrs. Helmer. I couldn't stop thinking about you all day. A cashier, a hack journalist, a—well, a man like me also has a little of what is commonly called heart, you know.

NORA Then show it. Think of my little children.

KROGSTAD   Have you or your husband given any thought to mine? But that's not the issue right now. I just wanted to tell you that you don't need to take this business too seriously. For the time being I'm not taking any action.

NORA   Oh, that's true, I was sure of it.

KROGSTAD   The whole thing can be settled amicably. No one else needs to know about it, just the three of us.

NORA   My husband can never find out.

KROGSTAD   How can you stop that? Can you pay off the balance?

NORA   No, not right now.

KROGSTAD   Maybe you can find a way to raise the money in a few days?

NORA   No way that I'd use.

KROGSTAD   Well, it wouldn't do you any good anyway. Even if you were standing there with a pile of cash in your hands you still wouldn't get your note back.

NORA   Tell me what you're going to do with it.

KROGSTAD   Just keep it—just hold it in my custody. No one else needs to know anything about it. So if you happen to be thinking of some desperate remedy—

NORA   Which I am.

KROGSTAD   If you're thinking of running away from home—

NORA   Which I am.

KROGSTAD   Or something worse—

NORA   How did you know?

KROGSTAD   Then give it up right now.

NORA   How could you know I was thinking of *that*?

KROGSTAD   Most of us think of *that* to begin with. I thought about it too— but I didn't have the courage.

NORA (*Lifelessly.*)   I don't either.

KROGSTAD (*Relieved.*)   That's true?

NORA   I don't have it; I don't have it.

KROGSTAD   It'd be pretty silly anyway. As soon as the first big storm blows over—I have here in my pocket a letter to your husband—

NORA   Which tells everything?

KROGSTAD   As nicely as possible.

NORA (*Quickly.*)   He must never get that letter. Tear it up. I'll get the money somehow.

KROGSTAD   Excuse me, Mrs. Helmer, but I think I just told you—

NORA   I'm not talking about what I owe you. Just let me know how much you demand from my husband and I'll get you the money.

KROGSTAD   I'm not demanding any money from your husband.

NORA   So what then?

KROGSTAD   I'll tell you. I want to get back on my feet, Mrs. Helmer; I want to move up. And your husband is going to help me. For the last year and a half I haven't gone near anything disreputable—all the time fighting to make ends meet—but I was happy to work my way up, step by step. Now I'm being driven out again and I'm not in a very forgiving mood, I'm ready to climb, I tell you. I'll get back in the bank, and in a higher position than before. Your husband will set me up.

NORA He'll never do that!

KROGSTAD He'll do it. I know him; he won't even dare to argue. And once I'm in there with him, you'll see how it goes. In a year I'll be the manager's right-hand man. Nils Krogstad will be running that bank, not Torvald Helmer.

NORA You'll never live to see that.

KROGSTAD You think you might—

NORA Now I have the courage.

KROGSTAD Forget it—a pampered, spoiled woman like you?

NORA You'll see—you'll see.

KROGSTAD Under the ice, maybe? Down in the freezing black water? Floating up in the spring, ugly, unrecognizable, your hair falling out—

NORA You don't frighten me.

KROGSTAD You don't frighten me either. People don't do such things, Mrs. Helmer. Besides, what would be the point? I'd have him in my pocket just the same.

NORA After—? Even when I'm no longer—?

KROGSTAD Are you forgetting? In that case I'll be in charge of your reputation. (*Nora stares speechless at him.*) Well, I've warned you. Don't do anything stupid. When Helmer gets my letter, I'll wait for a word from him. Just keep in mind that it's your husband who has forced me back onto these old roads of mine. I'll never forgive him for that. Goodbye, Mrs. Helmer. (*He goes out through the hallway.*)

NORA (*Goes to the hall door, opens it a fraction, and listens.*) Gone. He didn't leave the letter. No, no, no, that would be impossible! (*Opening the door farther.*) What? He's waiting outside. Not going downstairs. Changing his mind? Maybe he'll—?

(*A letter drops into the mailbox; then Krogstad's footsteps are heard receding as he walks downstairs. Nora, with a stifled cry, runs across the room to the sofa table; short pause.*)

NORA In the mailbox. (*Creeps cautiously to the hall door.*) Lying there. Torvald, Torvald—no saving us now!

(*Mrs. Linde enters with the costume from the room at the left.*)

MRS. LINDE Well, I think that's it for the repairs. Should we try it—

NORA (*In a low, hoarse voice.*) Kristine, come here.

MRS. LINDE (*Throws the dress onto the sofa.*) What's the matter—you're upset!

NORA Come here. See that letter? There—see it, through the window in the mailbox?

MRS. LINDE Yes, I see it.

NORA It's from Krogstad.

MRS. LINDE Nora—Krogstad's the one who lent you the money!

NORA Yes. And now Torvald will know everything.

MRS. LINDE Believe me, Nora, that's best for both of you.

NORA There's more to it. I forged a signature.

MRS. LINDE Oh for heaven's sake—

NORA I'm just telling you this, Kristine, so that you can be my witness.

MRS. LINDE What do you mean, witness? How can I—?

NORA   If I were to lose my mind—that could easily happen—

MRS. LINDE   Nora!

NORA   Or if anything else happened to me, if I couldn't be here—

MRS. LINDE   Nora, you're beside yourself!

NORA   And if someone wanted to try to take the whole thing onto himself, all the blame, you see—

MRS. LINDE   Yes, but how can you think—

NORA   You've got to swear it isn't true, Kristine. I'm in my perfect mind; I understand exactly what I'm saying; and I'm telling you: no one else knew about it. I did it all alone. Remember that.

MRS. LINDE   I will. But I don't understand any of it.

NORA   How could you understand? A wonderful thing is about to happen.

MRS. LINDE   Wonderful?

NORA   Yes, a wonderful thing. But also terrible, Kristine, and it just can't happen, not for all the world.

MRS. LINDE   I'm going to talk to Krogstad right away.

NORA   Don't: he'll only hurt you some way.

MRS. LINDE   Once upon a time he'd have gladly done anything for me.

NORA   Him?

MRS. LINDE   Where does he live?

NORA   How should I know? Wait—(*Searches her pocket.*)   Here's his card. But what about the letter, the letter—?

HELMER (*In his study, knocking on the door.*)   Nora!

NORA (*Screams in panic.*)   What is it? What do you want?

HELMER   Now, don't be frightened. We're not coming in. The door's locked; are you trying on your costume?

NORA   Yes, I'm trying it on. I'm going to be so beautiful, Torvald.

MRS. LINDE (*Having read the card.*)   He lives right around the corner.

NORA   Yes, but that's no help. We're lost. The letter's in the box.

MRS. LINDE   Your husband has the key?

NORA   Always.

MRS. LINDE   Krogstad will have to ask for his letter back unopened—he'll have to find some excuse—

NORA   But this is the time when Torvald usually—

MRS. LINDE   Stall him. Go in there and stay with him. I'll get back as fast as I can. (*She goes out hurriedly through the hall door. Nora goes to Helmer's door and opens it, looking in.*)

NORA   Torvald!

HELMER   Well—can I finally come back into my own living room? Come on, Rank, now we'll get to see—(*In the doorway.*) But—?

NORA   What, Torvald my dear?

HELMER   Rank had me all set for a great dress parade.

RANK (*In the doorway.*)   That's what I was expecting, but I guess I was wrong.

NORA   No one gets to bask in my full glory until tomorrow.

HELMER   But Nora, you look so tired. Have you been practicing too hard?

NORA   No, I haven't practiced at all yet.

HELMER   You know it's essential—

NORA   Absolutely essential. But I can't possibly do it without your help; I've forgotten everything.

HELMER   We'll get it back quick enough.

NORA   Yes, take care of me right to the end, Torvald. Do you promise? Ah, I'm so nervous. That big party—you have to give up everything for me tonight. Not one bit of business, don't even go near your work. All right, Torvald. Promise?

HELMER   I promise. Tonight I'll be completely at your service—you helpless little thing. Hmm—just one item to take care of first—(*Goes toward the hall door.*)

NORA   What do you want out there?

HELMER   Just seeing if there's any mail.

NORA   No, no, Torvald, don't do that!

HELMER   What now?

NORA   Torvald, please, there's nothing there.

HELMER   Just let me have a look. (*About to go; Nora, at the piano, plays the opening notes of the tarantella. Helmer stops at the door.*)

NORA   I can't dance tomorrow if I don't rehearse with you.

HELMER (*Going to her.*)   Nora, are you really so frightened of it?

NORA   Tremendously frightened. Let's rehearse right now; there's still time before dinner. Oh, Torvald, sit down and play for me. Show me how it goes; direct me, like you always do.

HELMER   I'd be glad to, if you want.
(*Nora snatches the tambourine out of the box, and also a long, multicolored shawl which she drapes ground herself; then she springs forward and calls out.*)

NORA   Play for me! Now I'll dance!
(*Helmer plays and Nora dances; Doctor Rank stands behind Helmer and watches.*)

HELMER (*Playing.*)   Slower, slower—

NORA   I can't help it.

HELMER   Not so violent, Nora!

NORA   That's how it has to be.

HELMER (*Stopping.*)   No, no—that's not it at all.

NORA (*Laughing, swinging the tambourine.*)   What did I tell you?

RANK   Let me play for her.

HELMER (*Getting up.*)   Yes, good idea. That way I can be a better teacher.

(*Rank sits at the piano and plays. Nora dances with increasing wildness. Helmer has placed himself by the stove, continually directing dancing instructions to her; she seems not to hear him; her hair loosens and falls over her shoulders; she doesn't notice, but keeps on dancing. Mrs. Linde enters.*)

MRS. LINDE (*As though spellbound in the doorway.*)   Ah—!

NORA (*Still dancing.*)   See, Kristine, what fun!

HELMER   But Nora, you're dancing as if your life were at stake.

NORA   It is, it is!

HELMER   Rank, stop. This is absolute madness. Stop it!
(*Rank stops playing and Nora suddenly comes to a halt.*)

HELMER (*Goes to her.*)   I would never have believed this—you've forgotten everything I taught you.

NORA (*Throwing down the tambourine.*)   As you can see.

HELMER   Some extra work's in order here.

NORA   Yes, you see how important it is. You've got to keep teaching me right up to the last minute. Promise, Torvald?

HELMER   Depend on it.

NORA   You can't even think—today or tomorrow—about anything but me— don't open any letters, don't even touch the mailbox—

HELMER   Ah—you're still afraid of that man.

NORA   Yes, yes, that too.

HELMER   Nora, I can see it in your face, there's a letter from him out there.

NORA   I don't know. I think there is. But you can't read things like that now; there can't be anything horrible between us till all this is over.

RANK (*Softly to Helmer.*)   You shouldn't go against her.

HELMER   The child will have its way. But tomorrow night—after you've danced—

NORA   Then you're free.

MAID (*In the doorway, right.*)   Ma'am, dinner's on the table.

NORA   We'll have champagne, Helene.

MAID   Very good, ma'am. (*Goes out.*)

HELMER   Hey, hey—a whole banquet?

NORA   Yes—a champagne supper right through till dawn! (*Calling out.*)   And some macaroons, Helene—lots of them—just this once.

HELMER (*Taking her hands.*)   There, there, there—not so wild, not so scared—be my little skylark again.

NORA   Oh, yes, I certainly will. But go to dinner—you too, Doctor Rank. Kristine, I need you to help me with my hair.

RANK (*Softly as they go.*)   There wouldn't be anything—anything on the way?

HELMER   No, my friend, not a thing; nothing more than these silly fears I've been telling you about. (*They go out, right.*)

NORA   Well?

MRS. LINDE   Gone to the country.

NORA   I saw it in your face.

MRS. LINDE   He gets back tomorrow night. I left him a note.

NORA   You shouldn't have done that. You can't stop it now. Behind it all there's this great joy—waiting for a wonderful thing to happen.

MRS. LINDE   What are you waiting for?

NORA   You can't understand that. Go in with them—I'll be there in a minute.

(*Mrs. Linde goes into the dining room, Nora stands for a moment as if to compose herself; then she looks at her watch.*)

NORA   Five. Seven hours to midnight. Then twenty-four hours to the next midnight. Then the tarantella will be done. Twenty-four plus seven— thirty-one hours to live.

HELMER (*In the doorway, right.*)   What happened to the skylark?

NORA (*Going to him with open arms.*)   Here's your skylark!

Act Three

Same room. The sofa-table, with chairs around it, has been moved to the middle of the room. A lamp is burning on the table. The door to the hall stands open. Dance music can be heard from the apartment above.

(Mrs. Linde is sitting by the table, desultorily turning the pages of the book; she attempts to read but seems unable to fix her attention. Once or twice she listens, tensely, for a sound at the door.)

MRS. LINDE   Not here yet. And it's now or never. If he'd only—(*Listens again.*) Ah—there he is. (*She goes out into the hall and cautiously opens the outer door; quiet footsteps are heard on the stairs. She whispers.*) Come in. Nobody's here.

KROGSTAD (*In the doorway.*)   I found a note from you at home. What does it mean?

MRS. LINDE   I had to talk to you.

KROGSTAD   Oh yes? And it had to be here, in this house?

MRS. LINDE   My place is impossible—there's no private entrance to my room. Come in; we're all alone. The maid's asleep and the Helmers are at a party upstairs.

KROGSTAD (*Comes into the room.*)   Well, well, well—so the Helmers are dancing tonight. How about that?

MRS. LINDE   Why shouldn't they?

KROGSTAD   True enough—why shouldn't they.

MRS. LINDE   Well, Krogstad, let's talk.

KROGSTAD   Do the two of us have anything more to talk about?

MRS. LINDE   We have a lot to talk about.

KROGSTAD   I wouldn't have thought so.

MRS. LINDE   No, because you've never really understood me.

KROGSTAD   What was there to understand, more than the usual thing? A heartless woman sends a man packing as soon as she gets a better offer.

MRS. LINDE   Do you think I'm that heartless? Do you think it was easy for me to break up with you?

KROGSTAD   Wasn't it?

MRS. LINDE   Krogstad, did you really think that?

KROGSTAD   Then how could you have written to me that way?

MRS. LINDE   I couldn't do anything else. If I had to make the break, it was my duty to try to stamp out whatever feelings you had for me.

KROGSTAD (*Clenching his hands.*)   So that was it! And this—all this for money's sake!

MRS. LINDE   Don't forget that I had a helpless mother and two little brothers. We couldn't wait for you, Krogstad; your prospects were so cloudy then.

KROGSTAD   Maybe. But you had no right to abandon me for somebody else's sake.

MRS. LINDE   Yes—I don't know. I've asked myself over and over if I had any right to do that.

KROGSTAD (*More quietly.*)   When I lost you I felt the ground dissolve under my feet. Look at me: I'm a man adrift on a wreck.

MRS. LINDE   Help could be close by.

KROGSTAD   It was—until you appeared and blocked the way.

MRS. LINDE   I didn't know, Krogstad. I only learned today that I'm replacing you at the bank.

KROGSTAD   Since you say so, I believe it. But now you know—so won't you pull out?

MRS. LINDE   No, because that wouldn't do you the least bit of good.

KROGSTAD   Oh, who cares? I'd do it anyway.

MRS. LINDE   I've learned to act rationally. Life and bitter necessity have taught me that.

KROGSTAD   And life has taught me not to believe in empty phrases.

MRS. LINDE   Then life has taught you a very rational lesson. But you do believe in deeds, don't you?

KROGSTAD   What do you mean?

MRS. LINDE   You said that you were like a man adrift, standing on a wreck.

KROGSTAD   I said that with good reason.

MRS. LINDE   Well I'm a woman adrift; I'm hanging on to a wreck as well.

KROGSTAD   That was your choice.

MRS. LINDE   There was no other choice at the time.

KROGSTAD   So?

MRS. LINDE   Krogstad, what if these two shipwrecks could reach across to one another?

KROGSTAD   What are you saying?

MRS. LINDE   Two on one raft stand a better chance than each one alone.

KROGSTAD   Kristine!

MRS. LINDE   Why do you suppose I came to town?

KROGSTAD   Were you really thinking about me?

MRS. LINDE   For me to go on living, I need to work. All my life, as long as I can remember, I've worked—it's given me my only real joy. But now I'm completely alone in the world, completely empty and desolate. Working for yourself—well, there's no joy in that. Krogstad: give me someone and something to work for.

KROGSTAD   I don't believe all this. This is just some hysterical feminine urge for self-sacrifice.

MRS. LINDE   Have you ever known me to be hysterical?

KROGSTAD   Can you really mean all this? Do you know about my past—the whole story?

MRS. LINDE   Yes.

KROGSTAD   And you know what people think of me here?

MRS. LINDE   You hinted just now that you thought you could have been a different person with me.

KROGSTAD   I know that for sure.

MRS. LINDE   Couldn't it still happen?

KROGSTAD   Kristine—you're serious about this? Yes, you are. I can see it in you. Do you have the courage as well?

MRS. LINDE   I need someone to be a mother to, and your children need a mother. The two of us need each other. Krogstad, I have faith in you, in what's there deep down in your heart. I could risk anything together with you.

KROGSTAD   (*Seizing her hands.*)   Thank you, Kristine, thank you—now I know I can bring myself up in people's eyes—ah, I forgot—

MRS. LINDE (*Listening.*)   The tarantella! Go, go, go!

KROGSTAD   What's going on?

MRS. LINDE   Do you hear the music up there? When it's over, they'll be down.

KROGSTAD   All right, I'll go. It's all pointless. Of course you don't know what I've done with the Helmers.

MRS. LINDE   Yes, Krogstad, I know all about it.

KROGSTAD   And you still have the courage to—

MRS. LINDE   I know very well how far despair can drive a man like you.

KROGSTAD   If I could only undo what I've done!

MRS. LINDE   That's easy. Your letter's still in the mailbox.

KROGSTAD   Are you sure?

MRS. LINDE   Absolutely. But—

KROGSTAD (*Looks searchingly at her.*)   Is that what this is all about? Would you save your friend at any price? Tell me honestly, tell me straight—is that it?

MRS. LINDE   Krogstad: when you've sold yourself *once* for someone else's sake, you don't do it a second time.

KROGSTAD   I'll demand my letter back.

MRS. LINDE   No, no.

KROGSTAD   Yes, of course I will. I'll stay here until Helmer comes down; I'll tell him to give me back my letter—that it's only about my dismissal—that he shouldn't read it.

MRS. LINDE   No, Krogstad. Don't take back your letter.

KROGSTAD   But wasn't that exactly why you got me over here?

MRS. LINDE   Yes, in the first panic. But in the twenty-four hours between then and now, I've seen some incredible things in this house. Helmer has to learn everything; this awful secret has to come to light; those two have to come to a clear understanding—they can't go on with all this hiding, all these lies.

KROGSTAD   Well, if you're willing to take the risk—. But there's one thing I can do right away.

MRS. LINDE (*Listening.*)   Hurry! Go, go! The dance is over. We're not safe another second!

KROGSTAD   I'll wait for you downstairs.

MRS. LINDE   Yes, do that. You'll have to see me home.

KROGSTAD   This incredible happiness—I've never felt anything like it!
(*He goes out by the front door; the door between the living room and the hall stays open.*)

MRS. LINDE (*Tidies the room a little and gets her outer garments ready.*)   What a change! What a change! People to work for, to live for—a home to make. That's something worth doing. If only they'd come soon. (*Listens.*) Ah—there they are. Get dressed.

(*Helmer's and Nora's voices are heard outside; a key is turned and Helmer leads Nora almost forcibly into the hall. She is wearing the Italian costume with a large black shawl over it; he is in evening dress with an open black domino over it.*)

NORA (*Still in the doorway, resisting.*)   No, no, no, not in there! I'm going up again. I don't want to leave so early!

HELMER   But Nora, my dearest—

NORA   Oh, I beg you, I implore you, from the bottom of my heart Torvald—just one more hour!

HELMER   Not another minute, Nora, my sweet. You know we had an agreement. Come on now, into the drawing room; you're catching cold out here. (*He leads her gently into the drawing room against her resistance.*)

MRS. LINDE   Good evening.

NORA   Kristine!

HELMER   Well, Mrs. Linde—here so late?

MRS. LINDE   Yes, forgive me. I really wanted to see Nora in her costume.

NORA   So you've been sitting here waiting for me?

MRS. LINDE   Yes, I didn't get here in time—you'd all gone upstairs. And I just thought I couldn't leave without seeing you.

HELMER (*Taking off Nora's shawl.*)   Well, get a good look at her. I think she's worth looking at. Isn't she lovely, Mrs. Linde?

MRS. LINDE   Yes, I have to say—

HELMER   Isn't she incredibly lovely? That was the general consensus at the party, too—but also incredibly stubborn, the sweet thing. What to do about that? Would you believe it, I almost had to use force to get her down here.

NORA   Ah, Torvald, you're going to regret that you didn't let me have my way just a half-hour more.

HELMER   Hear that, Mrs. Linde? She danced her tarantella to thunderous applause—well-deserved applause, too—even though there was something a little too naturalistic about the whole thing—I mean, something that went beyond the strict requirements of art. But so what? The main thing is, she was a success—a tremendous success. Should I let her stay around after that? Spoil the effect? No, thank you! I took my lovely Capri girl—my capricious little Capri girl, I could say—on my arm; made a quick trip around the ballroom—a curtsy to all sides—and as they say in novels, the lovely apparition vanished. Exits are tremendously important, Mrs. Linde—they should always be effective; but that's what I can't get Nora to see. Uch, it's hot in here. (*Throws his domino on a chair and opens the door to his room.*) What? it's dark—oh, yes, of course—excuse me—(*Goes in and lights candles.*)

NORA (*Whispering quickly and breathlessly.*)   Well?

MRS. LINDE (*Quietly.*)   I talked to him.

NORA   And—?

MRS. LINDE   Nora, you have to tell your husband everything.

NORA (*Dully.*)   I knew it.

MRS. LINDE   You've got nothing to worry about from Krogstad—but you have to speak out.

NORA   I won't do it.

MRS. LINDE   Then the letter will.

NORA   Thank you, Kristine. Now I know what I have to do. Sssh!—

HELMER (*Coming in again.*)   Now, Mrs. Linde—have you had a chance to admire her?

MRS. LINDE   Yes, and now I'll say good night.

HELMER   So soon? Is this yours, this knitting?

MRS. LINDE (*Taking it.*)   Oh yes.

HELMER   So you also knit.

MRS. LINDE Yes.

HELMER Know what? You should embroider instead.

MRS. LINDE Really? Why?

HELMER Much prettier. Want to see? You hold the embroidery like this with your left hand, and guide the needle with your right—like this—lightly, in and out, in a sweeping curve—right?

MRS. LINDE I suppose so—

HELMER Now knitting, on the other hand—so ugly to watch—see here, the arms jammed together, the needles going up and down—there's something Chinese about it. Ah—that was a tremendous champagne up there.

MRS. LINDE Well, Nora, good night! And no more stubbornness!

HELMER Well said, Mrs. Linde!

MRS. LINDE Good night, Mr. Helmer.

HELMER (*Following her to the door.*) Good night, good night. I hope you're all right getting home. I would, of course—but you don't have far to go. Good night, good night. (*She leaves; he closes the door after her and comes in again.*) Well, well. We finally got her out the door. What an incredible bore that woman is.

NORA Aren't you tired, Torvald?

HELMER No, not a bit.

NORA Not sleepy at all?

HELMER Absolutely not—in fact, I'm exhilarated! You, on the other hand, are looking very tired and sleepy.

NORA Yes, I'm tired. I'll go to sleep soon.

HELMER See, see! I was right! It was time to go home.

NORA Oh, everything you do is right.

HELMER (*Kisses her on the brow.*) Now my little lark is talking like a real person. Say—did you notice how lively Rank was tonight?

NORA Was he? I didn't get to talk to him.

HELMER I barely did myself, but I haven't seen him in such a good mood in a long time. (*Looks at Nora a while, then comes closer to her.*) Hmm—my God, it's glorious to be back in our own home again, completely alone with you—you enchanting young woman!

NORA Don't look at me like that, Torvald!

HELMER Shouldn't I look at my most precious possession? All this magnificence, and it's mine, mine alone, completely and utterly mine!

NORA You shouldn't talk this way to me tonight.

HELMER (*Following her.*) The tarantella's still in your blood. I understand. And that makes me want you even more. Listen! Now the guests are beginning to leave. (*More softly.*) Nora—soon the whole house will be silent.

NORA I hope so.

HELMER Yes, my own darling Nora, that's right. Ah—do you know why, whenever I'm out at a party with you—do you know why I barely speak to you, why I keep my distance, hardly even shoot you a stolen glance? Do you know why I do that? Because I'm imagining you're my secret lover, my young, secret sweetheart, and that no one in the room guesses there's anything going on between us.

NORA Oh yes, yes, yes—I know you're always thinking of me.

HELMER   And when it's time to go, and I place the shawl over your smooth young shoulders, around this wonderful curve of your neck—then I pretend you're my young bride, that we've come straight from the wedding, that I'm bringing you home for the first time, alone with you for the first time, completely alone with you, you young, trembling, delicious—ah, I've done nothing but long for you all night! When I saw you doing the tarantella—like a huntress, luring us all to your trap—my blood started to boil. I couldn't stand it any longer. That's why I got you down here so early—

NORA   Get away, Torvald! Please get away from me. I don't want all this.

HELMER   What are you saying? Still playing the lark with me, Nora? You want, you don't want? Aren't I your husband?

(*There's a noise outside.*)

NORA (*Startled.*)   Did you hear that?

HELMER (*Going to the door.*)   Who's there?

RANK (*Outside.*)   Just me. May I come in for a moment?

HELMER (*Softly, irritated.*)   What can he possibly want now? (*Aloud.*) Just a second. (*Goes to the door and opens it.*) I'm so glad you didn't pass us by on your way out.

RANK   I thought I heard voices, and I really wanted to stop in. (*Looking around.*) Oh, yes—the old haunts. What a warm little nest you've got here.

HELMER   Speaking of which, you were having a pretty warm time upstairs—almost hot, I'd say.

RANK   Absolutely. And why not? You have to get the most out of life—everything you can, anyway, for as long as you can. That was excellent wine.

HELMER   And the champagne!

RANK   You thought so too? My thirst for it was amazing—even to me.

NORA   Torvald also had his share of champagne tonight.

RANK   Oh yes?

NORA   Yes, and that makes him so entertaining.

RANK   And why shouldn't you enjoy an evening like this after a productive day?

HELMER   Productive? I can't exactly say that for myself.

RANK (*Slaps him on the back.*)   Ah, but you see, I can!

NORA   Doctor Rank, it sounds like you've done some medical research today.

RANK   That's right.

HELMER   Oh come on—here's little Nora talking about medical research!

NORA   And may I congratulate you on the results?

RANK   Yes indeed.

NORA   Were they good?

RANK   The best kind—for doctor and patient alike—certainty.

NORA (*Quickly, inquisitively.*)   Certainty.

RANK   Absolute certainty. So haven't I earned a festive night out?

NORA   Yes, Doctor Rank, you have.

HELMER   I'm all for that—as long as the morning after's not too bad.

RANK   Well, you never get something for nothing in this world.

NORA   Doctor Rank, do you like masquerade balls?

RANK   Oh yes—especially when the disguises are good and strange—

NORA   So tell me. At the next one, how should the two of us appear?

HELMER   You little noodlehead! You're already on to the next one?

RANK   The two of us? I can tell you that: you'll go as Charmed Life—

HELMER   All right, but what's the costume for that?

RANK   Your wife can go just as she always is.

HELMER   Well said. Now have you decided on something for yourself?

RANK   Yes, Helmer, my mind's made up.

HELMER   Well?

RANK   At the next masquerade, I will be—invisible.

HELMER   That's pretty funny.

RANK   I hear there's a hat—a huge, black hat—called the Hat of Invisibility. You put it on, and no one on earth can see you.

HELMER   (*Stifling a grin.*)   Oh, yes, of course.

RANK   But I've forgotten what I really came for. Helmer, how about a cigar—a dark Havana.

HELMER   With pleasure. (*Holds out the case to him.*)

RANK   Thanks. (*Takes one and cuts the tip.*)

NORA   Let me give you a light.

RANK   Thank you. (*She holds the match as he lights the cigar.*) Now, good-bye.

HELMER   Old friend—good-bye, good-bye.

NORA   Sleep well, Doctor.

RANK   Thank you for that wish.

NORA   Now wish me the same.

RANK   Wish you?—All right, if you want—sleep well. And thanks for the light. (*He exits, nodding to both of them.*)

HELMER   (*Quietly.*)   He's drunk.

NORA   (*Vaguely.*)   Maybe.

(*Helmer takes his keys from his pocket and goes out into the hall.*)

NORA   What are you doing, Torvald?

HELMER   I've got to empty the mailbox—it's so full, there's no room for the morning papers.

NORA   Are you working tonight?

HELMER   You know I'm not. What's this? Someone's been fiddling with the lock.

NORA   The lock?

HELMER   Yes, definitely. Who could it be? I can't believe the maids—? Wait, here's a broken hairpin—Nora, this is yours—

NORA   (*Quickly.*)   Then it must be the children.

HELMER   Well you've really got to break them of that. Hmm—there we go, finally got it open. (*Takes out the contents and shouts into the kitchen.*) Helene? Helene—put out the hall lamp. (*He comes back into the room and shuts the door. He holds the letters in his hand.*) Look—see how it piled up? (*Sorts through them.*)   What's this?

NORA   (*By the window.*)   The letter! No, no, Torvald!

HELMER   Two cards, from Rank.

NORA   From Doctor Rank?

HELMER   (*Looking at them.*)   Doctor Rank, Physician and Surgeon. They were on top. He must have dropped them in as he left.

NORA   Is there anything on them?

HELMER   There's a black cross over the name. Look. That's gruesome. It's like he's announcing his own death.

NORA   That's exactly what he's doing.

HELMER   What? Did he tell you anything?

NORA   Yes. He said that when these cards arrived, it meant he's saying good-bye to us. Now he'll shut himself in and die.

HELMER   My poor friend. Of course I knew I wouldn't have him for long. But so soon—and now he's hiding himself away like a wounded animal.

NORA   If it has to happen, it's best to let it happen quietly. Isn't that right, Torvald?

HELMER (*Pacing up and down.*)   He'd grown to be a part of us. I don't think I can imagine myself without him. His loneliness—his suffering was like a cloudy background to our sunlit happiness. Well, maybe it's best this way—at least for him. (*Stands still.*) And maybe for us too, Nora. Now we only have each other. (*Puts his arms around her.*) Ah, you—my darling wife. I don't think I'll ever be able to hold you close enough. You know, Nora—so many times I've wished that you were in some terrible danger, so I could risk my life, my blood, everything, everything for you.

NORA (*Tears herself free and says firmly and resolutely.*)   Read your mail now, Torvald.

HELMER   No, not tonight. Tonight I want to be with you—

NORA   With your friend's death on your mind?

HELMER   You're right. We're both a little shaken by this. This ugliness has come between us—thoughts of death and decay. We have to try to get rid of them; until then, we go our separate ways.

NORA (*Her arms around his neck.*)   Torvald—good night! Good night!

HELMER (*Kissing her forehead.*)   Good night, little songbird. Sleep well, Nora. Now I'll read the mail. (*He goes in with the letters, shuts the door behind him.*)

(*Nora, with wild eyes, fumbles around, seizes Helmer's domino, wraps it around herself, and whispers quickly, hoarsely, spasmodically.*)

NORA   Never see him again—never, never, never. (*Throws the shawl over her head.*)   Never see the children again either—not even the children—never, never—the icy black water—the bottomless—that—if only it weren't all over—now he has it, he's reading it now—no, no, not yet. Torvald, good-bye, children, good-bye—

(*She starts to go into the hall; at the same moment Helmer flings open his door and stands there, an open letter in his hand.*)

HELMER   Nora!

NORA (*Screams.*)   Ahh—!

HELMER   What is this? Do you know what's in this letter?

NORA   Yes. Yes I know. Let me go. Let me out!

HELMER (*Holding her back.*)   Where are you going?

NORA (*Trying to break loose.*)   Don't try to save me, Torvald!

HELMER (*Staggers back.*)   It's true?! What he said is the truth? Horrible! No—it's impossible—this can't be true.

NORA   It is true. I have loved you more than anything in the world.

HELMER   Don't start with your silly excuses.

NORA (*Taking a step toward him.*)   Torvald!

HELMER   You miserable—what have you done?

NORA   Let me go. You won't have to take the blame for me. You're not going to take it on yourself.

HELMER   No more playacting! (*Locking the hall door.*) You'll stay right here and explain yourself. Do you understand what you've done? Answer me! Do you understand?

NORA (*Looking fixedly at him, her face hardening.*)   Yes. Now I'm beginning to understand everything.

HELMER (*Pacing up and down.*)   Ah!—what a rude awakening for me! For eight years—my pride and joy, a hypocrite, a liar,—even worse, a criminal! There's so much ugliness at the bottom of all this—indescribable ugliness! Uccch! (*Nora remains silent, looking fixedly at him.*) I should have seen it coming. Every one of your father's disgusting values—quiet!—every disgusting value is coming out in you. No religion, no morals, no sense of duty— this is my punishment for being so easy on him up there. I did it for your sake; and you repay me like this!

NORA   Yes, like this.

HELMER   You've destroyed my happiness. My whole future—thrown away! It's horrible when you think about it. I'm totally at the mercy of some amoral animal who can do whatever he wants with me—demand anything he wants, order me around, command me however he pleases, and I can't so much as squeak in protest. And this is how I'll go down, right to the bottom, all for the sake of some frivolous woman.

NORA   When I'm gone from this world, then you'll be free.

HELMER   Stop playacting! You sound like your father—he always had one of those phrases on the tip of his tongue. How would it help me if you were gone from this world, as you put it? Not in the least. He can still reveal everything, and if he does I'd be suspected of being an accomplice to your crimes! People might think I was behind it all, that it was my idea! And I have you to thank for all this—after I've carried you along, taken you and led you by the hand ever since we were married. Do you understand what you have done to me?

NORA (*Coldly and calmly.*)   Yes.

HELMER   I cant grasp this—it's just unbelievable to me. But we have to try to set things right. Take off that shawl. I said take it off! I've got to find some way to appease him—this thing has to be covered up, whatever it costs. As for you and me, things will seem just like before. For public consumption only, of course. You'll stay in the house, that's understood. But I can't trust you to bring up the children. Oh God—to have to say that to the one I—even now—well, that's over. After today there's no happiness, only holding the wreckage together, the scraps and shards—(*The doorbell rings. Helmer starts.*) What's that? It's so late! Is this it? Is he going to—? Nora, hide yourself! Say you're sick. (*Nora stands motionless. Helmer goes and opens the hall door.*)

MAID (*Half-dressed in the hall doorway.*)   A letter for Mrs. Helmer.

HELMER   Give it here. (*Takes the letter and closes the door.*) Yes, it's from him. You're not getting it. I'll read it myself.

NORA   Read it.

HELMER (*By the lamp.*)   I hardly dare. It could be the end for both of us. I've got to know. (*Tears open the letter; scans a few lines; looks at an enclosed paper and gives a cry of joy.*) Nora! (*Nora looks enquiringly at him.*) Nora! No, let me read it again—yes, yes, it's true. I'm saved! Nora, I'm saved!

NORA   And I?

HELMER   You too, of course. We're both saved, both of us. See? He sent you back your note—he writes that he's sorry and ashamed—that a happy change in his life—oh, what does it matter what he writes? We're saved, Nora! Now no one can hurt you. Oh, Nora, Nora—no: first, let's get all this ugliness out of here. Let me see. (*Glances at the note for a moment.*) No, I won't look at it. It'll be nothing more than a dream I had. (*He tears both letters in pieces and throws them both into the stove, watching them burn.*) So, nothing left. He wrote that ever since Christmas Eve—God, these must have been three terrible days for you, Nora.

NORA   I have fought a hard battle these last three days.

HELMER   And suffered, not seeing any way out but—no, we won't think about this ugly thing any more. We'll just rejoice and keep telling ourselves "it's over—it's all over." Do you hear me, Nora? It seems like you haven't quite got it yet—it's over! What's this about, this cold stare? Ah, poor little Nora, I understand—you can't bring yourself to believe I've forgiven you. But I have, Nora, I swear. I've forgiven everything. I know perfectly well that you did all this out of love for me.

NORA   That's true.

HELMER   You've loved me like a wife should love her husband. You just couldn't judge how to do it. But do you think that makes me love you any the less, because you couldn't manage by yourself? No, no—just lean on me. I'll counsel you, I'll direct you. I wouldn't be much of a man if this female helplessness didn't make you doubly attractive to me. Forget what I said in those first few terrible moments, when I thought I was going to lose everything. I've forgiven you, Nora—I swear, I've forgiven you.

NORA   Thank you for your forgiveness. (*She goes out through the door on the right.*)

HELMER   No, stay—(*Looking in.*) What are you doing?

NORA   Taking off my costume.

HELMER   (*By the open door.*)   Yes, do that. Try to calm down, collect your thoughts, my little, shivering songbird. If you need protection, I have broad wings to shelter you with. (*Walks around near the door.*) Oh, Nora—our home is so snug, so cozy. This is your nest, where I can keep you like a dove that I've snatched, unharmed, from the falcon's claws; I'll bring peace and rest to your beating heart. Little by little it will happen, Nora, believe me. Tomorrow, this will all seem different to you; and soon everything will be back to normal. I won't need to keep saying I forgive you—you'll feel it, you'll know it's true. How could you ever think I could bring myself to disown you, or even punish you? You don't know how a man's heart works, Nora. There's something indescribably sweet and satisfying for a man in knowing he's forgiven his wife—forgiven her from the bottom of his heart. It's as if he possesses her doubly now—as if she were born into the world all over again—and she becomes, in a way, his wife and his child at the same time. And that's what you'll be for me from now on, you little, helpless, confused creature. Don't be frightened of anything—just open your heart to me and I'll be both your conscience and your will. What's this—? You've changed your dress?

NORA   Yes, Torvald, I've changed my dress.

HELMER   But why now, so late?

NORA   I'm not sleeping tonight.

HELMER   But Nora, dear—

NORA   (*Looking at her watch.*)   It's not all that late. Sit down, Torvald. We have a great deal to talk about together. (*She sits at one end of the table.*)

HELMER   Nora—what s going on? That hard expression—

NORA   Sit down. This will take time. I have a lot to say to you.

HELMER   (*Sits at table directly opposite her.*)   You're worrying me, Nora. I don't understand you.

NORA   No, that's just it. You don't understand me. And I have never understood you—not until tonight. No—no interruptions. You have to hear me out. We're settling accounts, Torvald.

HELMER   What do you mean by that?

NORA   (*After a short silence.*)   Doesn't *one* thing strike you about the way we're sitting here?

HELMER   What might that be?

NORA   We've been married for eight years. Doesn't it strike you that this is the first time that the two of us—you and I, man and wife—have ever talked seriously?

HELMER   Well—"seriously"—what does that mean?

NORA   In eight whole years—no, longer—right from the moment we met, we haven't exchanged one serious word on one serious subject.

HELMER   Should I constantly be involving you in problems you couldn't possibly help me solve?

NORA   I'm not talking about problems. I'm saying that we've never sat down together and seriously tried to get to the bottom of anything.

HELMER   But Nora, dearest—would you have wanted that?

NORA   Yes, of course, that's just it. You've never understood me. A great wrong has been done me, Torvald. First by Papa, then by you.

HELMER   What! By us—who've loved you more than anyone in the world.

NORA   (*Shaking her head.*)   You've never loved me. You just thought it was a lot of fun to be in love with me.

HELMER   Nora, how can you say that?

NORA   It's a fact, Torvald. When I was at home with Papa, he told me all his opinions; so of course I had the same opinions. And if I had any others, I kept them hidden, because he wouldn't have liked that. He called me his doll-child, and he played with me like I played with my dolls. Then I came to your house—

HELMER   What kind of way is that to describe our marriage?

NORA   (*Undisturbed.*)   I mean, I went from Papa's hands into yours. You set up everything according to your taste; so of course I had the same taste, or I pretended to, I'm not really sure. I think it was half-and-half, one as much as the other. Now that I look back on it, I can see that I've lived like a beggar in this house, from hand to mouth; I've lived by doing tricks for you, Torvald. But that's how you wanted it. You and Papa have committed a great sin against me. It's your fault that I've become what I am.

HELMER   Nora—this is unreasonable, and it's ungrateful! Haven't you been happy here?

NORA No, never. I thought so, but I never really was.

HELMER Not—not happy!

NORA No, just having fun. You've always been very nice to me. But our home has never been anything but a playpen. I've been your doll-wife here, just like I was Papa's doll-child at home. And my children, in turn, have been my dolls. It was fun when you came and played with me, just like they had fun when I played with them. That's what our marriage has been, Torvald.

HELMER There's some truth in this—as exaggerated and hysterical as it is. But from now on, things will be different. Playtime is over: now the teaching begins.

NORA Who gets this teaching? Me or the children?

HELMER Both you and the children, my dearest Nora.

NORA Ah, Torvald: you're not the man to teach me how to be a good wife to you.

HELMER You can say that!

NORA And me—how can I possibly teach the children?

HELMER Nora!

NORA Didn't you say that yourself, not too long ago? You didn't dare trust them to me?

HELMER In the heat of the moment! How can you take that seriously?

NORA Yes, but you spoke the truth. I'm not equal to the task. There's another task I have to get through first. I have to try to teach myself. And you can't help me there. I've got to do it alone. And so I'm leaving you.

HELMER (*Springing up.*) What did you say?

NORA If I'm going to find out anything about myself—about everything out there—I have to stand completely on my own. That's why I can't stay with you any longer.

HELMER Nora, Nora!

NORA I'll leave right away. Kristine can put me up for tonight—

HELMER You're out of your mind! I won't allow it—I forbid you!

NORA It's no use forbidding me anything any more. I'll take what's mine with me. I won't take anything from you, now or later.

HELMER What kind of madness is this?

NORA Tomorrow I'm going home—back to my old hometown, I mean. It'll be easier for me to find something to do up there.

HELMER You blind, inexperienced creature!

NORA I have to try to get some experience, Torvald.

HELMER Abandon your home, your husband, your children! Do you have any idea what people will say?

NORA I can't worry about that. I only know what I have to do.

HELMER It's grotesque! You're turning your back on your most sacred duties!

NORA What do you think those are—my most sacred duties?

HELMER I have to tell you? Aren't they to your husband and children?

NORA I have other duties, equally sacred.

HELMER No, you don't! Like what?

NORA Duties to myself.

HELMER   You're a wife and mother, first and foremost.

NORA   I don't believe that any more. I believe that, first and foremost, I'm a human being—just as much as you—or at least I should try to become one. I'm aware that most people agree with you, Torvald, and that your opinion is backed up by plenty of books. But I can't be satisfied any more with what most people say, or what's written in the books. Now I've got to think these things through myself, and understand them.

HELMER   What don't you understand about your place in your own home? Don't you have an infallible teacher for questions like this? Don't you have your religion?

NORA   Oh, Torvald, I really don't know what religion is.

HELMER   What are you saying?

NORA   I only know what Pastor Hansen said when I was confirmed. He told me that religion was this and that and the other thing. When I get away from here, when I'm alone, I'll look into that subject too. I'll see if what Pastor Hansen said is true—or at least, if it's true for me.

HELMER   These things just aren't right for a young woman to be saying. If religion can't get through to you, let me try your conscience. You do have some moral feeling? Or—answer me—maybe not?

NORA   Well, Torvald, it's not easy to answer that. I really don't know. I'm actually quite confused about these things. I only know that my ideas are totally different from yours. I find out that the law is not what I thought it was—but I can't get it into my head that the law is right. A woman has no right to spare her dying father's feelings, or save her husband's life! I just can't believe these things.

HELMER   You're talking like a child. You don't understand the society you live in.

NORA   No, I don't. But now I'm going to find out for myself. I've got to figure out who's right—the world or me.

HELMER   You're ill, Nora—you have a fever. I almost think you're out of your mind.

NORA   I've never been so clear—and so certain—about so many things as I am tonight.

HELMER   You're clear and certain that you'll desert your husband and children?

NORA   Yes, I will.

HELMER   There's only one explanation left.

NORA   What is it?

HELMER   You no longer love me.

NORA   No. That's precisely it.

HELMER   Nora!—you can say that!

NORA   Oh, it hurts so much, Torvald. Because you've always been so kind to me. But I can't help it. I don't love you any more.

HELMER   (*Struggling to control himself.*)   Are you also clear and certain about that?

NORA   Yes, absolutely clear and certain. That's why I can't live here any more.

HELMER   Can you tell me how I lost your love?

NORA   Yes, I can. It was this evening, when the wonderful thing didn't happen—then I saw that you weren't the man I thought you were.

HELMER   Say more—I'm not following this.

NORA   I've waited so patiently for ten years now—good Lord. I know that these wonderful things don't come along every day. Then this disaster broke over me, and I was absolutely certain: now the wonderful thing is coming. While Krogstad's letter was lying out there, I never imagined you'd give in to his terms, even for a minute. I was so certain you'd say to him: tell your story to the whole world! And when that was done—

HELMER   Yes, then what? When I'd given my wife up to shame and disgrace—!

NORA   When that was done, I was completely certain that you would step forward and take everything on yourself—you'd say "I am the guilty one."

HELMER   Nora!

NORA   You're thinking that I'd never accept such a sacrifice from you? No, of course I wouldn't. But what good would my protests be over yours? *That* was the wonderful thing I was hoping for, and in terror of. And to prevent it, I was willing to end my life.

HELMER   I'd work for you night and day, Nora—gladly—suffer and sacrifice for your sake. But no one gives up his honor even for the one he loves.

NORA   That's exactly what millions of women have done.

HELMER   Oh—! You're thinking and talking like an ignorant child.

NORA   Maybe. But you don't think—or talk—like the man I could choose to be with. When your big fright was over—not the danger I was in, but what might happen to you—when that threat was past, then it was like nothing happened to you. I was just what I was before, your little songbird, your doll, and you'd have to take care of it twice as hard as before, since it was so frail and fragile. In that moment, Torvald, it dawned on me that I'd been living with a stranger—that I'd borne three children with him—. Aah—I can't stand the thought of it! I could tear myself to pieces.

HELMER   (*Heavily.*)   I see. I see. A gulf has really opened up between us. But Nora, can't we fill it in somehow?

NORA   The way I am now, I'm no wife for you.

HELMER   I can transform myself—I have the strength for it.

NORA   Maybe—if your doll is taken away from you.

HELMER   To live without—without you! Nora, I can't bear the thought of it!

NORA   All the more reason it has to happen. (*Having gone in to the right, she returns with her outdoor clothes and a little traveling bag, which she sets on a chair by the table.*)

HELMER   Nora, Nora, not now! Wait until tomorrow.

NORA   (*Puts on her coat.*)   I can't spend the night in a strange man's house.

HELMER   Can't we live here like brother and sister?

NORA   (*Tying her hat.*)   You know very well how long that would last. (*Throws her shawl around her.*)   Good-bye, Torvald. I won't see the children. They're in better hands than mine, that much I know. The way I am now, I can't do anything for them.

HELMER   But some day, Nora—some day—?

NORA How do I know? I have no idea what will become of me.

HELMER But you're my wife, right now and always, no matter what becomes of you.

NORA Listen, Torvald; when a wife deserts her husband's house, as I'm doing now, I've heard that the law frees him from any responsibility to her. And anyway, I'm freeing you. From everything. Complete freedom on both sides. See, here's your ring. Give me mine.

HELMER Even that.

NORA Even that.

HELMER Here it is.

NORA So. Well, now it's finished. I'm putting the keys here. As far as the household goes, the maids know all about it—better than I do. Tomorrow, after I'm gone, Kristine will come and pack the things I brought from home. I'll have them sent.

HELMER All finished, all over! Nora—will you never think about me after this?

NORA Of course I'll think about you often—and the children, and the house—.

HELMER Could I write to you, Nora?

NORA No, never. You can't do that.

HELMER But I'll have to send you—

NORA Nothing; nothing.

HELMER —help you, if you need—

NORA No. I'm telling you, I accept nothing from strangers.

HELMER Nora—can't I ever be anything more than a stranger to you?

NORA (*Taking her traveling bag.*) Oh, Torvald—not unless the most wonderful thing of all were to happen—

HELMER Name it—what is this most wonderful thing?

NORA It's—both you and I would have to transform ourselves to the point that—oh, Torvald, I don't know if I believe in it any more—

HELMER But I will. Name it! Transform ourselves to the point that—

NORA That our living together could become a marriage. Good-bye. (*She goes through the hall door.*)

HELMER (*Sinking down into a chair by the door and burying his face in his hands.*) Empty. She's not here. (*A hope flares up in him.*) The most wonderful thing of all—?

(*From below, the sound of a door slamming shut.*)

END OF PLAY

1879

JAMES JOYCE
1882–1941

Araby

North Richmond Street, being blind, was a quiet street except at the hour when the Christian Brothers' School set the boys free. An uninhabited house of two storeys stood at the blind end, detached from its neighbours in a square ground. The other houses of the street, conscious of decent lives within them, gazed at one another with brown imperturbable faces.

The former tenant of our house, a priest, had died in the back drawingroom. Air, musty from having been long enclosed, hung in all the rooms and the waste room behind the kitchen was littered with old useless papers. Among these I found a few papercovered books, the pages of which were curled and damp: *The Abbot* by Walter Scott, *The Devout Communicant* and *The Memoirs of Vidocq*. I liked the last best because its leaves were yellow. The wild garden behind the house contained a central apple tree and a few straggling bushes under one of which I found the late tenant's rusty bicycle pump. He had been a very charitable priest; in his will he had left all his money to institutions and the furniture of his house to his sister.

When the short days of winter came dusk fell before we had well eaten our dinners. When we met in the street the houses had grown sombre. The space of sky above us was the colour of everchanging violet and towards it the lamps of the street lifted their feeble lanterns. The cold air stung us and we played till our bodies glowed. Our shouts echoed in the silent street. The career of our play brought us through the dark muddy lanes behind the houses where we ran the gantlet of the rough tribes from the cottages, to the back doors of the dark dripping gardens where odours arose from the ashpits, to the dark odorous stables where a coachman smoothed and combed the horse or shook music from the buckled harness. When we returned to the street light from the kitchen windows had filled the areas. If my uncle was seen turning the corner we hid in the shadow until we had seen him safely housed. Or if Mangan's sister came out on the doorstep to call her brother in to his tea we watched her from our shadow peer up and down the street. We waited to see whether she would remain or go in and if she remained we left our shadow and walked up to Mangan's steps resignedly. She was waiting for us, her figure defined by the light from the half-opened door. Her brother always teased her before he obeyed and I stood by the railings looking at her. Her dress swung as she moved her body and the soft rope of her hair tossed from side to side.

Every morning I lay on the floor in the front parlour watching her door. The blind was pulled down to within an inch of the sash so that I could not be seen. When she came out on the doorstep my heart leaped. I ran to the hall, seized my books and followed her. I kept her brown figure always in my eye and when we came near the point at which our ways diverged I quickened my pace and passed her. This happened morning after morning. I had never spoken to her except for a few casual words and yet her name was like a summons to all my foolish blood.

Her image accompanied me even in places the most hostile to romance. On Saturday evenings when my aunt went marketing I had to go to carry some of the parcels. We walked through the flaring streets, jostled by drunken men and bargaining women, amid the curses of labourers, the shrill litanies of shop boys who stood on guard by the barrels of pigs' cheeks the nasal chanting of street singers who sang a *come-all-you* about O'Donovan Rossa or a ballad about the troubles in our native land. These noises converged in a single sensation of life for me: I imagined that I bore my chalice safely through a throng of foes. Her name sprang to my lips at moments in strange prayers and praises which I myself did not understand. My eyes were often full of tears (I could not tell why) and at times a flood from my heart seemed to pour itself out into my bosom. I thought little of the future. I did not know whether I would ever speak to her or not or, if I spoke to her, how I could tell her of my confused adoration. But my body was like a harp and her words and gestures were like fingers running upon the wires.

One evening I went into the back drawingroom in which the priest had died. It was a dark rainy evening and there was no sound in the house. Through one of the broken panes I heard the rain impinge upon the earth, the fine incessant needles of water playing in the sodden beds. Some distant lamp or lighted window gleamed below me. I was thankful that I could see so little. All my senses seemed to desire to veil themselves and, feeling that I was about to slip from them, I pressed the palms of my hands together until they trembled, murmuring: *O love! O love!* many times.

At last she spoke to me. When she addressed the first words to me I was so confused that I did not know what to answer. She asked me was I going to *Araby.* I forget whether I answered yes or no. It would be a splendid bazaar, she said; she would love to go.

—And why can't you? I asked.

While she spoke she turned a silver bracelet round and round her wrist. She could not go, she said, because there would be a retreat that week in her convent. Her brother and two other boys were fighting for their caps and I was alone at the railings. She held one of the spikes, bowing her head towards me. The light from the lamp opposite our door caught the white curve of her neck, lit up the hair that rested there and, falling, lit up the hand upon the railing. It fell over one side of her dress and caught the white border of a petticoat, just visible as she stood at ease.

—It's well for you, she said.

—If I go, I said, I will bring you something.

What innumerable follies laid waste my waking and sleeping thoughts after that evening! I wished to annihilate the tedious intervening days. I chafed against the work of school. At night in my bedroom and by day in the classroom her image came between me and the page I strove to read. The syllables of the word *Araby* were called to me through the silence in which my soul luxuriated and cast an eastern enchantment over me. I asked for leave to go to the bazaar on Saturday night. My aunt was surprised and hoped it was not some freemason affair. I answered few questions in class. I watched my master's face pass from amiability to sternness; he hoped I was not beginning to idle. I could not call my wandering thoughts together. I had hardly any patience with the serious work of life which, now that it stood between me and my desire, seemed to me child's play, ugly monotonous child's play.

On Saturday morning I reminded my uncle that I wished to go to the bazaar in the evening. He was fussing at the hallstand, looking for the hatbrush, and answered me curtly:

—Yes, boy, I know.

As he was in the hall I could not go into the front parlour and lie at the window. I left the house in bad humour and walked slowly towards the school. The air was pitilessly raw and already my heart misgave me.

When I came home to dinner my uncle had not yet been home. Still it was early. I sat staring at the clock for some time and when its ticking began to irritate me I left the room. I mounted the staircase and gained the upper part of the house. The high cold empty gloomy rooms liberated me and I went from room to room singing. From the front window I saw my companions playing below in the street. Their cries reached me weakened and indistinct and, leaning my forehead against the cool glass, I looked over at the dark house where she lived. I may have stood there for an hour seeing nothing but the brownclad figure cast by my imagination, touched discreetly by the lamplight at the curved neck, at the hand upon the railings and at the border below the dress.

When I came downstairs again I found Mrs Mercer sitting at the fire. She was an old garrulous woman, a pawnbroker's widow who collected used stamps for some pious purpose. I had to endure the gossip of the teatable. The meal was prolonged beyond an hour and still my uncle did not come. Mrs Mercer stood up to go: she was sorry she couldn't wait any longer but it was after eight o'clock and she did not like to be out late as the night air was bad for her. When she had gone I began to walk up and down the room, clenching my fists. My aunt said:

—I'm afraid you may put off your bazaar for this night of Our Lord.

At nine o'clock I heard my uncle's latchkey in the halldoor. I heard him talking to himself and heard the hallstand rocking when it had received the weight of his overcoat. I could interpret these signs. When he was midway through his dinner I asked him to give me the money to go to the bazaar. He had forgotten.

—The people are in bed and after their first sleep now, he said.

I did not smile. My aunt said to him energetically:

—Can't you give him the money and let him go? You've kept him late enough as it is.

My uncle said he was very sorry he had forgotten. He said he believed in the old saying: *All work and no play makes Jack a dull boy.* He asked me where I was going and when I had told him a second time he asked me did I know *The Arab's Farewell to his Steed.* When I left the kitchen he was about to recite the opening lines of the piece to my aunt.

I held a florin tightly in my hand as I strode down Buckingham Street towards the station. The sight of the streets thronged with buyers and glaring with gas recalled to me the purpose of my journey. I took my seat in a third class carriage of a deserted train. After an intolerable delay the train moved out of the station slowly. It crept onward among ruinous houses and over the twinkling river. At Westland Row Station a crowd of people pressed at the carriage doors; but the porters moved them back, saying that it was a special train for the bazaar. I remained alone in the bare carriage. In a few minutes the train drew up beside an improvised wooden platform. I passed out on to the road and saw by the lighted dial of a clock that it was ten minutes to ten. In front of me was a large building which displayed the magical name.

I could not find any sixpenny entrance and, fearing that the bazaar would be closed, I passed in quickly through a turnstile, handing a shilling to a weary-looking man. I found myself in a big hall girdled at half its height by a gallery. Nearly all the stalls were closed and the greater part of the hall was in darkness. I recognised a silence like that which pervades a church after a service. I walked into the centre of the bazaar timidly. A few people were gathered about the stalls which were still open. Before a curtain over which the words *Café Chantant* were written in coloured lamps two men were counting money on a salver. I listened to the fall of the coins.

Remembering with difficulty why I had come I went over to one of the stalls and examined porcelain vases and flowered teasets. At the door of the stall a young lady was talking and laughing with two young gentlemen. I remarked their English accents and listened vaguely to their conversation.

—O, I never said such a thing!

—O, but you did!

—O, but I didn't!

—Didn't she say that?

—She did. I heard her.

—O, there's a . . . fib!

Observing me the young lady came over and asked me did I wish to buy anything. The tone of her voice was not encouraging: she seemed to have spoken to me out of a sense of duty. I looked humbly at the great jars that stood like eastern guards at either side of the dark entrance to her stall and murmured:

—No, thank you.

The young lady changed the position of one of the vases and went back to the two young men. They began to talk of the same subject. Once or twice the young lady glanced at me over her shoulder.

I lingered before her stall, though I knew my stay was useless, to make my interest in her wares seem the more real. Then I turned away slowly and walked down the middle of the bazaar. I allowed the two pennies to fall against the sixpence in my pocket. I heard a voice call from one end of the gallery that the light was out. The upper part of the hall was now completely dark.

Gazing up into the darkness I saw myself as a creature driven and derided by vanity: and my eyes burned with anguish and anger.

1914

SALMAN RUSHDIE

born 1947

The Courter

1

Certainly-Mary was the smallest woman Mixed-Up the hall porter had come across, dwarfs excepted, a tiny sixty-year-old Indian lady with her greying hair tied behind her head in a neat bun, hitching up her red-hemmed white sari in the front and negotiating the apartment block's front steps as if they were Alps. "No," he said aloud, furrowing his brow. What would be the right peaks. Ah, good, that was the name. "Ghats," he said proudly. Word from a schoolboy atlas long ago, when India felt as far away as Paradise. (Nowadays Paradise seemed even further away but India, and Hell, had come a good bit closer.) "Western Ghats, Eastern Ghats, and now Kensington Ghats," he said, giggling. "Mountains."

She stopped in front of him in the oak-panelled lobby. "But ghats in India are also stairs," she said. "Yes yes certainly. For instance in Hindu holy city of Varanasi, where the Brahmins sit taking the filgrims' money is called Dasashwamedh-ghat. Broad-broad staircase down to River Ganga. O, most certainly! Also Manikarnika-ghat. They buy fire from a house with a tiger leaping from the roof—yes certainly, a statue tiger, coloured by Technicolor, what are you thinking?—and they bring it in a box to set fire to their loved ones' bodies. Funeral fires are of sandal. Photographs not allowed; no, certainly not."

He began thinking of her as Certainly-Mary because she never said plain yes or no; always this O-yes-certainly or no-certainly-not. In the confused circumstances that had prevailed ever since his brain, his one sure thing, had let him down, he could hardly be certain of anything any more; so he was stunned by her sureness, first into nostalgia, then envy, then attraction. And attraction was a thing so long forgotten that when the churning started he thought for a long time it must be the Chinese dumplings he had brought home from the High Street carry-out.

English was hard for Certainly-Mary, and this was a part of what drew damaged old Mixed-Up towards her. The letter p was a particular problem, often turning into an f or a c; when she proceeded through the lobby with a wheeled wicker shopping basket, she would say, "Going shocking," and when, on her return, he offered to help lift the basket up the front ghats, she would answer, "Yes, fleas." As the elevator lifted her away, she called through the grille: "Oé, courter! Thank you, courter. O, yes, certainly." (In Hindi and Konkani, however, her p's knew their place.)

So: thanks to her unexpected, somehow stomach-churning magic, he was no longer porter, but courter. "Courter," he repeated to the mirror when she had gone. His breath made a little dwindling picture of the word on the glass.

"Courter courter caught." Okay. People called him many things, he did not mind. But this name, this courter, this he would try to be.

2

For years now I've been meaning to write down the story of Certainly-Mary, our ayah, the woman who did as much as my mother to raise my sisters and me, and her great adventure with her "courter" in London, where we all lived for a time in the early Sixties in a block called Waverley House; but what with one thing and another I never got round to it.

Then recently I heard from Certainly-Mary after a longish silence. She wrote to say that she was ninety-one, had had a serious operation, and would I kindly send her some money, because she was embarrassed that her niece, with whom she was now living in the Kurla district of Bombay, was so badly out of pocket.

I sent the money, and soon afterwards received a pleasant letter from the niece, Stella, written in the same hand as the letter from "Aya"—as we had always called Mary, palindromically dropping the "H." Aya had been so touched, the niece wrote, that I remembered her after all these years. "I have been hearing the stories about you folks all my life," the letter went on, "and I think of you a little bit as family. Maybe you recall my mother, Mary's sister. She unfortunately passed on. Now it is I who write Mary's letters for her. We all wish you the best."

This message from an intimate stranger reached out to me in my enforced exile from the beloved country of my birth and moved me, stirring things that had been buried very deep. Of course it also made me feel guilty about having done so little for Mary over the years. For whatever reason, it has become more important than ever to set down the story I've been carrying around unwritten for so long, the story of Aya and the gentle man whom she renamed—with unintentional but prophetic overtones of romance—"the courter." I see now that it is not just their story, but ours, mine, as well.

3

His real name was Mecir: you were supposed to say Mishirsh because it had invisible accents on it in some Iron Curtain language in which the accents had to be invisible, my sister Durré said solemnly, in case somebody spied on them or rubbed them out or something. His first name also began with an m but it was so full of what we called Communist consonants, all those z's and c's and w's walled up together without vowels to give them breathing space, that I never even tried to learn it.

At first we thought of nicknaming him after a mischievous little comic-book character, Mr Mxyztplk from the Fifth Dimension, who looked a bit like Elmer Fudd and used to make Superman's life hell until ole Supe could trick him into saying his name backwards, Klptzyxm, whereupon he disappeared back into the Fifth Dimension; but because we weren't too sure how to say Mxyztplk (not to mention Klptzyxm) we dropped that idea. "We'll just call you Mixed-Up," I told him in the end, to simplify life. "Mishter Mikshed-Up Mishirsh." I was fifteen then and bursting with unemployed cock and it meant I could say things like that right into people's faces, even people less accommodating than Mr Mecir with his stroke.

What I remember most vividly are his pink rubber washing-up gloves, which he seemed never to remove, at least not until he came calling for Certainly-Mary . . . At any rate, when I insulted him, with my sisters Durré and Muneeza cackling in the lift, Mecir just grinned an empty good-natured grin, nodded, "You call me what you like, okay," and went back to buffing and polishing the brasswork. There was no point teasing him if he was going to be like that, so I got into the lift and all the way to the fourth floor we sang *I Can't Stop Loving You* at the top of our best Ray Charles voices, which were pretty awful. But we were wearing our dark glasses, so it didn't matter.

4

It was the summer of 1962, and school was out. My baby sister Scheherazade was just one year old. Durré was a beehived fourteen; Muneeza was ten, and already quite a handful. The three of us—or rather Durré and me, with Muneeza trying desperately and unsuccessfully to be included in our gang—would stand over Scheherazade's cot and sing to her. "No nursery rhymes," Durré had decreed, and so there were none, for though she was a year my junior she was a natural leader. The infant Scheherazade's lullabies were our cover versions of recent hits by Chubby Checker, Neil Sedaka, Elvis and Pat Boone.

"Why don't you come home, Speedy Gonzales?" we bellowed in sweet dis-harmony: but most of all, and with actions, we would jump down, turn around and pick a bale of cotton. We would have jumped down, turned around and picked those bales all day except that the Maharaja of B—— in the flat below complained, and Aya Mary came in to plead with us to be quiet.

"Look, see, it's Jumble-Aya who's fallen for Mixed-Up," Durré shouted, and Mary blushed a truly immense blush. So naturally we segued right into a quick me-oh-my-oh; son of a gun, we had big fun. But then the baby began to yell, my father came in with his head down bull-fashion and steaming from both ears, and we needed all the good luck charms we could find.

I had been at boarding school in England for a year or so when Abba took the decision to bring the family over. Like all his decisions, it was neither explained to nor discussed with anyone, not even my mother. When they first arrived he rented two adjacent flats in a seedy Bayswater mansion block called Graham Court, which lurked furtively in a nothing street that crawled along the side of the ABC Queensway cinema towards the Porchester Baths. He commandeered one of these flats for himself and put my mother, three sisters and Aya in the other; also, on school holidays, me. England, where liquor was freely available, did little for my father's *bonhomie*, so in a way it was a relief to have a flat to ourselves.

Most nights he emptied a bottle of Johnnie Walker Red Label and a soda-siphon. My mother did not dare to go across to "his place" in the evenings. She said: "He makes faces at me."

Aya Mary took Abba his dinner and answered all his calls (if he wanted anything, he would phone us up and ask for it). I am not sure why Mary was spared his drunken rages. She said it was because she was nine years his senior, so she could tell him to show due respect.

After a few months, however, my father leased a three-bedroom fourth-floor apartment with a fancy address. This was Waverley House in Kensington Court, W8. Among its other residents were not one but two Indian Maharajas, the sporting Prince P—— as well as the old B—— who has already been mentioned. Now we were jammed in together, my parents and Baby Scare-zade (as her siblings had affectionately begun to call her) in the master bedroom, the three of us in a much smaller room, and Mary, I regret to admit, on a straw mat laid on the fitted carpet in the hall. The third bedroom became my father's office, where he made phone-calls and kept his *Encyclopaedia Britannica*, his *Reader's Digests*, and (under lock and key) the television cabinet. We entered it at our peril. It was the Minotaur's lair.

One morning he was persuaded to drop in at the corner pharmacy and pick up some supplies for the baby. When he returned there was a hurt, schoolboyish look on his face that I had never seen before, and he was pressing his hand against his cheek.

"She hit me," he said plaintively.

"Hai! Allah-tobah! Darling!" cried my mother, fussing. "Who hit you? Are you injured? Show me, let me see."

"I did nothing," he said, standing there in the hall with the pharmacy bag in his other hand and a face as pink as Mecir's rubber gloves. "I just went in with your list. The girl seemed very helpful. I asked for baby compound, Johnson's powder, teething jelly, and she brought them out. Then I asked did she have any nipples, and she slapped my face."

My mother was appalled. "Just for that?" And Certainly-Mary backed her up. "What is this nonsense?" she wanted to know. "I have been in that chemist's shock, and they have flenty nickels, different sizes, all on view."

Durré and Muneeza could not contain themselves. They were rolling round on the floor, laughing and kicking their legs in the air.

"You both shut your face at once," my mother ordered. "A madwoman has hit your father. Where is the comedy?"

"I don't believe it," Durré gasped. "You just went up to that girl and said," and here she fell apart again, stamping her feet and holding her stomach, "'*have you got any nipples?*'"

My father grew thunderous, empurpled. Durré controlled herself. "But Abba," she said, at length, "here they call them teats."

Now my mother's and Mary's hands flew to their mouths, and even my father looked shocked. "But how shameless!" my mother said. "The same word as for what's on your bosoms?" She coloured, and stuck out her tongue for shame.

"These English," sighed Certainly-Mary. "But aren't they the limit? Certainly-yes; they are."

I remember this story with delight, because it was the only time I ever saw my father so discomfited, and the incident became legendary and the girl in the pharmacy was installed as the object of our great veneration. (Durré and I went in there just to take a look at her—she was a plain, short girl of about seventeen, with large, unavoidable breasts—but she caught us whispering and glared so fiercely that we fled.) And also because in the general hilarity I was able to conceal the shaming truth that I, who had been in England for so long, would have made the same mistake as Abba did.

It wasn't just Certainly-Mary and my parents who had trouble with the English language. My schoolfellows tittered when in my Bombay way I said "brought-up" for upbringing (as in "where was your brought-up?") and "thrice" for three times and "quarter-plate" for side-plate and "macaroni" for pasta in general. As for learning the difference between nipples and teats, I really hadn't had any opportunities to increase my word power in that area at all.

5

So I was a little jealous of Certainly-Mary when Mixed-Up came to call. He rang our bell, his body quivering with deference in an old suit grown too loose, the trousers tightly gathered by a belt; he had taken off his rubber gloves and there were roses in his hand. My father opened the door and gave him a withering look. Being a snob, Abba was not pleased that the flat lacked a separate service entrance, so that even a porter had to be treated as a member of the same universe as himself.

"Mary," Mixed-Up managed, licking his lips and pushing back his floppy white hair. "I, to see Miss Mary, come, am."

"Wait on," Abba said, and shut the door in his face.

Certainly-Mary spent all her afternoons off with old Mixed-Up from then on, even though that first date was not a complete success. He took her "up West" to show her the visitors' London she had never seen, but at the top of an up escalator at Piccadilly Circus, while Mecir was painfully enunciating the words on the posters she couldn't read—*Unzip a banana*, and *Idris when I's dri*—she got her sari stuck in the jaws of the machine, and as the escalator pulled at the garment it began to unwind. She was forced to spin round and round like a top, and screamed at the top of her voice, "O BAAP! BAAPU-RÉ! BAAP-RÉ-BAAP-RÉ-BAAP!" It was Mixed-Up who saved her by pushing the emergency stop button before the sari was completely unwound and she was exposed in her petticoat for all the world to see.

"O, courter!" she wept on his shoulder. "O, no more escaleater, courter, nevermore, surely not!"

My own amorous longings were aimed at Durré's best friend, a Polish girl called Rozalia, who had a holiday job at Faiman's shoe shop on Oxford Street. I pursued her pathetically throughout the holidays and, on and off, for the next two years. She would let me have lunch with her sometimes and buy her a Coke and a sandwich, and once she came with me to stand on the terraces at White Han Lane to watch Jimmy Greaves's first game for the Spurs. "Come on you whoi-oites," we both shouted dutifully. "Come on you *Lily-whoites.*" After that she even invited me into the back room at Faiman's, where she kissed me twice and let me touch her breast, but that was as far as I got.

And then there was my sort-of-cousin Chandni, whose mother's sister had married my mother's brother, though they had since split up. Chandni was eighteen months older than me, and so sexy it made you sick. She was training to be an Indian classical dancer, Odissi as well as Natyam, but in the meantime she dressed in tight black jeans and a clinging black polo-neck jumper and took me, now and then, to hang out at Bunjie's, where she knew most of the folk-music crowd that frequented the place, and where she answered to the name of Moonlight, which is what *chandni* means. I chain-smoked with the folkies and then went to the toilet to throw up.

Chandni was the stuff of obsessions. She was a teenage dream, the Moon River come to Earth like the Goddess Ganga, dolled up in slinky black. But for her I was just the young greenhorn cousin to whom she was being nice because he hadn't learned his way around.

She-E-rry, won't you come out tonight? yodelled the Four Seasons. I knew exactly how they felt. *Come, come, come out toni-yi-yight.* And while you're at it, love me do.

6

They went for walks in Kensington Gardens. "Pan," Mixed-Up said, pointing at a statue. "Los' boy. Nev' grew up." They went to Barkers and Pontings and Derry & Toms and picked out furniture and curtains for imaginary homes. They cruised supermarkets and chose little delicacies to eat. In Mecir's cramped lounge they sipped what he called "chimpanzee tea" and toasted crumpets in front of an electric bar fire.

Thanks to Mixed-Up, Mary was at last able to watch television. She liked children's programmes best, especially *The Flintstones.* Once, giggling at her daring, Mary confided to Mixed-Up that Fred and Wilma reminded her of her Sahib and Begum Sahiba upstairs; at which the courter, matching her audaciousness, pointed first at Certainly-Mary and then at himself, grinned a wide gappy smile and said, "Rubble."

Later, on the news, a vulpine Englishman with a thin moustache and mad eyes declaimed a warning about immigrants, and Certainly-Mary flapped her hand at the set: "Khali-pili bom marta," she objected, and then, for her host's benefit translated: "For nothing he is shouting shouting. Bad life! Switch it off."

They were often interrupted by the Maharajas of B—— and P——, who came downstairs to escape their wives and ring other women from the call-box in the porter's room.

"Oh, baby, forget that guy," said sporty Prince P——, who seemed to spend all his days in tennis whites, and whose plump gold Rolex was almost lost in the thick hair on his arm. "I'll show you a better time than him, baby; step into my world."

The Maharaja of B—— was older, uglier, more matter-of-fact. "Yes, bring all appliances. Room is booked in name of Mr Douglas Home. Six forty-five to seven fifteen. You have printed rate card? Please. Also a two-foot ruler, must be wooden. Frilly apron, plus."

This is what has lasted in my memory of Waverley House, this seething mass of bad marriages, booze, philanderers and unfulfilled young lusts; of the Maharaja of P—— roaring away towards London's casinoland every night, in a red sports car with fitted blondes, and of the Maharaja of B—— skulking off to Kensington High Street wearing dark glasses in the dark, and a coat with the collar turned up even though it was high summer; and at the heart of our little universe were Certainly-Mary and her courter, drinking chimpanzee tea and singing along with the national anthem of Bedrock.

But they were not really like Barney and Betty Rubble at all. They were formal, polite. They were . . . courtly. He courted her, and, like a coy, ringleted ingénue with a fan, she inclined her head, and entertained his suit.

7

I spent one half-term weekend in 1963 at the home in Beccles, Suffolk of Field Marshal Sir Charles Lutwidge-Dodgson, an old India hand and a family friend who was supporting my application for British citizenship. "The Dodo," as he was known, invited me down by myself, saying he wanted to get to know me better.

He was a huge man whose skin had started hanging too loosely on his face, a giant living in a tiny thatched cottage and forever bumping his head. No wonder he was irascible at times; he was in Hell, a Gulliver trapped in that rose-garden Lilliput of croquet hoops, church bells, sepia photographs and old battle-trumpets.

The weekend was fitful and awkward until the Dodo asked if I played chess. Slightly awestruck at the prospect of playing a Field Marshal, I nodded; and ninety minutes later, to my amazement, won the game.

I went into the kitchen, strutting somewhat, planning to boast a little to the old soldier's long-time housekeeper, Mrs Liddell. But as soon as I entered she said: "Don't tell me. You never went and won?"

"Yes," I said, affecting nonchalance. "As a matter of fact, yes, I did."

"Gawd," said Mrs Liddell. "Now there'll be hell to pay. You go back in there and ask him for another game, and this time make sure you lose."

I did as I was told, but was never invited to Beccles again.

Still, the defeat of the Dodo gave me new confidence at the chessboard, so when I returned to Waverley House after finishing my O levels, and was at once invited to play a game by Mixed-Up (Mary had told him about my victory in the Battle of Beccles with great pride and some hyperbole), I said: "Sure, I don't mind." How long could it take to thrash the old duffer, after all?

There followed a massacre royal. Mixed-Up did not just beat me; he had me for breakfast, over easy. I couldn't believe it—the canny opening, the fluency of his combination play, the force of his attacks, my own impossibly cramped, strangled positions—and asked for a second game. This time he tucked into me even more heartily. I sat broken in my chair at the end, close to tears. *Big girls don't cry*, I reminded myself, but the song went on playing in my head: *That's just an alibi.*

"Who are you?" I demanded, humiliation weighing down every syllable. "The devil in disguise?"

Mixed-Up gave his big, silly grin. "Grand Master," he said. "Long time. Before head."

"You're a Grand Master," I repeated, still in a daze. Then in a moment of horror I remembered that I had seen the name Mecir in books of classic games. "Nimzo-Indian," I said aloud. He beamed and nodded furiously.

"That Mecir?" I asked wonderingly.

"That," he said. There was saliva dribbling out of a corner of his sloppy old mouth. This ruined old man was in the books. He was in the books. And even with his mind turned to rubble he could still wipe the floor with me.

"Now play lady," he grinned. I didn't get it. "Mary lady," he said. "Yes yes certainly."

She was pouring tea, waiting for my answer. "Aya, you can't play," I said, bewildered.

"Learning, baba," she said. "What is it, na? Only a game."

And then she, too, beat me senseless, and with the black pieces, at that. It was not the greatest day of my life.

8

From *100 Most Instructive Chess Games* by Robert Reshevsky, 1961:

M. Mecir - M. Najdorf
Dallas 1950, Nimzo-Indian Defense

The attack of a tactician can be troublesome to meet—that of a strategist even more so. Whereas the tactician's threats may be unmistakable, the strategist confuses the issue by keeping things in abeyance. He threatens to threaten!

Take this game for instance: Mecir posts a Knight at Q6 to get a grip on the center. Then he establishes a passed Pawn on one wing to occupy his opponent on the Queen side. Finally he stirs up the position on the King-side. What does the poor bewildered opponent do? How can he defend everything at once? Where will the blow fall?

Watch Mecir keep Najdorf on the run, as he shifts the attack from side to side!

Chess had become their private language. Old Mixed-Up, lost as he was for words, retained, on the chessboard, much of the articulacy and subtlety which had vanished from his speech. As Certainly-Mary gained in skill—and she had learned with astonishing speed, I thought bitterly, for someone who couldn't read or write or pronounce the letter p—she was better able to understand, and respond to, the wit of the reduced maestro with whom she had so unexpectedly forged a bond.

He taught her with great patience, showing-not-telling, repeating openings and combinations and endgame techniques over and over until she began to see the meaning in the patterns. When they played, he handicapped himself, he told her her best moves and demonstrated their consequences, drawing her, step by step, into the infinite possibilities of the game.

Such was their courtship. "It is like an adventure, baba," Mary once tried to explain to me. "It is like going with him to his country, you know? What a place, baap-ré! Beautiful and dangerous and funny and full of fuzzles. For me it is a big-big discovery. What to tell you? I go for the game. It is a wonder."

I understood, then, how far things had gone between them. Certainly-Mary had never married, and had made it clear to old Mixed-Up that it was too late to start any of that monkey business at her age. The courier was a widower, and had grown-up children somewhere, lost long ago behind the ever-higher walls of Eastern Europe. But in the game of chess they had found a form of flirtation, an endless renewal that precluded the possibility of boredom, a courtly wonderland of the ageing heart.

What would the Dodo have made of it all? No doubt it would have scandalised him to see chess, chess of all games, the great formalisation of war, transformed into an art of love.

As for me: my defeats by Certainly-Mary and her courter ushered in further humiliations. Durré and Muneeza went down with the mumps, and so, finally, in spite of my mother's efforts to segregate us, did I. I lay terrified in bed while the doctor warned me not to stand up and move around if I could possibly help it. "If you do," he said, "your parents won't need to punish you. You will have punished yourself quite enough."

I spent the following few weeks tormented day and night by visions of grotesquely swollen testicles and a subsequent life of limp impotence—finished before I'd even started, it wasn't fair!—which were made much worse by my sisters' quick recovery and incessant gibes. But in the end I was lucky; the illness didn't spread to the deep South. "Think how happy your hundred and one girlfriends will be, bhai," sneered Durré, who knew all about my continued failures in the Rozalia and Chandni departments.

On the radio, people were always singing about the joys of being sixteen years old. I wondered where they were, all those boys and girls of my age having the time of their lives. Were they driving around America in Studebaker convertibles? They certainly weren't in my neighbourhood. London, W8 was Sam Cooke country that summer. *Another Saturday night* . . . There might be a mop-top love-song stuck at number one, but I was down with lonely Sam in the lower depths of the charts, how-I-wishing I had someone, etc., and generally feeling in a pretty goddamn dreadful way.

<h1 style="text-align:center">9</h1>

"Baba, come quick."

It was late at night when Aya Mary shook me awake. After many urgent hisses, she managed to drag me out of sleep and pull me, pajama'ed and yawning, down the hall. On the landing outside our flat was Mixed-Up the courter, huddled up against a wall, weeping. He had a black eye and there was dried blood on his mouth.

"What happened?" I asked Mary, shocked.

"Men," wailed Mixed-Up. "Threaten. Beat."

He had been in his lounge earlier that evening when the sporting Maharaja of P—— burst in to say, "If any-body comes looking for me, okay, any tough-guy type guys, okay, I am out, okay? Oh you tea. Don't let them go upstairs, okay? Big tip, okay?"

A short time later, the old Maharaja of B—— also arrived in Mecir's lounge, looking distressed.

"Suno, listen on," said the Maharaja of B——. "You don't know where I am, samajh liya? Understood? Some low persons may inquire. You don't know. I am abroad, achha? On extended travels abroad. Do your job, porter. Handsome recompense."

Late at night two tough-guy types did indeed turn up. It seemed the hairy Prince P—— had gambling debts. "Out," Mixed-Up grinned in his sweetest way. The tough-guy types nodded, slowly. They had long hair and thick lips like Mick Jagger's. "He's a busy gent. We should of made an appointment," said the first type to the second. "Didn't I tell you we should of called?"

"You did," agreed the second type. "Got to do these things right, you said, he's royalty. And you was right, my son, I put my hand up, I was dead wrong. I put my hand up to that."

"Let's leave our card," said the first type. "Then he'll know to expect us."

"Ideal," said the second type, and smashed his fist into old Mixed-Up's mouth. "You tell him," the second type said, and struck the old man in the eye. "When he's in, You mention it."

He had locked the front door after that; but much later, well after midnight, there was a hammering. Mixed-Up called out, "Who?"

"We are close friends of the Maharaja of B——" said a voice. "No, I tell a lie. Acquaintances."

"He calls upon a lady of our acquaintance," said a second voice. "To be precise."

"It is in that connection that we crave audience," said the first voice.

"Gone," said Mecir. "Jet plane. Gone."

There was a silence. Then the second voice said, "Can't be in the jet set if you never jump on a jet, eh? Biarritz, Monte, all of that."

"Be sure and let His Highness know," said the first voice, "that we eagerly await his return."

"With regard to our mutual friend," said the second voice. "Eagerly."

What does the poor bewildered opponent do? The words from the chess book popped unbidden into my head, *How can he defend everything at once? Where will the blow fall? Watch Mecir keep Najdorf on the run, as he shifts the attack from side to side!*

Mixed-Up returned to his lounge and on this occasion, even though there had been no use of force, he began to weep. After a time he took the elevator up to the fourth floor and whispered through our letterbox to Certainly-Mary sleeping on her mat.

"I didn't want to wake Sahib," Mary said. "You know his trouble, na? And Begum Sahiba is so tired at end of the day. So now you tell, baba, what to do?"

What did she expect me to come up with? I was sixteen years old. "Mixed-Up must call the police," I unoriginally offered.

"No, no, baba," said Certainly-Mary emphatically. "If the courter makes a scandal for Maharaja-log, then in the end it is the courter only who will be out on his ear."

I had no other ideas. I stood before them feeling like a fool, while they both turned upon me their frightened, supplicant eyes.

"Go to sleep," I said. "We'll think about it in the morning." *The first pair of thugs were tacticians*, I was thinking. *They were troublesome to meet. But the second pair were scarier; they were strategists. They threatened to threaten.*

Nothing happened in the morning, and the sky was clear. It was almost impossible to believe in fists, and menacing voices at the door. During the course of the day both Maharajas visited the porter's lounge and stuck five-pound notes in Mixed-Up's waistcoat pocket. "Held the fort, good man," said Prince P——, and the Maharaja of B—— echoed those sentiments: "Spot on. All handled now, achha? Problem over."

The three of us—Aya Mary, her courter, and me—held a council of war that afternoon and decided that no further action was necessary. The hall porter was the front line in any such situation, I argued, and the front line had held. And now the risks were past. Assurances had been given. End of story.

"End of story," repeated Certainly-Mary doubtfully, but then, seeking to reassure Mecir, she brightened. "Correct," she said. "Most certainly! All-done, finis." She slapped her hands against each other for emphasis. She asked Mixed-Up if he wanted a game of chess; but for once the courter didn't want to play.

10

After that I was distracted, for a time, from the story of Mixed-Up and Certainly-Mary by violence nearer home.

My middle sister Muneeza, now eleven, was entering her delinquent phase a little early. She was the true inheritor of my father's black rage, and when she lost control it was terrible to behold. That summer she seemed to pick fights with my father on purpose; seemed prepared, at her young age, to test her strength against his. (I intervened in her rows with Abba only once, in the kitchen. She grabbed the kitchen scissors and flung them at me. They cut me on the thigh. After that I kept my distance.)

As I witnessed their wars I felt myself coming unstuck from the idea of family itself. I looked at my screaming sister and thought how brilliantly self-destructive she was, how triumphantly she was ruining her relations with the people she needed most.

And I looked at my choleric, face-pulling father and thought about British citizenship. My existing Indian passport permitted me to travel only to a very few countries, which were carefully listed on the second right-hand page. But I might soon have a British passport and then, by hook or by crook, I would get away from him. I would not have this face-pulling in my life.

At sixteen, you still think you can escape from your father. You aren't listening to his voice speaking through your mouth, you don't see how your gestures already mirror his; you don't see him in the way you hold your body, in the way you sign your name. You don't hear his whisper in your blood.

On the day I have to tell you about, my two-year-old sister Chhoti Scheherazade, Little Scare-zade, started crying as she often did during one of our family rows. Amma and Aya Mary loaded her into her push-chair and made a rapid getaway. They pushed her to Kensington Square and then sat on the grass, turned Scheherazade loose and made philosophical remarks while she tired herself out. Finally, she fell asleep, and they made their way home in the fading light of the evening. Outside Waverley House they were approached by two well-turned-out young men with Beatle haircuts and the buttoned-up, collarless jackets made popular by the band. The first of these young men asked my mother, very politely, if she might be the Maharani of B——.

"No," my mother answered, flattered.

"Oh, but you are, madam," said the second Beatle, equally politely. "For you are heading for Waverley House and that is the Maharaja's place of residence."

"No, no," my mother said, still blushing with pleasure. "We are a different Indian family."

"Quite so," the first Beatle nodded understandingly, and then, to my mother's great surprise, placed a finger alongside his nose, and winked. "Incognito, eh. Mum's the word."

"Now excuse us," my mother said, losing patience. "We are not the ladies you seek."

The second Beatle tapped a foot lightly against a wheel of the push-chair. "Your husband seeks ladies, madam, were you aware of that fact? Yes, he does. Most assiduously, may I add."

"Too assiduously," said the first Beatle, his face darkening.

"I tell you I am not the Maharani Begum," my mother said, growing suddenly alarmed. "Her business is not my business. Kindly let me pass."

The second Beatle stepped closer to her. She could feel his breath, which was minty. "One of the ladies he sought out was our ward, as you might say," he explained. "That would be the term. Under our protection, you follow. Us, therefore, being responsible for her welfare."

"Your husband," said the first Beatle, showing his teeth in a frightening way, and raising his voice one notch, "damaged the goods. Do you hear me, Queenie? He damaged the fucking goods."

"Mistaken identity, fleas," said Certainly-Mary. "Many Indian residents in Waverley House. We are decent ladies; *fleas*."

The second Beatle had taken out something from an inside pocket. A blade caught the light. "Fucking wogs," he said. "You fucking come over here, you don't fucking know how to fucking behave. Why don't you fucking fuck off to fucking Wogistan? Fuck your fucking wog arses. Now then," he added in a quiet voice, holding up the knife, "unbutton your blouses."

Just then a loud noise emanated from the doorway of Waverley House. The two women and the two men turned to look, and out came Mixed-Up, yelling at the top of his voice and windmilling his arms like a mad old loon.

"Hullo," said the Beatle with the knife, looking amused. "Who's this, then? Oh oh fucking seven?"

Mixed-Up was trying to speak, he was in a mighty agony of effort, but all that was coming out of his mouth was raw, unshaped noise. Scheherazade woke up and joined in. The two Beatles looked displeased. But then something happened inside old Mixed-Up; something popped, and in a great rush he gabbled, "Sirs sirs no sirs these not B—— women sirs B—— women upstairs on floor three sirs Maharaja of B—— also sirs God's truth mother's grave swear."

It was the longest sentence he had spoken since the stroke that had broken his tongue long ago.

And what with his torrent and Scheherazade's squalls there were suddenly heads poking out from doorways, attention was being paid, and the two Beatles nodded gravely. "Honest mistake," the first of them said apologetically to my mother, and actually bowed from the waist. "Could happen to anyone," the knife-man added, ruefully. They turned and began to walk quickly away. As they passed Mecir, however, they paused. "I know you, though," said the knife-man "'*Jet plane. Gone.*'" He made a short movement of the arm, and then Mixed-Up the courter was lying on the pavement with blood leaking from a wound in his stomach. "All okay now," he gasped, and passed out.

11

He was on the road to recovery by Christmas; my mother's letter to the landlords, in which she called him a "knight in shining armour," ensured that he was well looked after, and his job was kept open for him. He continued to live in his little ground-floor cubby-hole, while the hall porter's duties were carried out by shift-duty staff. "Nothing but the best for our very own hero," the landlords assured my mother in their reply.

The two Maharajas and their retinues had moved out before I came home for the Christmas holidays, so we had no further visits from the Beatles or the Rolling Stones. Certainly-Mary spent as much time as she could with Mecir; but it was the look of my old Aya that worried me more than poor Mixed-Up.

She looked older, and powdery, as if she might crumble away at any moment into dust.

"We didn't want to worry you at school," my mother said. "She has been having heart trouble. Palpitations. Not all the time, but."

Mary's health problems had sobered up the whole family. Muneeza's tantrums had stopped, and even my father was making an effort. They had put up a Christmas tree in the sitting-room and decorated it with all sorts of baubles. It was so odd to see a Christmas tree at our place that I realised things must be fairly serious.

On Christmas Eve my mother suggested that Mary might like it if we all sang some carols. Amma had made song-sheets, six copies, by hand. When we did O come, all ye faithful I showed off by singing from memory in Latin. Everybody behaved perfectly. When Muneeza suggested that we should try Swinging on a Star or I Wanna Hold Your Hand instead of this boring stuff, she wasn't really being serious. So this is family life, I thought. This is it.

But we were only play-acting.

A few weeks earlier, at school, I'd come across an American boy, the star of the school's Rugby football team, crying in the Chapel cloisters. I asked him what the matter was and he told me that President Kennedy had been assassinated. "I don't believe you," I said, but I could see that it was true. The football star sobbed and sobbed. I took his hand.

"When the President dies, the nation is orphaned," he eventually said, brokenheartedly parroting a piece of cracker-barrel wisdom he'd probably heard on Voice of America.

"I know how you feel," I lied. "My father just died, too."

Mary's heart trouble turned out to be a mystery; unpredictably, it came and went. She was subjected to all sorts of tests during the next six months, but each time the doctors ended up by shaking their heads: they couldn't find anything wrong with her. Physically, she was right as rain; except that there were these periods when her heart kicked and bucked in her chest like the wild horses in The Misfits, the ones whose roping and tying made Marilyn Monroe so mad.

Mecir went back to work in the spring, but his experience had knocked the stuffing out of him. He was slower to smile, duller of eye, more inward. Mary, too, had turned in upon herself. They still met for tea, crumpets and The Flintstones, but something was no longer quite right.

At the beginning of the summer Mary made an announcement.

"I know what is wrong with me," she told my parents, out of the blue. "I need to go home."

"But, Aya," my mother argued, "homesickness is not a real disease."

"God knows for what-all we came over to this country," Mary said. "But I can no longer stay. No. Certainly not." Her determination was absolute.

So it was England that was breaking her heart, breaking it by not being India. London was killing her, by not being Bombay. And Mixed-Up? I wondered. Was the courter killing her, too, because he was no longer himself? Or was it that her heart, roped by two different loves, was being pulled both East and West, whinnying and rearing, like those movie horses being yanked this way by

Clark Gable and that way by Montgomery Clift, and she knew that to live she would have to choose?

"I must go," said Certainly-Mary. "Yes, certainly. *Bas.* Enough."

That summer, the summer of '64, I turned seventeen. Chandni went back to India. Durré's Polish friend Rozalia informed me over a sandwich in Oxford Street that she was getting engaged to a "real man," so I could forget about seeing her again, because this Zbigniew was the jealous type. Roy Orbison sang *It's Over* in my ears as I walked away to the Tube, but the truth was that nothing had really begun.

Certainly-Mary left us in mid-July. My father bought her a one-way ticket to Bombay, and that last morning was heavy with the pain of ending. When we took her bags down to the car, Mecir the hall porter was nowhere to be seen. Mary did not knock on the door of his lounge, but walked straight out through the freshly polished oak-panelled lobby, whose mirrors and brasses were sparkling brightly; she climbed into the back seat of our Ford Zodiac and sat there stiffly with her carry-on grip on her lap, staring straight ahead. I had known and loved her all my life. *Never mind your damned courier*, I wanted to shout at her, *what about me?*

As it happened, she was right about the homesickness. After her return to Bombay, she never had a day's heart trouble again; and, as the letter from her niece Stella confirmed, at ninety-one she was still going strong.

Soon after she left, my father told us he had decided to "shift location" to Pakistan. As usual, there were no discussions, no explanations, just the simple fiat. He gave up the lease on the flat in Waverley House at the end of the summer holidays, and they all went off to Karachi, while I went back to school.

I became a British citizen that year. I was one of the lucky ones, I guess, because in spite of that chess game I had the Dodo on my side. And the passport did, in many ways, set me free. It allowed me to come and go, to make choices that were not the ones my father would have wished. But I, too, have ropes around my neck, I have them to this day, pulling me this way and that, East and West, the nooses tightening, commanding, *choose, choose.*

I buck, I snort, I whinny, I rear, I kick. Ropes, I do not choose between you. Lassoes, lariats, I choose neither of you, and both. Do you hear? I refuse to choose.

A year or so after we moved out I was in the area and dropped in at Waverley House to see how the old courter was doing. Maybe, I thought, we could have a game of chess, and he could beat me to a pulp. The lobby was empty, so I knocked on the door of his little lounge. A stranger answered.

"Where's Mixed-Up?" I cried, taken by surprise. I apologised at once, embarrassed. "Mr Mecir, I meant, the porter."

"I'm the porter, sir," the man said. "I don't know anything about any mix-up."

1994

JOY HARJO
born 1951

Remember

Remember the sky that you were born under,
know each of the star's stories.
Remember the moon, know who she is.
Remember the sun's birth at dawn, that is the
strongest point of time. Remember sundown   5
and the giving away to night.
Remember your birth, how your mother struggled
to give you form and breath. You are evidence of
her life, and her mother's, and hers.
Remember your father. He is your life, also.   10
Remember the earth whose skin you are:
red earth, black earth, yellow earth, white earth
brown earth, we are earth.
Remember the plants, trees, animal life who all have their
tribes, their families, their histories, too. Talk to them,   15
listen to them. They are alive poems.
Remember the wind. Remember her voice. She knows the
origin of this universe.
Remember you are all people and all people
are you.   20
Remember you are this universe and this
universe is you.
Remember all is in motion, is growing, is you.
Remember language comes from this.
Remember the dance language is, that life is.   25
Remember.

1983

New Orleans

This is the south. I look for evidence
of other Creeks, for remnants of voices,
or for tobacco brown bones to come wandering
down Conti Street, Royale, or Decatur.
Near the French Market I see a blue horse   5
caught frozen in stone in the middle of
a square. Brought in by the Spanish on
an endless ocean voyage he became mad
and crazy. They caught him in blue

rock, said   10
      don't talk.

I know it wasn't just a horse
         that went crazy.

Nearby is a shop with ivory and knives.
There are red rocks. The man behind the   15
counter has no idea that he is inside
magic stones. He should find out before
they destroy him. These things
have memory,
        you know.   20

I have a memory.
          It swims deep in blood,
a delta in the skin. It swims out of Oklahoma,
deep the Mississippi River. It carries my
feet to these places: the French Quarter,   25
stale rooms, the sun behind thick and moist
clouds, and I hear boats hauling themselves up
and down the river.

My spirit comes here to drink.
My spirit comes here to drink.   30
Blood is the undercurrent.

There are voices buried in the Mississippi
mud. There are ancestors and future children
buried beneath the currents stirred up by
pleasure boats going up and down.   35
There are stories here made of memory.

I remember DeSoto. He is buried somewhere in
this river, his bones sunk like the golden
treasure he traveled half the earth to find,
came looking for gold cities, for shining streets   40
of beaten gold to dance on with silk ladies.

He should have stayed home.

        Creeks knew of him for miles
          before he came into town.
            Dreamed of silver blades   45
           and crosses.
And knew he was one of the ones who yearned
for something his heart wasn't big enough
to handle.
        (And DeSoto thought it was gold.)   50

The Creeks lived in earth towns,
                    not gold,
            spun children, not gold.
That's not what DeSoto thought he wanted to see.
The Creeks knew it, and drowned him in   55
            the Mississippi River
                so he wouldn't have to drown himself.

Maybe his body is what I am looking for
as evidence. To know in another way
that my memory is alive.   60
But he must have got away, somehow,
because I have seen New Orleans,
the lace and silk buildings,
trolley cars on beaten silver paths,
graves that rise up out of soft earth in the rain,   65
shops that sell black mammy dolls
holding white babies.

And I know I have seen DeSoto,
            having a drink on Bourbon Street,
            mad and crazy   70
            dancing with a woman as gold
            as the river bottom.

                                        1983

She Had Some Horses

She had some horses.

She had horses who were bodies of sand.
She had horses who were maps drawn of blood.
She had horses who were skins of ocean water.
She had horses who were the blue air of sky.   5
She had horses who were fur and teeth.
She had horses who were clay and would break.
She had horses who were splintered red cliff.

She had some horses.

She had horses with eyes of trains.   10
She had horses with full, brown thighs.
She had horses who laughed too much.
She had horses who threw rocks at glass houses.
She had horses who licked razor blades.

She had some horses.   15

She had horses who danced in their mothers' arms.
She had horses who thought they were the sun and their
bodies shone and burned like stars.

She had horses who waltzed nightly on the moon.
She had horses who were much too shy, and kept quiet
in stalls of their own making.
20

She had some horses.

She had horses who liked Creek Stomp Dance songs.
She had horses who cried in their beer.
She had horses who spit at male queens who made
them afraid of themselves.
25
She had horses who said they weren't afraid.
She had horses who lied.
She had horses who told the truth, who were stripped
bare of their tongues.
30

She had some horses.

She had horses who called themselves, "horse."
She had horses who called themselves, "spirit," and kept
their voices secret and to themselves.
She had horses who had no names.
35
She had horses who had books of names.

She had some horses.

She had horses who whispered in the dark, who were afraid to speak.
She had horses who screamed out of fear of the silence, who
carried knives to protect themselves from ghosts.
40
She had horses who waited for destruction.
She had horses who waited for resurrection.

She had some horses.

She had horses who got down on their knees for any saviour.
She had horses who thought their high price had saved them.
45
She had horses who tried to save her, who climbed in her
bed at night and prayed.

She had some horses.

She had some horses she loved.
She had some horses she hated.
50

These were the same horses.

1983

I Give You Back

I release you, my beautiful and terrible
fear. I release you. You were my beloved

and hated twin, but now, I don't know you
as myself. I release you with all the
pain I would know at the death of   5
my children.

You are not my blood anymore.

I give you back to the soldiers
who burned down my home, beheaded my children,
raped and sodomized my brothers and sisters.   10
I give you back to those who stole the
food from our plates when we were starving.

I release you, fear, because you hold
these scenes in front of me and I was born
with eyes that can never close.   15

I release you
I release you
I release you
I release you

I am not afraid to be angry.   20
I am not afraid to rejoice.
I am not afraid to be black.
I am not afraid to be white.
I am not afraid to be hungry.
I am not afraid to be full.   25
I am not afraid to be hated.
I am not afraid to be loved.

to be loved, to be loved, fear.

Oh, you have choked me, but I gave you the leash.
You have gutted me but I gave you the knife.   30
You have devoured me, but I laid myself across the fire.

I take myself back, fear.
You are not my shadow any longer,
I won't hold you in my hands.
You can't live in my eyes, my ears, my voice   35
my belly, or in my heart my heart
my heart my heart

But come here, fear
I am alive and you are so afraid
                                          of dying.   40

                                                          1983

SHERMAN ALEXIE
born 1966

Class

She wanted to know if I was Catholic.

I was completely unprepared to respond with any degree of clarity to such a dangerous question. After all, we had been talking about the shrimp appetizers (which were covered with an ambitious pesto sauce) and where they fit, in terms of quality, in our very separate histories of shrimp appetizers in particular and seafood appetizers in general. I'd just been describing to her how cayenne and lobster seemed to be mortal enemies, one of the more secular and inane culinary observations I'd ever made, when she'd focused her blue eyes on me, really looked at me for the first time in the one minute and thirty-five seconds we'd known each other, and asked me if I was Catholic.

How do you answer a question like that, especially when you've just met the woman at one of those house parties where you'd expected to know everybody in attendance but had gradually come to realize that you knew only the host couple, and then only well enough to ask about the welfare of the two kids (a boy and a girl or two boys) you thought they parented? As far as I could tell, there were no priests, ministers, or pastors milling about, so I had no easy visual aids in guessing at the dominant denomination in the room. If there'd been a Jesuit priest, Hasidic rabbi, or Tibetan monk drinking a pale ale over by the saltwater aquarium, I might have known the best response, the clever, scintillating answer that would have compelled her to take me home with her for a long night of safe and casual sex.

"Well," she asked again, with a musical lilt in her voice. "Are you Catholic?"

Her left eye was a significantly darker blue than the right.

"Your eyes," I said, trying to change the subject. "They're different."

"I'm blind in this one," she said, pointing to the left eye.

"Oh, I'm sorry," I said, mortified by my lack of decorum.

"Why? It was my big brother who stabbed me with the pencil. He didn't mean it, though."

She told the story as if she'd only skinned a knee or received a slight concussion, as if the injury had been temporary.

"He was aiming for my little sister's eye," she added. "But she ducked. She was always more athletic than me."

"Where's your sister now?"

"She's dead. Car wreck. Bang, bang, bang."

So much pain for such a white woman. I wondered how often a man can say the wrong thing during the course of a particular conversation.

"What about your brother?" I asked, praying that he had not been driving the car that killed her sister.

"He's right over there," she said and pointed at a handsome man, taller than everybody else in the room, who was sitting on the carpeted stairs with a woman whose red hair I'd been admiring all evening. Though engaged in what appeared to be a passionate conversation, the brother sensed his sister's attention and looked up. Both of his eyes were the same shade of blue as her good eye.

"He's the one who did it," she said and tapped her blind eye.

In response, the brother smiled and tapped his left eye. He could see perfectly.

"You cruel bastard," she mouthed at him, though she made it sound like an affectionate nickname, like a tender legacy from childhood.

"You cruel bastard," she repeated. Her brother could obviously read her lips because he laughed again, loud enough for me to hear him over the din of the party, and hugged the redhead in a tender but formal way that indicated they'd made love only three or four times in their young relationship.

"Your brother," I said, trying to compliment her by complimenting the family genetics. "He's good-looking."

"He's okay," she said.

"He's got your eyes."

"Only one of them, remember," she said and moved one step closer to me. "Now, quit trying to change the subject. Tell me. Are you Catholic or are you not Catholic?"

"Baptized," I said. "But not confirmed."

"That's very ambiguous."

"I read somewhere that many women think ambiguity is sexy."

"Not me. I like men who are very specific."

"You don't like mystery?"

"I always know who did it," she said and moved so close that I could smell the red wine and dinner mints on her breath.

I took a step back.

"Don't be afraid," she said. "I'm not drunk. And I just chewed on a few Altoids because I thought I might be kissing somebody very soon."

She could read minds. She was also drunk enough that her brother had already pocketed the keys to her Lexus.

"Who is this somebody you're going to be kissing?" I asked. "And why just somebody? That sounds very ambiguous to me."

"And very sexy," she said and touched my hand. Blond, maybe thirty-five, and taller than me, she was the tenth most attractive white woman in the room. I always approached the tenth most attractive white woman at any gathering. I didn't have enough looks, charm, intelligence, or money to approach anybody more attractive than that, and I didn't have enough character to approach the less attractive. Crassly speaking, I'd always made sure to play ball only with my equals.

"You're Indian," she said, stretching the word into three syllables and nearly a fourth.

"Do you like that?"

"I like your hair," she said, touching the black braids that hung down past my chest. I'd been growing the braids since I'd graduated from law school. My hair impressed jurors but irritated judges. Perfect.

"I like your hair, too," I said and brushed a pale strand away from her forehead. I counted three blemishes and one mole on her face. I wanted to kiss the tips of her fingers. Women expected kisses on the parts of their bodies hidden

by clothes, the private places, but were often surprised when I paid more attention to their public features: hands, hairline, the soft skin around their eyes.

"You're beautiful," I said.

"No, I'm not," she said. "I'm just pretty. But pretty is good enough."

I still didn't know her name, but I could have guessed at it. Her generation of
white women usually carried two-syllable names, like Becky, Erin, and Wendy, or
monosyllabic nicknames that lacked any adornment. Peg, Deb, or Sam. Efficient
names, quick-in-the-shower names, just-brush-it-and-go names. Her mother
and her mother's friends would be known by more ornate monikers, and if she
had daughters, they would be named after their grandmothers. The country was
filling up with little white girls named Rebecca, Elizabeth, and Willamena.

"Sara," I guessed. "Your name is Sara."

"With or without an *h*?" she asked.

"Without," I said, pleased with my psychic ability.

"Actually, it's neither. My name is Susan. Susan McDermott. Without the
h."

"I'm Edgar Eagle Runner," I said, though my driver's license still read Edgar
Joseph.

"Eagle Runner," she repeated, feeling the shape of my name fill her mouth,
then roll past her tongue, teeth, and lips.

"Susan," I said.

"Eagle Runner," she whispered. "What kind of Indian are you?"

"Spokane."

"Never heard of it."

"We're a small tribe. Salmon people."

"The salmon are disappearing," she said.

"Yes," I said. "Yes, they are."

Susan McDermott and I were married in a small ceremony seven months
later in St. Therese Catholic Church in Madrona, a gentrified neighborhood
ten minutes from downtown Seattle. She'd been baptized at St. Therese as a
toddler by a Jesuit who many years later went hiking on Mount Rainier and
vanished. Father David or Joseph or Father Something Biblical. She didn't
remember anything about him, neither the color of his hair nor the exact shape
of his theology, but she thought that his disappearance was a metaphor for her
love life.

"One day, many years ago," she said, "my heart walked into the snow and
vanished. But then you found it and gave it heat."

"Is that a simile or a metaphor?" I asked.

"It might be an analogy," she said.

Our vows were witnessed by three dozen of Susan's best friends, along with
most of her coworkers at the architecture firm, but Susan's handsome brother
and parents stayed away as a protest against my pigmentation.

"I can understand fucking him," her brother had said upon hearing the
news of our engagement. "But why do you want to share a checking account?"

He was so practical.

Half of the partners and all of my fellow associates from the law firm
showed up to watch me tie the knot.

Velma, my dark-skinned mother, was overjoyed by my choice of mate. She'd
always wanted me to marry a white woman and beget half-breed children who

would marry white people who would beget quarter-bloods, and so on and so on, until simple mathematics killed the Indian in us.

When asked, my mother told white people she was Spanish, not Mexican, not Hispanic, not Chicana, and certainly not Spokane Indian with a little bit of Aztec thrown in for spice, even though she was all of these things.

As for me, I'd told any number of white women that I was part Aztec and I'd told a few that I was completely Aztec. That gave me some mystery, some ethnic weight, a history of glorious color and mass executions. Strangely enough, there were aphrodisiacal benefits to claiming to be descended from ritual cannibals. In any event, pretending to be an Aztec warrior was a lot more impressive than revealing I was just some bright kid who'd fought his way off the Spokane Indian Reservation in Washington State and was now a corporate lawyer in Seattle who pretended to have a lot more money that he did.

I'd emptied my meager savings account to pay for the wedding and reception, refusing to allow Susan to help, though she made twice what I did. I was living paycheck to paycheck, a bizarre circumstance for a man whose monthly wage exceeded his mother's yearly income as a social worker in the small city of Spokane, Washington.

My mother was an Indian woman who taught drunk white people not to drink, stoned whites not to smoke, and abusive whites not to throw the punch. A simple and honorable job. She was very good at it and I loved her. She wore a black dress to the wedding, nearly funeral wear, but brightened it with a salmon-colored scarf and matching shoes.

I counted seventeen white women at the wedding. On an average day, Susan would have been the fourth or fifth most attractive. On this, her wedding day, dressed in an ivory gown with plunging neckline, she was easily the most beautiful white woman in the chapel; she was more serene, sexy, and spiritual than the wooden Mary hanging on the west wall or the stained-glassed Mary filling up one of the windows.

Susan's niece, an eighteen-year-old, served as her maid of honor. She modeled teen wear for Nordstrom's. I tried not to stare at her. My best man was one of the partners in the law firm where I worked.

"Hey, Runner," he had said just before the ceremony began. "I love you, man."

I'd hugged him, feeling guilty. My friendship with him was strictly professional.

During the ceremony, he cried. I couldn't believe it. I'm not one of those men who believe tears are a sign of weakness. On the contrary, I believe it's entirely appropriate, even attractive, for a man to cry under certain circumstances, but my wedding was not tearworthy. In fact, there was a decided lack of emotion during the ceremony, mostly due to the absence of Susan's immediate family.

My mother was the only member of my family sitting in the pews, but that didn't bother or surprise me. She was the only one I had invited.

The ceremony itself was short and simple, because Susan believed brevity was always more elegant, and more sexy, than excess. I agreed with her.

"I will," she said.

"I will," I said.

We did.

▲

During the first two years of our marriage, we attended thirty-seven cocktail parties, eighteen weddings, one divorce, seven Christmas parties, two New Year's Eve parties, three New Year's Day parties, nine birthday parties—only one of them for a child under the age of eighteen—six opera performances, nine literary readings, twelve museum openings, one museum closing, three ballets, including a revival of *Swan Lake* in New York City, one spouse-swapping party we left before we took off our coats, and thirty-two films, including most of those nominated for Oscars and two or three that had screened at the Sundance Film Festival.

I attended business lunches Monday through Friday, and occasionally on Saturdays, while Susan kept her Friday lunches free so she could carry on an affair with an architect named Harry. She'd begun the affair a few days after our first anniversary and it had gone on for seven months before she'd voluntarily quit him, never having known that I'd known about the tryst, that I'd discovered his love letters hidden in a shoe box at the bottom of her walk-in closet.

I hadn't been snooping on her when I'd found the letters and I didn't bother to read any of them past the salutation that began each. "My love, my love, my love," they'd read, three times, always three times, like a chant, like a prayer. Brokenhearted, betrayed, I'd kept the letters sacred by carefully placing them back, intact and unread, in the shoe box and sliding the box back into its hiding place.

I suppose I could have exacted revenge on her by sleeping with one or more of her friends or coworkers. I'd received any number of subtle offers to do such a thing, but I didn't want to embarrass her. Personal pain should never be made public. Instead, in quiet retaliation, I patronized prostitutes whenever I traveled out of town. Miami, Los Angeles, Boston. Chicago, Minneapolis, Houston.

In San Francisco for a deposition hearing, I called the first service listed in the Yellow Pages.

"A-1 Escorts," said the woman. A husky voice, somehow menacing. I'm sure her children hated the sound of it, even as I found myself aroused by its timbre.

"A-1 Escorts," she said again when I did not speak.

"Oh," I said. "Hi. Hello. Uh, I'm looking for some company this evening."

"Where you at?"

"The Prescott."

"Nice place."

"Yeah, they have whirlpool bathtubs."

"Water sports will cost you extra."

"Oh, no, no, no. I'm, uh, rather traditional."

"Okay, Mr. Traditional, what are you looking for?"

I'd slept with seventeen prostitutes, all of them blond and blue-eyed. Twelve of them had been busty while the other five had been small-breasted. Eight of them had claimed to be college students; one of them even had a chemistry textbook in her backpack.

"Do you employ any Indian women?" I asked.

"Indian? Like with the dot in the forehead?"

"No, no, that's East Indian. From India. I'm looking for American Indian. You know, like Tonto."

"We don't have any boys."

"Oh, no, I mean, I want an Indian woman."

There was a long silence on the other end. Was she looking through some kind of catalogue? Searching her inventory for the perfect woman for me? Was she calling other escort companies, looking for a referral? I wanted to hang up the phone. I'd never had intercourse with an Indian woman.

"Yeah, we got somebody. She's a pro."

"What do you mean by pro?"

"She used to work pornos."

"Pornos?"

"Dirty movies? X-rated? You got them right there on the pay-per-view in your room, buddy."

"What's her name?"

"She calls herself Tawny Feather."

"You're kidding."

"I never kid."

I wondered what kind of Indian woman would call herself Tawny Feather. Sexually speaking, Indian women and men are simultaneously promiscuous and modest. That's a contradiction, but it also happens to be the truth. I just couldn't imagine an Indian woman who would star in pornographic movies.

"Well, you want a date or not?" asked the husky-voiced woman.

"How much?"

"How much you got?"

"How much you want?"

"Two hundred."

"Sold," I said.

"What room?"

"1216."

"Who should she ask for?"

"Geronimo."

"Ha, ha," she said and hung up the phone.

Less than an hour later, there was a knock on the door. I peered through the peephole and saw her.

Tawny Feather.

She wore a conservative tan suit and a string of fake pearls. Dream-catcher earrings, turquoise rings, a stainless-steel eagle pinned to her lapel. Good camouflage. Professional but eccentric. She looked like a woman on her way to or from a meeting. She looked like a woman with an Individualized Retirement Account.

She was also a white woman wearing a black wig over her short blond hair.

"You're not Indian," I said when I opened the door.

She looked me up and down.

"No, I'm not," she said. "But you are."

"Mostly."

"Well," she said as she stepped into the room and kissed my neck. "Then you can mostly pretend I'm Indian."

She stayed all night, which cost me another five hundred dollars, and ordered eggs and toast for breakfast, which cost me another twenty.

"You're the last one," I said as she prepared to leave.

"The last what?"

"My last prostitute."

"The last one today?" she asked. "Or the last one this month? What kind of time period are we talking about here?"

She swore she was an English major.

"The last one forever," I said.

She smiled, convinced that I was lying and/or fooling myself, having heard these same words from any number of customers. She knew that she and her coworkers were drugs for men like me.

"Sure I am," she said.

"No, really," I said. "I promise."

She laughed.

"Son," she said, though she was ten years younger than me. "You don't have to make me any damn promises."

She took off her black wig and handed it to me.

"You keep it," she said and gave me a free good-bye kiss.

▲

Exactly three years after our wedding, Susan gave birth to our first child, a boy. He weighed eight pounds, seven ounces, and was twenty-two inches long. A big baby. His hair was black and his eyes were a strange gray. He died ten minutes after leaving Susan's body.

▲

After our child died, Susan and I quit having sex. Or rather, she stopped wanting to have sex. I just want to tell the whole story. For months I pressured, coerced, seduced, and emotionally blackmailed her into sleeping with me. At first, I assumed she'd been engaged in another affair with another architect named Harry, but my private detective found only evidence of her grief: crying jags in public rest rooms, aimless wandering in the children's departments of Nordstrom's and the Bon Marche, and visits to a therapist I'd never heard about.

She wasn't touching anybody else but me. Our lives moved on.

After a year of reluctant sex, I believed her orgasms were mostly due to my refusal to quit touching her until she did come, the arduous culmination of my physical endeavors rather than the result of any emotional investment she might have had in fulfillment. And then, one night, while I was still inside her, moving my hips in rhythm with hers, I looked into her eyes, her blue eyes, and saw that her good eye held no more light in it than her dead eye. She wasn't literally blind, of course. She'd just stopped seeing me. I was startled by the sudden epiphany that she'd been faking her orgasms all along, certainly since our child had died, and probably since the first time we'd made love.

"What?" she asked, a huge question to ask and answer at any time in our lives. Her hands never left their usual place at the small of my back.

"I'm sorry," I told her, and I was sorry, and left her naked and alone in bed while I quickly dressed and went out for a drink.

I don't drink alcohol, never have, mostly because I don't want to maintain and confirm any of my ethnic stereotypes, let alone the most prevalent one, but also because my long-lost father, a half-breed, is still missing somewhere in the bottom of a tequila bottle. I had always wondered if he was a drunk because he was Indian or because he was white or because he was both.

Personally, I like bottled water, with gas, as the Europeans like to say. If I drink enough of that bubbly water in the right environment, I can get drunk. After a long night of Perrier or Pellegrino, I can still wake up with a vicious hangover. Obviously, I place entirely too much faith in the power of metaphor.

When I went out carousing with my fellow lawyers, I ended up in fancy hotel lounges, private clubs, and golf course cigar rooms, the places where the alcoholics adhere to a rigid dress code, but after leaving my marriage bed I wanted to drink in a place free from lawyers and their dress codes, from emotional obligations and beautiful white women, even the kind of white woman who might be the tenth most attractive in any room in the world.

I chose Chuck's, a dive near the corner of Virginia and First.

I'd driven by the place any number of times, had seen the Indians who loitered outside. I assumed it was an Indian bar, one of those establishments where the clientele, through chance and design, is mostly indigenous. I'd heard about these kinds of places. They are supposed to exist in every city.

"What can I get you?" asked the bartender when I sat on the stool closest to the door. She was an Indian woman with scars on her face and knuckles. A fighter. She was a woman who had once been pretty but had grown up in a place where pretty was punished. Now, twenty pounds overweight, on her way to forty pounds more, she was most likely saving money for a complete move to a city yet to be determined.

"Hey, handsome," she asked again as I stared blankly at her oft-broken nose. I decided that her face resembled most of the furniture in the bar: dark, stained by unknown insults, and in a continual state of repair. "What the fuck would you like to drink?"

"Water," I said, surprised that the word "fuck" could sound so friendly.

"Water?"

"Yeah, water."

She filled a glass from the tap behind her and plunked it down in front of me. "A dollar," she said.

"For tap water?"

"For space rental."

I handed her a five-dollar bill.

"Keep the change," I said and took a big drink.

"Cool. Next time, you get a clean glass," she said and waited for my reaction.

I swallowed hard, kept my dinner down, and smiled.

"I don't need to know what's coming next," I said. "I like mysteries."

"What kind of mysteries?"

"Hard-boiled. The kind where the dog gets run over, the hero gets punched in the head, and the bad guy gets eaten by sharks."

"Not me," she said, "I got too much blood in my life already. I like romances."

I wondered if she wanted to sleep with me.

"You want something else," she said, "just shout it out. I'll hear you."

She moved to the other end of the bar where an old Indian man sipped at a cup of coffee. They talked and laughed. Surprisingly jealous of their camaraderie, I turned away and looked around the bar. It was a small place, maybe fifty feet long by twenty feet wide, with one pinball machine, one pool table, and two bathrooms. I supposed the place would be packed on a weekend.

As it was, on a cold Thursday, there were only five Indians in the bar, other than the bartender, her old friend, and me.

Two obese Indian women shared a table in the back, an Indian couple danced in front of a broken jukebox, and one large and muscular Indian guy played pool by himself. In his white T-shirt, blue-jean jacket, tight jeans, and cowboy boots, he looked like Chief Broom from *One Flew Over the Cuckoo's Nest.* I decided he could have killed me with a flick of one finger.

He looked up from his pool cue when he felt my eyes on him.

"What the fuck are you looking at?" he asked. His eyes were darker than the eight ball. I had no idea that "fuck" could be such a dangerous word.

"Nothing," I said.

Still holding his cue stick, he walked a few paces closer to me. I was afraid, very afraid.

"Nothing?" he asked. "Do I look like nothing to you?"

"No, no, that's not what I meant. I mean, I was just watching you play pool. That's all."

He stared at me, studied me like an owl might study a field mouse.

"You just keep your eyes to yourself," he said and turned back to his game.

I thought I was safe. I looked down to the bartender, who was shaking her head at me.

"Because I just, I just want to know," sputtered the big Indian. "I just want to know who the hell you think you are."

Furious, he shouted, a primal sort of noise, as he threw the cue stick against the wall. He rushed at me and lifted me by the collar.

"Who are you?" he shouted. "Who the fuck are you?"

"I'm nobody," I said, wet with fear. "Nobody. Nobody."

"Put him down, Junior," said the bartender.

Junior and I both turned to look at her. She held a pistol down by her hip, not as a threat, but more like a promise. Junior studied the bartender's face, estimated the level of her commitment, and dropped me back onto the stool.

He took a few steps back, pointed at me.

"I'm sick of little shits like you," he said. "Fucking urban Indians in your fancy fucking clothes. Fuck you. Fuck you."

I looked down and saw my denim jacket and polo shirt, the khakis and brown leather loafers. I looked like a Gap ad.

"I ever see you again," Junior said. "I'm going to dislocate your hips."

I flinched. Junior obviously had some working knowledge of human anatomy and the most effective means of creating pain therein. He saw my fear, examined its corners and edges, and decided it was large enough.

"Jesus," he said. "I don't know why I'm even talking to you. What are you going to do? You fucking wimp. You're not worth my time. Why don't you get the fuck out of here? Why don't you just get in your BMW, that's what you drive, enit? Why don't you get in your fucking BMW and get out of here before I change my mind, before I pop out one of your eyes with a fucking spoon, all right?"

I didn't drive a BMW; I drove a Saab.

"Yeah, fuck you," Junior said, thoroughly enjoying himself now. "Just drive back to your fucking mansion on Mercer Island or Edmonds or whatever white fucking neighborhood you live in. Drive back to your white wife. She's white, enit? Yeah, blond and blue-eyed, I bet. White, white. I bet her pussy hair is blond, too. Isn't it? Isn't it?"

I wanted to hate him.

"Go back to your mansion and read some fucking Teletubbies to your white fucking kids."

"What?" I asked.

"I said, go home to your white fucking kids."

"Fuck you," I said and completely surprised Junior. Good thing. He hesitated for a brief moment before he rushed at me again. His hesitation gave the bartender enough time to vault the bar and step in between Junior and me. I couldn't believe how fast she was.

She pressed the pistol tightly against Junior's forehead.

"Let it go, Junior," said the bartender.

"Why are you protecting him?" Junior asked.

"I don't give a shit about him," she said. "But I do care about you. You get into trouble again and you're going to jail forever. You know that."

Junior smiled.

"Sissy," he said to the bartender. "In another world, you and I are Romeo and Juliet."

"But we live in this world, Junior."

"Okay," said Sissy. "This is what's going to happen, Junior. You're going to walk over behind the bar, get yourself another Diet Pepsi, and mellow out. And Mr. Tap Water here is going to walk out the front door and never return. How does that sound to the both of you?"

"Make it two Pepsis," said Junior.

"Deal," said Sissy. "How about you, Polo?"

"Fuck him," I said.

Junior didn't move anything except his mouth.

"Sissy," he said. "How can you expect me to remain calm, how can you expect me to stay reasonable, when this guy so obviously wants to die?"

"I'll fight you," I said.

"What?" asked Sissy and Junior, both amazed.

"I'll fight you," I said again.

"All right, that's what I want to hear," said Junior. "Maybe you do have some balls. There's an alley out back."

"You don't want to do this," Sissy said to me.

"I'll meet you out there, Junior," I said.

Junior laughed and shook his head.

"Listen up, Tommy Hilfiger," he said. "I'm not stupid. I go out the back door and you're going to run out the front door. You don't have to make things so complicated. You want to leave, I'll let you leave. Just do it now, man."

"He's giving you a chance," Sissy said to me. "You better take it."

"No," I said. "I want to fight. I'll meet you out there. I promise."

Junior studied my eyes.

"You don't lie, do you?"

"I lie all the time," I said. "Most of the time. But I'm not lying now. I want to fight."

"All right, then, bring your best," he said and walked out the back door.

"Are you out of your mind?" Sissy asked. "Have you ever been in a fight?"

"I boxed a little in college."

"You boxed a little in college? You boxed a little in college? I can't believe this. Do you have any idea who Junior is?"

"No, why should I?"

"He's a pro."

"What? You mean, like a professional boxer?"

"No, man. A professional street fighter. No judges, no ring, no rules. The loser is the guy who don't get up."

"Isn't that illegal?"

"Illegal? Illegal? What, you think you're a lawyer now?"

"Actually, I am a lawyer."

Sissy laughed until tears ran down her face.

"Sweetheart," she said after she'd finally calmed down. "You need to leave. Please. Junior's got a wicked temper but he'll calm down soon enough. Hell, you come in a week from now and he'll probably buy you some water."

"Really?"

"No, not at all. I'm lying. You come in a week from now and Junior will break your thumbs."

She laughed again, laughed until she had to lean against the bar for support.

"Stop it," I said.

She kept laughing.

"Stop it," I shouted.

She kept laughing.

"Sweetheart," she said, trying to catch her breath. "I could kick your ass."

I shrugged off my denim jacket and marched for the back door. Sissy tried to stop me, but I pulled away from her and stepped into the alley.

Junior was surprised to see me. I felt a strange sense of pride. Without another word, I rushed at Junior, swinging at him with a wide right hook, with dreams of connecting with his jaw and knocking him out with one punch.

Deep in the heart of the heart of every Indian man's heart, he believes he is Crazy Horse.

My half-closed right hand whizzed over Junior's head as he expertly ducked under my wild punch and then rose, surely and accurately, with a left uppercut that carried with it the moon and half of every star in the universe.

▲

I woke up with my head in Sissy's lap. She was washing my face with a cold towel.

"Where are we?" I asked.

"In the storeroom," she said.

"Where is he?"

"Gone."

My face hurt.

"Am I missing any teeth?"

"No," said Sissy. "But your nose is broken."

"Are you sure?"

"Trust me."

I looked up at her. I decided she was still pretty and pretty was good enough. I grabbed her breast.

"Shit," she said and shoved me away.

I sprawled on the floor while she scrambled to her feet.

"What's wrong with you?" she asked. "What is wrong with you?"

"What do you mean? What?"

"Did you think, did you somehow get it into your crazy head that I was going to fuck you back here? On the goddamn floor in the goddamn dirt?"

I didn't know what to say.

"Jesus Christ, you really thought I was going to fuck you, didn't you?"

"Well, I mean, I just . . ."

"You just thought because I'm an ugly woman that I'd be easy."

"You're not ugly," I said.

"Do you think I'm impressed by this fighting bullshit? Do you think it makes you some kind of warrior or something?"

She could read minds.

"You did, didn't you? All of you Indian guys think you're Crazy Horse."

I struggled to my feet and walked over to the sink. I looked in the mirror and saw a bloody mess. I also noticed that one of my braids was missing.

"Junior cut it off," said Sissy. "And took it with him. You're lucky he liked you. Otherwise, he would have taken a toe. He's done that before."

I couldn't imagine what that would have meant to my life.

"Look at you," she said. "Do you think that's attractive? Is that who you want to be?"

I carefully washed my face. My nose was most certainly broken.

"I just want to know, man. What are you doing here? Why'd you come here?"

My left eye was swelling shut. I wouldn't be able to see out of it in the morning.

"I wanted to be with my people," I said.

"Your people?" asked Sissy. "Your people? We're not your people."

"We're Indians."

"Yeah, we're Indians. You, me, Junior. But we live in this world and you live in your world."

"I don't like my world."

"You pathetic bastard," she said, her eyes swelling with tears that had nothing to do with laughter. "You sorry, sorry piece of shit. Do you know how much I want to live in your world? Do you know how much Junior wants to live in your world?"

Of course I knew. For most of my life, I'd dreamed about the world where I currently resided.

"Junior and me," she said. "We have to worry about having enough to eat. What do you have to worry about? That you're lonely? That you have a mortgage? That your wife doesn't love you? Fuck you, fuck you. *I have to worry about having enough to eat.*"

She stormed out of the room, leaving me alone.

I stood there in the dark for a long time. When I walked out, the bar was nearly empty. Another bartender was cleaning glasses. He didn't look at me. Sissy was gone. The front door was wide open. I stepped into the street and saw her sitting at the bus stop.

"I'm sorry," I said.

"Whatever."

"Can I give you a ride somewhere?"

"Do you really want to do that?" she asked.

"No," I said.

"Finally, you're being honest."

I stared at her. I wanted to say the exact right thing.

"Go home," she said. "Just go home."

I walked away, stopped halfway down the block.

"Do you have any kids?" I shouted back at her.

"Three," she said.

Without changing my clothes, I crawled back into bed with Susan. Her skin was warm to the touch. The house ticked, ticked, ticked. In the morning, my pillow would be soaked with my blood.

"Where did you go?" Susan asked me.

"I was gone," I said. "But now I'm back."

2000

PERMISSIONS ACKNOWLEDGMENTS